Is This OK?

Harriet Gibsone

PICADOR

First published 2023 by Picador
an imprint of Pan Macmillan
The Smithson, 6 Briset Street, London ECIM 5NR
EU representative: Macmillan Publishers Ireland Ltd, 1st Floor,
The Liffey Trust Centre, 117–126 Sheriff Street Upper,
Dublin 1, DOI YC43
Associated companies throughout the world
www.panmacmillan.com

ISBN 978-1-0350-0099-9

1 3 5 7 9 8 6 4 2

A CIP catalogue record for this book is available from the British Library.

Typeset by Palimpsest Book Production Ltd, Falkirk, Stirlingshire
Printed and bound by CPI Group (UK) Ltd, Croydon, CRO 4YY

Visit **www.picador.com** to read more about all our books
and to buy them. You will also find features, author interviews and
news of any author events, and you can sign up for e-newsletters
so that you're always first to hear about our new releases.

For Mum, Dad and Mark

Some names and details pertaining to a number of the people mentioned in this memoir have been amended to protect their privacy. Arguably I should have done more to protect my own privacy, but here we are.

Contents

CHAPTER ONE

Am I OK?

It takes two weeks to fall in love with my new neighbour Tanya. I am nine years old at the time and she is three years my senior. Tanya is a wildly creative and prodigal musician; I watch her do her scales and exam pieces on the clarinet, flute and piano most nights. She plays like a professional tap dancer and part-time sniper – with poise, urgent precision and intensity, the tips of her soft strawberry-blonde hair whipping with vigour in the final throes of a particularly fraught arpeggio. When her sad, vast rabbit begins to urinate on the freshly installed carpet of her bedroom floor one Saturday afternoon, my knee-jerk reaction is to pick up the pet with one hand and hold my dress out like a net with the other. I am grateful that she seeks my company and try to prove it at any cost – often at the expense of my gingham school uniform.

While we possess a mutual passion for Sylvanian Families, *Jagged Little Pill* and watching *Ricky Lake*, our relationship is crystallized by the obsessive, illicit hobby we both share. Most weekends and some afternoons after school, we meet on the sandpaper roof of her rotting wooden playhouse, where we whittle sticks or lick the sourness off Irn Bru bars, while staring intently into the front room of the elderly couple who live over the fence. Our view partially obscured by spindly trees, we study them for hours, rejoicing whenever we are rewarded with the smallest gesture – a sneeze, or a lean in for the remote. It is a connection to a very adult world, an exercise in anthropology. To follow the couple's every move, even though they aren't the demographic of people we are typically interested in – aka the respective casts of *Fresh Prince*, *Party of Five*, *Boy Meets World* and *Eerie Indiana*, along with the whole of Year 10 – is mesmerizing. It is an ambient, almost meditative experience that creates a silent sense of camaraderie between the two of us.

Those weekends remain some of the most pleasurable of my life: our private form of light entertainment is a relief from the rest of the world and its pressures, her clarinet practice put on hold while we lose ourselves in the scenes playing out from just over the fence. After a springtime accompanied by a constant thick spritz of rain, the roof of the playhouse begins to dip in the middle, so we put our hobby on hold for a few months, only to return in the summer to find the old man slumped in his seat but his wife's chair empty, save for the outline of her torso in the sagging grey leather fabric. We wait and watch for a short while longer, but she never comes back, and our watching is never the same again.

As Tanya enters her teens, she begins to spend more time with girls her own age, and our days observing the elderly are now truly over. I would climb to the top of a tree in my garden and look at her as she lay on the grass with her new friend

Donna, trading gossip and makeup, two luxury goods I was still too young to acquire. I am hooked on sneaky observation, only unlike the playhouse days I'd return from the excursion wracked with wistfulness rather than soothed. Viewing them from the tree, sprawled on their backs, making daisy chains and swapping shag bands and laughing in the unhinged way that only teenagers can, I believed that it was only through surveying them that I might learn how to be a worthier friend, a savvier lady, and a better person in the process.

Then comes the arrival of hormones, those infamous and insistent chemical messengers that send the body instructions, whether it wishes to receive them or not. Hormones make my propensity to wallow and fixate even more heightened. It is the start of a lifelong battle with them – the unpredictable inferno of thoughts that arrived out of nowhere, the pills and potions I would soon begin to take to regulate them that, if anything, poured gasoline onto the fire. And who could forget Menstrual Blood – my narcissistic prankster sidekick who shows up in abundance for a medically concerning amount of months on end for many years, then one day vanishes completely, just when I need her. Hormones are a super-villain of sorts, and it is here they begin to take hold: aged fourteen and walking home from school, where they are telling me to visit the butcher's.

In front of the butcher's is a sports shop – Joggers! – and within that shop is a person named Tim. Tim is a grown man with grey specks in his hair, and the hollow eyes and slack cheekbones of a weed-smoker slash hopeless romantic. He is thirty years old and I know this because my good friend's mum plays tennis with his girlfriend on Thursday nights. On that day of the week I linger outside a little longer, just in case I can detect a frisson of excitement from him about a night decompressing at home alone. Alone and away from *her*.

At this point you might hastily, if understandably, assume I am some form of voyeur. But that's a label that doesn't sit right with me: my own personal experience of 'voyeurs' are a puce-faced man with the nickname Dave The Dagger rustling in the bushes of an alleyway next to my primary school, or a leathery middle-aged landlord who has installed pinhole cameras into the showerheads of the student accommodation. Those, to me, are voyeurs, not a lachrymose tween sucking the chlorine water from her wet ponytail after a swimming lesson, whose only true form of excitement comes from watching an adult male unload Quicksilver t-shirts from a cardboard box.

But back to the butcher's. Outside the shop front and cloaked in the sad, dull stench of dead animal flesh, I am still, silent, and nowhere near initiating contact with Tim; in fact, I am repulsed by the prospect of an actual conversation with him. I feel I don't yet qualify as a human of any intellectual value and my patter revolves around subjects such as rare cat breeds, mood rings and trinkets covered in astrological symbols. No: I'm chasing pure cinematic sensation, and I find that I can absorb and maintain euphoric levels of titillation through the sight of Tim's hair alone, something that I relive over and over again as I sit beneath a table in my bedroom and listen to Sheryl Crow singing songs about alleged loverat Eric Clapton on my Discman. It gives me great pleasure to visit a future world in which I ascend from my present state – a sixty-three-year-old spiritualist who runs a weekend build-your-own dreamcatcher workshop, trapped inside the body of a child – and become the mysterious seductress I know I truly am.

If I had known back then that something would enter my world and amplify my inherent lurk-mode compulsion to quite such a seismic degree, I would have cultivated an occupation for a more wholesome hobby instead, like BMXing, Brazilian jiu-jitsu or fracking. But instead, the internet arrived and became the ultimate facilitator of escapism and warped intimacy in the form of truly one-sided relationships.

Naturally, my preoccupations would expand to include those with a public profile too – people on TV, in films, musicians and, in later years, influencers. I'd come to discover this had a name: parasocial relationships, the dynamic where a 'normal' person feeling strongly towards a famous person, or, in some severe cases, a cartoon character. The term originated in 1956 to refer to the relationship between viewers and television personalities, and has become more widespread over the past decade due to fanatical 'stan culture' and the superficial notion that we have 24-hour access to the lives of public figures via social media and reality shows. There's a troubling delusion that comes with parasocial relationships – a sense that as fans or casual followers we are entitled to know everything; or that we already do via rigorous detail gathering and FBI levels of digital sleuthing. Some devolve into trolls to defend their beloved celebrity icons at any cost, while others are so dedicated to uncovering the truth, to making the object of their lust their entire identity, that they spend their spare time making memes and conspiracy videos about potential inter-band love affairs and rifts.

Mine, however, is a private, meaningful, near spiritual kind of reverence, that I return to again and again, particularly in times of need. It can be something in the way the celebrity sings, or speaks, or the way their fringe falls or top lip curls, that then leads me to believe we are soul mates. A tiny fragment of my internal world feels acknowledged by whatever art they're making, and in seeing myself reflected back in a big room or on a stage I am lifted from the existential loneliness that generic human existence brings. Other times, admittedly, they're just really hot and I want to bang them.

There is, however, another subset of parasocial relationships that is less discussed when it comes to obsessing over people on the internet; ones that exist firmly on the raw and humiliating end of the spectrum. These fixations extend beyond the lives of the rich and famous, to ex-lovers, new friends and colleagues, or just some person you stumble across and end up dedicating your entire life to. They're people that you could feasibly see in the flesh, should you walk past their nearby coffee shop before work, or loiter by their sister-in-law's food truck at a festival, or visit their regular Reformer Pilates class on Sunday morning, even though it's fifty-five minutes west of where you live and when you arrive she's not even there, it's just fifteen women who all somehow look like Emily Ratajkowski, and you leave with a hole in the central butt-zone of your leggings and discover you need to get a rail replacement service on the way back home, and the whole ordeal costs £45.

6

That is not to say I have lived a life of alienation and misery. If anything, I have been incredibly fortunate – as a music journalist, I have travelled the world with artists, met every low- to mid-tier indie band of the 2000s, some legitimate pop stars and Nick Grimshaw. Yet somehow the lure of online snooping and the onslaught of insecurity that it brings plagues my every move. From my frantic free-wheeling twenties, I pulled up to my thirties like a clapped out car, my body and brain in a perpetual malfunctioning state that would open me up to a new era of all-encompassing online obsessions.

These people, these fixations and fantasies, have defined my life. I have a habit of getting lost for days, months, years in these unrequited trysts – a devotion that is fundamental to my navigation of life. Just like hiding up a tree or skulking by a butcher's shop, I have used the internet to observe and escape when reality has become either too tedious or too painful, in order to cultivate some form of connection with another person, even if it is an artificial one played out from within the safety of my own mind. This isn't a self-help guide about how to stop using social media, or the chronicles of an unlucky online dater: it is the gradual unfurling of a private pastime that has coincided with each stage of my cumbersome coming-of-age climb towards womanhood – even if that is more of an ever-changing discourse, rather than a tangible destination. It's an experience that has been both twisted and magnificent, one that has provided sweet relief and also demonstrated the clear capacity to destroy me completely. Now, it's time to stop.

But first, I need to bring you up to speed.

CHAPTER TWO

Hello Boys

Most of the morning was spent whipping myself into a frenzy but I am finally here, alert and anxious in the underwear section of Eaden Lilley, an oppressively old-fashioned department store in the centre of mid-sized Essex market town Saffron Walden. My intention is to leave Eaden Lilley a transformed fifteen-year-old, as a sexually liberated owner of a Wonderbra.

It is spring 2001, and the bra ads are inescapable. The brand's provocative marketing over the last few years – big cleavages on big billboards – has forged them a reputation as the edgy, controversial lingerie brand. I want to buy into this glamorous world too – I want to burst into a room and turn heads with my devilish wit and coquettish charm. I want to know my way around a bikini and underarm wax strip. I want to hand-wash my gusset with one hand in the bathroom sink with a sliver of soap.

While I'm not totally rough, I'm no vixen, either. So far I've accrued an abundance of black hair under my armpits, a greasy T-zone and lacklustre breasts, although this hasn't stopped anyone from noticing them: the first-ever text message I received read *get your tits out*, from a guy named Rob who

I barely spoke to but sat behind in Religious Studies. And some girls in the changing room after netball once said my nipples were like burgers. I still haven't figured out if that's a compliment or criticism, but I'm leaning towards the latter and keen to cover the alleged meat discs with satin pads.

Keen is perhaps an understatement; my heart is pounding so hard my whole body is pulsing. To see these bras in the flesh is like witnessing a row of sex toys in a library; misplaced decadence and deviance. As a result, there's a tiny bit of tension between the woman adjusting a mannequin – a sixty-year-old retail worker whose hair is assembled like a croissant made of candy floss – and me, technically a child, quivering across the purple carpeted floor. We share a polite smile and for a few minutes I finger the rack of Sloggi pants and sensible nighties to give off the air of casual perusal. But now it's time. No more playing. I nonchalantly reach for one of the red bras, as if to say: 'Oh nice, yeah, I heard about these! I may as well touch them with my trembling, soaking-wet hands while I happen to be here.'

I flip the tag to reveal its price: £40. The tight-smiling shop assistant – let's call her Judy – might as well have slapped me around the face and called me a slut. I don't have that kind of money, Judy. Do you really want me to lose my virginity in my battered old M&S bra that's gone off-white in the wash, Judy? Judy doesn't care. Judy just wants me gone and out of her way so she can kiss that dummy with tongues while no one's watching. Judy, Judy, Judy.

With that savage punch to the head comes another from behind: the waft of instant coffee and oven-baked cake from the cafe upstairs. It reminds me of golden afternoons spent with my mum one floor up, sitting by the window, the optimal position for spying on shoppers milling around the market square. This was my favourite pastime, fuelled by our greed for salacious gossip ('Look, there's that woman who works at the school – and she's bought pears'), our fondness for being near one another and the shared buzz from observing humans without the intensity of having to function adequately alongside them. Now I am alone and nearly crying in anxious anticipation of breaking my hymen. And whose fault is that? It's MSN Messenger's fault. And Rory's.

In retrospect, life before MSN and Rory seems innocent and bucolic: all climbing trees and screaming in playgrounds. It was going to shopping centres on a Saturday, purchasing one top in the Kookaï sale with a mysterious bloodstain on the arm, and then not having enough money to buy lunch. It was going round to my best friend Laura's after school and her little brother finding a dead rat at the bottom of the garden, and him throwing it onto a bonfire, and him coming in to tell us that he'd burned a dead rat, and him smelling so much of dead rat that Laura and I throw up together in the bathroom. It was me, Laura and her little brother who burned the dead rat playing 'tag', but instead of tapping each other we spat, and sometimes the texture of the spit was so nasty we all ended up being sick again, together. It was me cutting out a photo of the cover of *The Good Sex Guide* from an advert on the back of the *Radio Times* and my mum finding it hidden under my pillow, and me trying to frame my thirteen-year-old sister, even though I'd asked my mum an hour ago if I could borrow the scissors so I could cut a photo out of the *Radio*

Times. It was making my Barbies have sex, clanging their plastic bodies together as I made lapping noises with my mouth. It was expressing my undying love for a boy in my form – 'I love Andrew Carter' – on a piece of paper, written using symbols of my own creation, ripping it into shreds, putting the shreds inside a piece of clay and burying it in my neighbour's garden, then not sleeping for weeks out of sheer fear that someone might unearth it. Life was rancid, full of spiritual abandon and humiliation – but at least it was relatively low-stakes and private in its quotidian horrors.

My relationship with the internet: honestly, a fairly typical one for anyone coming of age in the early 2000s. Shared family computer, a disgustingly loud dial-up modem that takes ten minutes to connect, and a strictly limited online slot due to Dad needing to call Uncle Nick on the house phone. The whole logistical ordeal resulted in a clunky and occasional poke on one or two websites, rather than the mind-rotting, six-hour carousel I am stuck on many years later.

The first time I go online, I panic. It's a few months before I turn fifteen and I am in limbo; the rabid teen feelings are pulsing under the surface but I still wear a flannel nightie to bed. When it comes to the internet, I'm stuck between wanting to play fun computer games and exploring mature, meaningful connections.

Laura and I are addicted to the game *Tomb Raider II*. Every day is a struggle to resist using the infamous cheat code that makes Lara Croft nude. I want to support Lara as a friend and fellow woman but the innate lure to get her out of that green cargo vest top is almighty. I'm wondering if there are similar fantastical gaming universes online, preferably ones in which I must navigate treacherous landscapes and potentially shoot Bengal tigers in the face. Unfortunately, despite much searching, I am only able to find quirky versions of Hangman, and no matter how much you tart up the backdrop, it's still just some poor thin guy in a desert getting murdered because I can't spell 'necessary'. So I move on to loftier ambitions, logging in to the first chatroom I find, and giving myself the username Lara Croft.

The initial hit of whatever this website is, is noxious; far too full-on for a fourteen-year-old and yet the danger is what I am drawn to. I sit and watch as people log in and out – a ceaseless tidal wave of strangers to engage with, any one of which could be a future husband. I'll be in a lot of trouble if anyone catches me doing this so I move fast, rapidly picking up the lingo as I go. This doesn't take too long: all that's essential is how desirable you are and where your house is, all of which can be neatly surmised with the abbreviation a/s/l (age/sex/location). Naturally I am a twenty-year-old woman with olive skin, green eyes, thick long hair, and I am living it up in London. It rolls off the tongue far better than 'pasty Essex dweeb'.

One man, using the name Garfield (real name Elon), is in his thirties and from Germany. We go from vital stats to talking about the weather, confiding that we are both a bit tired, and sharing email addresses, before discussing our hopes and dreams. I tell him I want to present music documentaries, while Elon would like to foster children. It's scintillating to speak to this amorphous German character and – thankfully – far from sexually charged, despite the obvious allure of my username. Eventually my internet cuts out, so I head back into the world and attempt to follow the *Neighbours* plotline as my head throbs with a post-chatroom comedown.

A few weeks later I am sent a chainmail with a warning that I must forward the message on to ten friends to avoid being blighted with seven years of bad luck. Only a few people I know have email addresses, so I decide to lean on my old pal Elon in a time of crisis and send it to him. He replies, almost immediately: 'Cut the crap, Hattie, I'm in love with you'.

It's becoming clear that emotions move fast on the World Wide Web.

When I'm not talking to men alone after school, Laura and I do it together, and I feel empowered whenever entering the chatroom with my friend. Laura and I are frightened by but also deeply curious about sex. We've spent a lot of time observing writhing balls of frogs mating in her pond, fervent and entwined, desperate and violent, and often poke at them – it – with a stick in horror. We're grossed out by leering men and have made up our own catchy jingle for the tabloid newspaper *The Sun*, satirizing the publication's insatiable appetite for topless pics of young women. 'Curries are nice, with lots of spice, and of course, extra sauce on page three,' Laura sings, before I chime in, with the vocal style of a tough male New York taxi driver: 'Get a stiff upper lip . . . and *something else*, with *The Sun*!'

Combining our passion for gaming, digital socializing and increasingly morbid intrigue around sex, we spark up conversations with guys on chat rooms, lead them into believing that we're instigating a dirty exchange, then share with them whatever scatological exploits spring to mind first. *I'm sat in a bath full of poo, I bet you've got poo all over your fingers, do you fancy eating poo* etc. Before they get time to reply, our fingers, already poised on a Force Quit shortcut, slam down on the keyboard. Neither of us admit it, because we are straight off into the crisp drawer to eat our way out of the adrenaline spike, but our dalliance with the men in the chat room, the predatory nature of us versus them, and vice versa, is thrilling.

Chucking obscenities into the ether gets boring, however, and my friends quickly migrate to MSN, a new chat service that we all come to use after school, so we can talk about school (having just walked home together from school). As a teen, your life force depends on your proximity to people of the same age – a frustrating proposition for grown-ups, who require cooperation and help around the house. Therefore MSN chats are often littered with abbreviations – 'be right back' (brb) and 'got to go' (g2g) – fast new ways with which to say: 'My mum is now in the room. Do not message me about that thing I just said I wanted to do to our English teacher Mr Dolan.'

The catharsis I get from these computer sessions is sensational. I've got a lot to say all of a sudden, a lot of hysteria to expunge, as my journey into high school has become quite an event. The route involves walking past a huge gothic grey house, the type of place with an AGA in the kitchen and a Victorian poltergeist in the attic. The boy who lives here – along with his mum, brother and two stepsisters – is Rory: eighteen years old, dazzling teeth, handsome nose, confident gait, big navy hoodies and baggy skater jeans.

As students of the same primary and secondary schools, I have known of Rory for most of my life, but he remained blurry, boring. He was to me like a shop selling brooms; there on every high street corner, but a peripheral factor of my every day. Now, all of a sudden, I urgently need a broom. I'm banging on that window demanding to see a broom. Sickly infatuation numbs my mind every time I catch a glance of him getting into his car for his seven-minute commute to sixth form. Just a flash of his wide-legged denim and new hair – a French-crop with a slight quiff set firm in seven layers of wet gel – reduces me to a puff of glitter.

It is utterly one-sided at first, but that's not a problem. I'm quite happy getting lost in my own angsty narrative about our imagined love. I time my enormous iPod to play the most cinematic moments of an All Saints album as I walk past his front door, taking in the delicate fragrance of the wallflowers in his front garden while imagining us chucking bags of salt at each other in the kitchen, or kneeling down naked in front of each other in a shallow bath, or whatever else happens on a Friday night at home in a committed adult relationship.

After a few weeks of observing him from afar, the mood shifts. Perhaps it's a mating call that I have been subconsciously emitting since turning fifteen and having my braces wrenched from my face, my huge shark teeth shoved into a more elegant place in my head. His eyes begin to catch mine for a split second and I wonder if he's also on board with this fantasy, perhaps running the bath a little deeper so we can kneel for a while longer in our tormented desire. I haven't felt such a severe spike of serotonin since Len dropped 'Steal My Sunshine'.

While the entry of Rory into my life is major, seminal, crushing was nothing new to me. Anyone and everyone was a potential object of lust, and had been since I was just out of nappies. One of my first proper memories is tottering into my parents' kitchen in a pair of red stiletto heels from the fancy-dress box. My motivation being that if Sahil, my extremely cool seventeen-year-old brother's best friend, could see me, a four-year-old, in a different light, he might want to take me out on a date, or just walk around the garden with me, sing a couple of songs and hold my hand. The aforementioned Andrew Carter was another one of the big crushes, a guy who had a sexy anxious habit of sucking the corner of his t-shirt during lessons, and with whom I shared a mutual love of Jamiroquai's *Return of the Space Cowboy* album. We grew close in the last year of primary school and slow-danced to Jay Kay's ballad 'Spend a Lifetime' ('Touch me in the night-time / All I want from you is love') at his summer party, before his family moved to the other side of the Atlantic. Or maybe it was Norfolk. I don't remember, but I do still remember vividly the close-up musk of that spitty t-shirt. There was also Tim, the old stoned guy I stared at after school, and my steady crush Dane at the start of high school, and my first proper kiss, a premeditated experiment which turned into an almost ticketed event in front of twenty discerning thirteen-year-olds outside Boots. I think they clapped afterwards but it's one of many core memories tarnished by trauma.

All of that – all of the giggling and hand-holding and slow-dancing – pales in comparison to my ephemeral moments of eye-contact with Rory, however. One morning, I arrive at my classroom and sit by the window waiting for my lesson to begin. There on the horizon is his boxy white Ford Fiesta MkII pulling into the car park twenty metres away. Rory steps out, shuts the door and swings his backpack on, his biceps flexing as he grips the strap with one arm. Such spellbinding chore-ography for a man caught unaware. From up in this window, I have become accustomed to feeling as if I am watching Rory on a TV screen – but this morning he turns to look up at me; purposeful, as if he's always known I've been there. With my body frozen, he begins to stroll closer to the window, somehow maintaining the gaze. I smile meekly like a Victorian maid. He smiles, cinematically cool, like a cowboy coming home. It is the start of several scintillating days of retinal interplay.

After a giddy week, I head back to my friend Helen's house for the evening. I'm expecting another night of assessing the new ways in which we felt insecure in the girls' toilets and playing fast tennis in her room using two books as a bat and a scrunchie as a ball, but as soon as her older sister Jamie gets home it's clear something more seismic is on the horizon. Jamie is in Rory's year, and says that Rory knows I have a crush on him. She says that he wants to talk.

With frantic deep breaths to quash the hysteria, Helen and I share a swivel chair and log on to MSN – where a notification alerts me to Rory's request to add me. I accept and wait. I suddenly believe as if I could make anything happen; as if I hold too much power. Our first interaction is a simple, classic 'hi :)'. That's enough action for me for one day. Sadly, he has ambitions beyond the idle back-and-forth I'm used to, and jumps straight in to see if I want to go to the cinema during half-term.

I'm too scared to have a conversation with him at school, a neutral zone, let alone spend time with him in a dark room with a closed door. I am a little bereft that this has graduated to a stage way beyond my social means already. So I say that I can't. But maybe soon? It buys me time – so I can find out a bit more about him and therefore figure out who I need to be.

In the weeks that follow, MSN becomes an urgent state of being. As soon as I get home from school I log on and spend the hours before dinner talking to Rory, learning how to be provocative using primitive emojis while simultaneously down-loading poor-quality versions of popular songs on Limewire. To the low bitrate sounds of 'Girls Dem Sugar' by Beenie Man (feat. Mya), he confides in me about sixth-form stresses and tells me that our conversations are helping him to get over 'Ellie'. Ellie's house is on my route into school. Before, she was just a girl with nice hair. Now, she's the enemy. From that day onwards I peer in at her family's kitchen as I walk past in a bid to learn more about this mystical witch. All I see are brief fragments of her life – placing a pencil case in a backpack or tipping the last of her tea into her mouth – but it's quite clear she's Saffron Walden's Lady of Shalott. She's dainty, mesmerically so: a cinched waist and long, silky fingers. I imagine they broke up at midnight in the pouring rain and that she spends her weekends reading Brontë beneath a weeping willow tree, the absolute fucking bitch.

With every MSN session, interactions between Rory and me escalate in sentimentality, expectation burgeoning with every chat. His present temperament is 'tortured soul': on top of the

Ellie stuff, there have been disruptive family fallouts and at a young age he has encountered a type of fury and tension that is foreign to me. It sounds like a traumatic few years. What's my story so far? Awful at maths. Odd undiagnosed condition whereby every time I go for a vigorous jog I bleed in my pants then do a tiny poo. Shall I tell him about my braces?

One Saturday night, Helen has a free house, so I head round for a sleepover. No more bat and ball – we immediately drink four huge glasses of vodka and orange juice and decide the best thing to do while we have the courage is to go to Rory's house, which is twelve minutes away if we run – which we do. Pounding those suburban streets that night, I've never felt more free. I feel so physically competent on vodka – like I could run like this forever; I could run while giving birth, and addressing the nation. Eventually we arrive; we catch our breath and he greets us at the door as if it's no big deal.

I can't believe I am in this house, in front of real-life Rory. His mum is out of town and he has a friend round. It's the stuff of parental nightmares. Helen and I knock around and laugh at each other for being so drunk. I can't tell if they're horrified by us or enjoying the girlish spectacle. Every time I sit still the alcohol clumps me in the face, so I keep moving. I'm given a glass of whatever happens to be left in his mother's drinks cabinet, which is unfortunately sake, and I am immediately sick. Sick on the way to the loo. In the loo. Outside his house. It's all a blur but at one point my head is in his lap and he strokes my face tenderly.

The next thing I know, Helen and I are walking home. The nightmare is over. My memories of the past hour are utterly chaotic: extreme nervousness, retching, stomach acid, unfamiliar bathroom floors and tissue mopping up spoiled carpets. I am thankful for the cold air, a beautiful contrast to the oppressive four walls of his house. But we are back at Helen's and I am inconsolable. There is nothing less sensual than regurgitated Salsa & Mesquite Kettle Chips on peach-coloured carpet. Inexplicably, however, before I sleep, I get a text from Rory. He says he wants to talk tomorrow and we arrange to meet on MSN.

It's there in the tiny chatbox the next evening that I experience romance more profound than slow-dancing to Jamiroquai in a marquee. He says there were moments in between vomiting where he got to properly look at me, hold me in his arms. He tells me I am perfect. There is a pause. 'Will you go out with me, Hattie?'

I feel sick. My first ever pang of commitment fear.

It's the weight of obligation: inevitable sex.

I type 'Yes :-)' and press send.

Pop culture has entered a period of febrile teen sexuality. The teens in *The OC* and in Abercrombie and Fitch dominate my thoughts, along with movies like *Scary Movie*, *American Pie* and *Coyote Ugly*. Think long hair, nice abs and former Disney stars newly conscious of their groins. When I'm not taping Coldplay off the radio, I am watching MTV obsessively, and I am absorbing every second. When 9/11 happens, Laura calls my house phone to tell me to turn on the news, and I do so reluctantly. Completely unable to process the image of the two burning towers, and what it all means for the future, I quickly slide back into the flashy universe of early 2000s music videos.

Right now, I cannot get over Britney's video for 'I'm A Slave 4 U'. The dark feminine energy of a twenty-year-old megastar controlling the sexual tension of the room. How in-the-moment she and all the dancers are during the orgasmic panting sauna scene. The dimples on her lower back, her sweaty neck, the tummy button piercing, sticky lip gloss and that unflappable facial expression that speaks to a sexual proficiency and steadiness in the face of the oily body-rolling that surrounds her.

The early stages of the new millennium are a post-'Thong Song' planet where anything goes. Videos are cartoonish and cinematic; Eminem has arrived like a bleach-blonde grenade, detonating the sentimental, sweetheart pop of the late 1990s; pop punk videos feature alt-guys lusting over *Playboy*-grade hot girls, while R&B and hip-hop are exploding with experimentation. Missy Elliott, Ludacris, NERD: their videos are as sexy as they are innovative (and if you stay up late enough you can catch the uncensored version of NERD's 'Lapdance', which is essentially porn in a damp-looking shed). Then there's Kylie Minogue and the gold hot pants. That said, I'm also ingesting a lot of sincere and orthopaedic-shoe-wearing singer-songwriters: Dido, David Grey and Macy Gray. I'm open to anything really, from Toploader's 'Achilles Heel' to Aphex Twin's 'Come To Daddy', heaven and hell consumed in quick succession as I flit across the multitude of MTV channels. It's a habit that permanently shrinks my ability to focus but establishes my two preferred aesthetics in both art and life: desperate longing or shiny bum cheeks in tiny pants.

Nine days after we make things official, Rory tells me he loves me. He's frustrated my parents won't let me stay at his house, though, and is nudging me towards questioning their authority. As my parents were art students during the Swinging Sixties, I assumed they'd be encouraging of free love and exploring new horizons, but there's no convincing them on the subject of a sleepover at Rory's. I think my dad finds the whole scenario agonizing – his youngest daughter, who can often be seen ragging around town in a rattling car decked out with subwoofers. My mum and I are falling out for the first time too.

'It's not fair,' I yell at her. 'You and Dad sleep in a bed together every night – why can't we?'

Both incandescent and on the cusp of laughter, she replies: 'We've been married for thirty years, and I'm not doing my GCSEs.'

'It's just mocks!'

'No.'

'Well, he's the love of my life so you'll have to get used to—'

She cuts me off to spare me the indecency. 'Nope, not happening I'm afraid.'

One last weasely wail from me: 'I don't see why it's such a big deal!?!'

I raise my middle finger and mouth the words 'Fuck off' to her turned back as she leaves the room and heads into the kitchen to make my dinner from scratch before crafting one hundred Roman shields out of toilet-roll tubes for the primary school students she's teaching the next day.

In a short space of time, a new mode of resisting my parents' power has been unlocked. Not that I take to the approach naturally, and every stab at rebellion, such as bunking off, sits a little awkwardly. On a wet Wednesday morning I knock on Rory's door so we can walk to school together. The sensation of damp tights and a sodden kilt makes me itchy and uptight. Rory tells me to come inside as he's not ready yet and, following his lead, I sink into a stupor watching an ITV talk show on a tiny TV screen in his attic bedroom. Thirty-seven minutes later I realize I am still waiting for him to give us the green light to get on our way to school, and I cautiously suggest we ought to be leaving.

'Hattie,' he says with his arch smirk, 'I have a free period. And you're late for school.'

In a panic I sprint down the familiar roads leading me to school; the streets without their usual ant stream of dawdling teens trudging their way to lessons. I am a lone species, the only surviving character at the end of a zombie apocalypse. Every step I now take is illegal. Ten minutes into my race towards the finish line, I realize it is futile. I'm already too late; I'd be punished; it'd go on my record. So I decide to turn around, and spend the guilty stroll back to my parents' house in a state of frantic paranoia and joyful anticipation of a day spent watching the video for Vanessa Carlton's 'A Thousand Miles' as many times as possible. I can make this work! I can be bad!

Turning the corner to our cul-de-sac, I am devastated to find that my dad is still at home, his blue Ford parked in the drive. Think quick. There is an alley behind our house – dubbed 'poo alley' by my mum on account of it being a dumping ground for local dogs – so I head there to hide. I spend three hours and forty-five minutes in that alley, a thin pathway flanked by a brutalist concrete wall and a ditch filled with the pages of top-shelf magazines. For a while I squat and rest, gormlessly staring at a photo of a pair of big circular breasts that lie on the mud before me, the porno paper semi-pulped by the rain. Gradually I realize the indignity of this stance will make my excuse of being 'en route to a doctor's appointment' look untrustworthy, should I come face to face with a neighbour or passer-by. So I decide to pace up and down, back and forth. Eventually, I bravely walk back to my home and collapse on the sofa, frightened but revived by the spirit of manic, bloodthirsty anarchy.

This spirit lives on in my pursuit of spending time alone with Rory. Although I am not allowed round his house in the evenings, we still have our ways of seeing each other. I live in a bungalow, which makes it very easy for him to find me whenever he likes. One night, I am taking a break from homework and lip-syncing to the Cranberries' 'Linger' while looking in the mirror, as if I am the girl in the video. He taps on the window, smiling at my extraordinary vanity. It's great to have such easy access to the man I love, but I never fully commit to my mirror-self ever again.

We also hang out after school, and at weekends. The more time we spend together, the more I am beginning to adore his character beyond this fireball of romantic emotion. He is sarcastic and quite quirky, especially when it comes to his relationship with his mum's dog. I get the feeling I'll never get to the bottom of him; he definitely has some issues. Yet his unpredictability and autonomy over his life gives him an unshakable confidence that impresses me and threatens the boys in my year.

Hanging out with him is never easy. I am on edge a lot. Not from what he might do to me, but more the insecurity of following the script on my first proper sexual relationship correctly, and also from the spectre of my parents, who'd hate to think of their youngest daughter snogging so aggressively most afternoons of the week. Being with him in any capacity is an enormous experience. Big feelings, all the time. Sitting on the sofa is two weeks away in the Seychelles – string quartets and a bed of roses. Everything suddenly makes sense. The culture. The Foo Fighters video for 'Walking After You' where Dave Grohl and a woman are both crying and pounding windows because they love each other so much. At one point she eats a dried cracker from a plate and coughs it up because she's so distressed by love. I get it now. Rory squeezes my hand when an advert for a holiday package soundtracked by Savage Garden's 'Truly Madly Deeply' comes on and I feel as if I might combust entirely, as if I am on the brink of choking. I'm dizzy, and while I don't enjoy it as much as I do spitting and yelling with Laura, I keep coming back for more.

When things move on, I first find it incredibly overwhelming, suffocating – the eye contact, bare skin, saliva, friction. But gradually I find genuine pleasure in it all. This is when I start thinking about underwear, the Wonderbras, the thongs, pubic hair. Being a child is inherently gross out of joyful unselfconsciousness and proximity to the ground, but now I'm doing everything I can to be the opposite of that. I'm preening and preparing for something major. I have read that Britney does

1,000 stomach crunches a day, so I'm doing the same, only less committed as I do it on my bed and give up after fifty. I keep having awful periods that last for four weeks. The doctor prescribes me the contraceptive pill Microgynon without any real consideration. I'm ecstatic. While my mum is uncertain about synthetic hormones, I urge her to give it the green light. My initial hopes are that popping it every day will fast-track me to womanliness, but in reality it just makes me unhinged. Beyond the surges of sadness, symptoms mainly include an accelerated interest in food and carbs, and a body that expands at a rapid rate despite three hours of PE a week and numerous after-school clubs. One Saturday afternoon I eat so many Doritos I have to go into his bathroom and make myself sick so I have room for the meal he's making for us. Garlic bread and ricotta-and-spinach-filled pasta. The archetypal 2001 dinner of romance. He later points out that my torso is changing – where once was a lean child is now a woman, one compromised by 'love handles', which sounds like something red and rubber you might see in a sex shop on an episode of *Eurotrash*. Nevertheless, he grabs onto them as we walk around town, and I can't tell if he's proud or mocking me.

His friends who are in couples are now having proper sex; not just foreplay. We discuss it. I say I am more than happy to graduate to this stage. We do it, eventually, me in my grey bra, and it is fairly fine, which comes as a great surprise to me as I've been under the impression we've been doing it for weeks. I even told Helen. Who can blame me for getting it so wrong? I had one sex education lesson: an hour of a sheathing a banana with a condom and trying not to laugh. Other than that, my Barbies taught me everything there was to know about making love. Which was: genitalia does not exist and you can keep your tiny pink heels on if you're in a rush.

Throughout our relationship, now eight months in – five years in adult metrics – Rory flits between extremes. As well as overwhelming waves of affection, he also breaks my heart constantly, and always on MSN. The first time is the worst. I've just come back from seeing relatives in Edinburgh when he tells me it's not working any more. I sit under my desk backlit by the tiny red light of the long plug adaptor, crying and listening to Jeff Buckley – a complex set-up to justify when my mum walks in and asks me to feed the cat. Rory and I get back together a week later, but it's never the same again. I am constantly paranoid that I'll do something wrong, like visiting Edinburgh.

Looking aloof on MSN is now integral to regaining dignity in this relationship and as such, my experience of the messaging service becomes torturous. I go back to my watching; set my status to 'appear offline' and wait for him to log on. Wonder who he is talking to. The longer he is online without me there makes me realize he's finding entertainment elsewhere.

My fear of getting dumped is now amplified by ten. I fire up the Boots-brand ghds and prepare for war. I've noticed the bad patches in our relationship often coincide with my tresses being slightly fluffy, possibly reminding him of the formerly feral, childlike aesthetic that came before. It doesn't help that the girls his age look more put-together, with more access to money and shops. There's a new one who's just joined sixth form. She has a sharp blonde bob, pearly-white teeth, tight jeans, and wears thick makeup to conceal her acne scars. I hide 'offline' on MSN and watch Rory log on, which he does a lot more often, and late into the night.

On my way home from netball practice I pop over to Rory's to say hello. He is using his mum's computer in her bedroom. A message bloops out from the PC. It's MSN and the girl with the bob.

'Saw u at the weekend,' she writes.

Rory decides to reply. 'Oh really? Was I walking the dog?'

'I wouldn't say she's the best looking – but that's no way to speak about your girlfriend.'

He snorts and tells me to calm down.

A week later I run the 200 metres at Sports Day. I try so hard, pelt down that straight strip of grass, and bust my guts out to come first. Bent over and panting at the finish line, I look up to the maths block where a group of sixth formers are watching from afar. My triumph must seem so trivial to them. Rory salutes me sarcastically, while the bob girl claps slowly. The evil president and his First Lady.

The months roll on and the sudden changes of heart continue. I've stopped telling my family about our fickle love affair. As far as they know we are together and fine. I'm doing my GCSEs and they want me to focus on my education. Plus I'd rather they didn't hate him.

Because of the age gap we've become quite a controversial couple, like Angelina Jolie and Billy Bob Thornton but without the leather flares. The girls in sixth form often make snide comments about me when I walk past them in the corridor. They think I'm a slut; it doesn't help that he goes to parties and tells them all my secrets.

My friends, meanwhile, are confused about the chaos of my new life. They think it's like something out of a soap opera. I'm always crying at parties because he's changing his mind about if I'm fit or not. A boy in my year and frontman of a ska punk band writes a song about me with the lyrics: 'She is all alone / When she gets home / And she don't know why / But she's so high'. It's nice to be immortalized in a song but odd to go to a gig and see the people I love skanking along to a story about me weeping.

Annoyingly, I still love Rory and yearn to make things more simple, to run away with him, live somewhere away from the chatter and other girls. Inspired by the music of Dido, I jot my confused thoughts down, pressing record and singing into my Dictaphone incredibly quietly so my parents don't hear:

> Today, I'm not feeling quite so bad.
> Today, you looked inside and saw what I had.
> And right now, I can't see all that clear
> Today, I fought a battle and faced my fear . . .
> Do you know just how I feel?
> I'd like you to know that these words are real
> So if you have the time, please step inside my mind,
> You are the truth I've been searching for.

I press the playback button. I am gobsmacked by the frailty of my voice and vow never to sing again.

The break-ups continue until we hit a year. Things start to get surreal. One time he cites suspected testicular cancer as the reason. The next one feels like the last, because I initiate it. I just can't handle the incessant turbulence any more.

We are at his house on a Sunday and I tell Rory that it's over. His eyes are wide, panicked. He says, 'Thanks, cool', and shows me the door. That went better than expected. Although he does seem disconcertingly wired – as if his fight-or-flight mode has just kicked in and he might go off and punch a wall.

For a moment I feel free. But in the following days, the calls and texts start flooding in, telling me I am perfect, that he will love me for ever. He was going to ask me to marry him but now his future's ruined and he won't let me forget it. If I don't write back, he drives to the top of my parents' drive and honks his horn until I come outside.

Sometimes he comes over very late when everyone is asleep, turns his lights off and waits silently. I've come to dread bedtime, the slow sound of tyre on gravel, a flashing headlight. Other times he will park his car and come down to my bedroom window. Tap, tap, tap. *Wake up, Hattie.*

Under the eerie glow of the moon, he can see me pretending to sleep through a crack in the curtain. He just wants to talk, he says. Sometimes it's easier to comply. On the times that I do, I climb out of my window and he either drives me to a temple on the estate of a stately home and sobs, or we just sit in his car. One way to guarantee I will get up is to phone the landline relentlessly, so I begin to unplug it before bed.

Other times I kick back at his advances, try to implement some distance between us. On one particular night I ignore his taps and knocks on the window. Eventually he gets so frustrated with me he headbutts the pane of glass. It leaves a huge crack down the middle like a lightning bolt. I tell my mum it must have been a branch.

During the day, if I don't return his calls, he'll crawl along the streets in his car looking for me. One time he sees me walk past his house, comes out, smashes his phone on the ground, drags me in by the arm and locks the front door. The back door. He takes me into his bedroom and shouts and cries. Nothing serious happens – nothing incriminating; we're just navigating a weird grey area in which I am frightened and unsure of the protocol. It's all too chaotic for me to process, and I'm too inexperienced to soothe him. I get quite good at tapping out of my emotions and stepping into a fuzzy spaced-out state.

It's the end of the summer and I've done OK in my GCSEs despite the fact I spent a lot of revision time tweezing my leg hair and dealing with a vulnerable young man having a break-down. Rory's passed his exams too and is going to university. I should get some respite then. Before he goes, he leaves one of his notes for me in the garden. This one, like the others, tells me how I *was* perfect but now he sees the truth. I'm not clever or kind; I'm arrogant and like everyone else. Ugly. Reading it makes me cry, as I have no idea who I am yet, and maybe this is true. I bring the note inside, into my bedroom to hide it in a box where I have been keeping memorabilia from this epic period of my life. Growing up in a bungalow has its perks but it's also impossible to have any kind of privacy; my mum, who was a few seconds ago mashing potatoes in the kitchen, is now standing in my bedroom after a mandatory warning knock. She asks why I am crying. I show the letter to her. She is furious with an instinctive maternal rage, and immediately goes to his house to speak to his mum. She is worried too. He left his Hotmail inbox open on her computer and she read an alarming email meant for me. She tells my mum not to worry. He won't be contacting me again.

Just like that, he disappears. The bright heat of the summer slips into the hazy newness of autumn – I am now in sixth form and Rory has left town. I still get a lot of mysterious calls on my phone. Heavy breathing and no words. It should be scary but it's not. Six months later I get in a car crash and he is the first person I want to tell. For better or worse we are still cosmically connected.

I remain in and out of his orbit for many years – he adds me on Facebook, deletes me, adds me again. I am still compliant to his every need and respond willingly with a haunting type of affection. In my early twenties I even agree to meet him one last time. Drawn to the temptation of being so intoxicating to him that he comes undone again, I wear a short summer dress and we go for a drink on the Southbank. I don't feel that same flip in my stomach when I see him as I did at the height of puberty, and I worry that I might have lost my effervescence in age too. We flirt but mostly pretend nothing ever happened, that things didn't get extremely weird. A year later he sends a Facebook message saying he is 'sorry for everything'. I accept his apology, reassure him that it was no big deal and with that he stops heavy breathing down the phone at 3 a.m. Instead I decide to dip in and out of his profiles online. On a good day I am looking at them to ensure he's happy, moved on and at arm's length. On the gloomier ones I am hoping to find a sign that I still mean something to him – a reference to sprinting or Edinburgh. Of which there are none.

The confused memories of this exhilarating period become a blight on my life. Not only did Rory establish my capability to be loved beyond the obligatory family unit and push my evolution from amoeba to adolescent, it also coincided with my addiction to the internet. The distance, the screen between us, gave me an extraordinary ability to exceed myself. As a woman prone to slow reaction times and meekness in real life, I now could partake in meaningful conversations and have an instant connection to someone without the threat of tending to them physically. The melancholy gratification of being able to watch his movements online when we'd lost that closeness in reality was even more seductive.

Rory goes on to live an active, outdoorsy life in Australia. He gets really, really ripped, losing the skatewear immediately, and turns into a kind of corporate hulk in wraparound sunglasses who might glamp or enjoy a gun. His mum moves to Scotland. He gets a girlfriend (it's not Ellie – fuck you, Ellie). He really deserves some kindness and stability, and she looks like she could give it to him – at least via bodycon dresses, gilets on a Sunday, and her ability to make a huge roast dinner once a week. But then he leaves. His Twitter stops. His Facebook is gone. Not on Instagram. He is on LinkedIn but the information is sparse and I'm not prepared to upgrade to

Premium until I have graduated into the FitFlop-wearing era of my life. Instead I check in on his brothers. No sign of Rory but they both seem good. Living their lives. Married, happy.

I really hope he is too. That he is successful and happy, thriving in whatever it is he does that LinkedIn will only partially let me see. Because he was the start of everything. While I had a litany of brand-new insecurities by the time I left him – unsure of whether I was an ugly, arrogant idiot or a perfect angel – I also became a woman who had unlocked an almighty understanding. An assumption that I could control the world. That I knew the thoughts of others just through subtle observation. I learned all of that, for better or worse. But mostly I learned that my mum is always right.

CHAPTER THREE

The Fittest Girl in Year 11

I've been clicking around for ages in search of a photo of Mike that provides some indication of his body shape or bone structure. In the handful of images he's uploaded onto the indie music forum, he's either in a wicker trilby, obscured by others, or distorted entirely by arty digital camera effects, like a slash of squiggly red and yellow striking the centre of his face. Is he an enigma? Some sort of cult-like figure? Or hiding a physical defect?

If it's the latter, I'd guess it's a mildly curvaceous backside; nothing to be ashamed of. It's just crucial for me to know either way so I can cast him in my pre-bed story: our imagined first meeting, soundtracked by Crazy Town's 'Butterfly', in which I am him, watching me move through a busy crowd at a gig. There's a band on stage, Snow Patrol tonight, but I'm the real star; so much so, the bassist is making awestruck eye-contact with me as I smoke and snake around the audience; mystery and mischief embodied. Who is this girl?

Mike – just a fuzzy, expressionless oblong wearing a wicker trilby – begins to approach me. I try to project noses, voices and mannerisms onto him but nothing sticks, nothing fits his frame.

I can't make love to this inaudible shape. This incubus could never sustain a whole sex scene. So Mike's journey stops here, the bass player steps in and I whip my knickers off for him down an alleyway, for the third time this week. Annoying really.

If only Mike would feed the messageboard something – a tooth or a leg. I really don't care what's going on. From my limited experience of the world, everyone generally looks completely great or totally fine, especially if you're funny. Apart from me, that is.

Most people carry some form of trauma from youth into adulthood that threatens to eat away at their self-belief. Startling incidents that rewire the brain: abuse, divorce, illness, death. I have friends who were neglected by their parents; friends who were bullied for their sexuality or the colour of their skin; friends who lived off food banks. They all survived and rebuilt themselves in spite of such hardships. Some people, however, never shake the spectre of that formative ordeal. Sadly I am one of them. Here is my story.

At the age of sixteen, approximately 150 pupils from my school year voted in the majority that I was the best-looking pupil attending my high school. As an annual ritual, our school would hold a kind of popularity census in which teenagers were forced to vote for the class clown, the girl with the shortest skirt, the best couple and, the most coveted titles of all, the Fittest Girl and Fittest Boy in the year. I had to go up on stage and collect the paper certificate from the PE teacher presenting it to me. Crowned in a public ceremony to rounds of applause, and plastered in our yearbook for eternity, I was congratulated for being so incredibly fit by fellow pupils in the corridors for the rest of the week.

I'd like to say my victory happened exclusively because of being conventionally attractive, but there were plenty more beautiful women at school than me. There was Grace, who used to stun assembly audiences with her performance of Mariah Carey's 'Hero'; Annabel, who looked like Nina from the Cardigans; and Kate, whose farts were so cute they made the boys laugh and literally smelt like biscuits. I was conscious of the competition and worked hard. It needed to take off more effectively than my last campaign trail. Year 7, lobbying to become a year prefect, I ran with the slogan 'Don't Be Batty – Vote For Hatty!', and . . . lost?

Not this time. This time around I went on a not-so-subtle rampage. I flirted, both with the guys at the top of the food chain – naughty boys who were fast at sprinting and had earrings and cool trainers – and those . . . I don't want to say the bottom, but the guys who went to Farm Club and didn't brush their teeth that often. If that makes me sound calculated and brutal then please bear in mind toxic noughties culture, 9/11 etc.

Somehow the girl who pined for the Wonderbra momentarily weaponized her assets to gain remarkable mainstream appeal; a brief collision of youthful innocence and risqué adulthood. I felt my allure falling into place: silky, clean, untainted. My legs were toned, exfoliated and tanned. My hair was huge, dangerous in a 'messy bun'. I did citrus peel-off face masks every evening before bed and picked my blackheads every Sunday morning instead of going to church with my mum. The school kilt was rolled up short and midi heels were worn. Silver eyeshadow and peach lip gloss, a chemical fug of peach deodorant and Body Shop White Musk perfume followed me like chemtrails.

In hindsight I did perhaps push my manifesto a little too aggressively at Jimmy Winwood's house party a few weeks before the big vote, where during the evening I repeatedly exposed my breasts to bewildered fellow students. They debuted in a group viewing around 9 p.m., and on request to anyone else milling around the corridors who missed the initial show thereafter. The sound of Christina Low muttering, 'They're not even that big' to Ellen Smith as they looked on in disdain will visit me long into my thirties, and most nights before I drift off to sleep, until I die. I even thought of it as I got dressed on my wedding day.

I'm pretty sure Omar Begg, winner of the Fittest Boy award, wasn't defined by this moment. It didn't hang over him like an albatross, a forever-symbol of one's youth and vitality at its peak. By the looks of his Facebook, he's aged well and is living a fulfilled life as a father of three and driving instructor. I can tell he's never given it a second thought. Because he never craved such superficial validation in the first place.

The ramifications of winning the Fittest Girl in the Year are immediately evident. My first week at sixth form should have been straightforward. The same group of friends and in the same school building I'd been attending for five years. The fundamental framework is all there. However, the main difference – the issue – is the lack of school uniform. Childhood's great equalizer removed.

Until college, the boys I knew were unaware that I didn't wear hotpants to exercise in, or short kilts and tight shirts on a day-to-day basis. The sexy corporate minx they knew and loved was all a mirage.

'Didn't know you were a greebo, Hattie!' Dan Roberts barks at me as I walk through the common room on my first day. It's a stark change from his former calls of 'Get your tits out!' across the assembly hall and my heart aches for this sweet refrain.

I hadn't ever considered myself as 'alternative', but when I'm back home and in the privacy of my bedroom that night I consider how I've evolved over the summer since Rory. Maybe there is an edge to me that I have yet to acknowledge. Maybe I have rebelled – rejected that shiny perfect girl in favour of being a socially oppressed outsider. I wear baggy black hoodies, vast skater trainers entirely engulfed by saggy chords that are ragged and weathered in an arc at the hem. Plus I like cutting-edge alternative music, like Biffy Clyro, Cooper Temple Clause, Hundred Reasons, Electric Soft Parade and Athlete. I've been eking out a spliff's worth of weed for a month and smoking it in the garden when my parents are at the supermarket, then going to bed and worrying about what might happen if they find all the roaches I've buried in the flowerbeds. I guess I'd just leave home and bum around with the rest of the kooks and punks in Camden. Fuck everyone. People = shit.

In reality I have no actual identity beyond having brown hair, and as a result I am having an existential crisis. I'm also not the only one experiencing a shocking rebirth after the post-school summer of transformation. A lot of bullies have dropped out and the nerds have taken over. Not only are they intelligent but they've accrued the requisite physical attributes to shirk the baggage of their gawky early teen years. As well as girls from nearby Essex high schools who've joined and are making valiant efforts to stake their claim as the year's premier babes – the gentle muscular ripples of Stacey's stomach in her casual crop-tops, Chantelle's low-key confidence and cleavage – there are former shy girls unshackled by the freedom of a uniform-less institution. Martha spent her school years covered up in bulky fabrics and living in the library, but has emerged from the summer holidays a real woman. The guys who once winced at being paired with her in science now refer to her as 'The Body'. I didn't realize the nerdy girl makeover existed beyond teen movies but here it is in the flesh – a geek reborn as Jessica Simpson. I wonder if I ought to frame my certificate before it bursts into flames.

While my status has lowered in terms of desirability, being out of the rat race does allow for more time to focus on academia. There's a lot to cherish now I've removed all the brain-mangling maths, science and geography lessons that once gave me so much strife and academic shame. I am studying English Literature, a class that I love, that I've also imbued with an extra sprinkle of *Inbetweeners*-styled titillation thanks to a secret game Laura and I play, whereby we pretend every word or phrase in whatever book we are reading out loud to the class actually refers to wanking. Then there's Theatre Studies, during which I star in a series of challenging, prob-lematic roles – the part of a seven-year-old child with schizophrenia, a woman dying from cancer, Alan Strang from

Equus, who in one act exposes his penis, and for one brief yet regretful scene, 'woman from a remote tribe finds can of Coke in desert'.

Last of all there is History. Good old-fashioned straight-forward learning and hard work, with a touch too much emphasis on UK kings. While I've been predicted mediocre grades based on my mediocre GCSE results and rejected for my top three university preferences as a result, I am for the first time ever keeping up with classes. In my down time from intellectualism I have also found a new and exciting online social group run by dangerously horny music dorks. What could possibly go wrong?

We Love Indie Gigs is a website about loving indie gigs. Set on a black backdrop with garish green font, it's written with a gonzo spirit and is updated every week with cheeky, unor-thodox ideas that would never get past the big-wig editors at the *NME*. It specializes in celebrating the underdog and short, pithy reviews of recent shows and new music – of which there are plenty, and all for free due to the explosion of illegal downloading.

The writers are by and large wannabe music journalists holding a grudge – to whom I'm not sure: the popular kids at school or the people who do it professionally. The tone is generally petty and superior but raw enough for it to be infinitely readable. Extra silly and scandalous, the logo has an illustration of a middle finger in the place of one of the I's and one of its regular features is the 'Indie Mascot' – a woman called Lisa with big boobs who poses almost nude with a band-related slogan emblazoned across her chest. It has the feel of SuicideGirls meets *Viz*. What with the tits and trivial or fetishized descriptions of female musicians (i.e. Björk is an 'Icelandic minx!'), I can't quite tell if the misogyny is ironic, satirizing mainstream media. Surely it's not just a bunch of pervy Manic Street Preacher fans posturing as subversive feminists? I'm sure there's clever commentary about gender in there somewhere. I stare a little harder at the tits. Somewhere.

The risqué reviews are fun but the main lure of We Love Indie Gigs is its 'forum': a hovel for scathing, cliquey music nerds. In 2002, forums are the ultimate way to connect to culturally like-minded people across the world. It's the ideal time to broaden my horizon; I'm feeling claustrophobic in my small town, bored of MSN chats with people I see every day; and while there is a large cohort of 'alt' students in my college (lots of white boys who are into Muse and Rage Against the Machine with stinking matted hair they refer to as dreadlocks, flame shirts, balloon pants or rainbow-coloured headbands), I'm after a more aspirational peer group to satiate my developing tastes.

After sixth form I love to kick back, eat a Babybel and catch up on whatever gossip is flying about on the forum. I marvel at the sheer consistency and energy expunged in this place; its users have so many opinions, all the time, about everything. Whereas I am on the fence mostly. About the new Stills single, why the Libertines are better than the Datsuns, and everything in between. Occasionally I'll consider posting a response to one of the more generic threads about what people are listening to – but I know that 'newbies' get trashed by the core forum group members if they say something too try-hard. There's no way I'm ready to compete.

So I watch for a while. Taking notes. I learn what its main players like and dislike, how to make a subtle entrance that assures you're not berated by the board. It's brutal on there; similar to walking into the sixth form common room and being jeered at for being a greebo. Only here the humiliation is permanent and something you can revisit; worse still, it's about what's going on in your brain; who you really are, rather than whatever you look like that day.

One person who escapes all criticism and navigates every conversation with grace and ease is a popular user named Mike. Swept away by his authoritative and witty posts, I begin to have deep, profound feelings for him; blasting out the Delays' 'Nearer Than Heaven' while combing the forum for previous interactions with former love interests, of which there are many. While he keeps his image concealed, his taste in music and creativity quickly leads me to believe that we are kindred spirits. One evening, emboldened by an A in an essay about *Tess of the d'Urbervilles*, I decide to send him a direct message:

I just wanted to say well done for your posts . they are so funny. it was about time to email the man behind the mouse! Don't get me wrong im not the sort of girl who's only form of friendship emerges from message boards. P.S Glad the genious that was Jeff Buckley's getting the recognition he deserves in your recent post about damien rice!!!!!!!!

No spell-check, eight exclamation marks. How could he resist? Mike replies the next day and is courteous and humble, but it's clear I haven't unlocked a forever friendship. How else can I get him to notice me, if not for my dazzling way with words? It is then I realize my only power to attract attention and respect. By being The Fittest Girl in Year 11.

Among the conversations about Billy Corgan and the latest Glastonbury line-up news, there is a huge, ongoing thread entitled Newbies in which members are free to post images and introduce themselves. It's aggressively flirtatious there; each member poised on the edge of their swivel chairs, waiting for the next image to upload and the cattle market to begin. There's a woman called Astralgirl who has captivated the entire forum with her cool backcombed emo hair and angelic face. She's already a forum celebrity, even though I suspect she's at most fourteen. Most of the images on the thread are kind of tragic – gawky and awkward. But we'll take it; anything. Just knowing there's any kind of human face behind the endless, daily banter, even if it's covered in pimples or loose in the jowl, is enough to allow its users to form an all-encompassing attraction to one another.

I've decided to go with the username 'Mojo_Pin1' – after the first track on Jeff Buckley's album *Grace*. I also toyed with 'Grace1' and 'Lilac_Wine86' – and I have whittled it down to the ideal image to get Mike's attention. He's talked a lot about his love for the band the Pipettes, three hyped female musicians inspired by 1950s girl groups who wear polka-dot dresses. One of its members, Rose, has dark hair, pale skin and blue eyes, and I am thrilled to find a photo from last summer in which I vaguely resemble her. It is taken outside my parents' house in an off-the-shoulder striped French top with a sideways ponytail, lots of eyeliner and an expression of melancholy. Let's not mince words: it's forum dynamite. Using Dad's computer I scan the photo, attach it to an email, download it, crop it in Photoshop. A few Force Quits, restarts and two hours of solid IT later, I upload it onto the forum with a cute caption. *'Hi y'all, this is me.'*

I enjoy the last few seconds of my anonymity before the rush of dread kicks in. Refresh the page. Nothing. A few more minutes pass, refresh the page. My mum needs to use the house phone so I log out and sit in the living room for a while, plucking my leg hair and imagining the worst. Derision or, even more devastating, totally ignored. Once Mum's done I rush back to check my status and there it is. A reply from Mike, who thinks I look lovely, and has sent me his personal email address. I've broken through – I'm in the mainframe and I want more. Still buzzing to the extent I feel sick with euphoria, I decide to scan in another photo and send a follow-up email, keeping things casual:

ello sexy Mike. Heres another picture of me of wot i look like now. Im the hardcore 1 with my middle finger up. If you look closely it looks like my heads coming out of the girl in the middles ear. Hope ur good. Im cold. Nipples like bullets. Need a hug!!!!!!!!!!!!

Mike replies quickly to say that the photo hasn't been attached; I can't figure out what I've done wrong. My dad is the master of computers but I can't ask him to help as it's likely he will very slowly and silently read the entire email chain as I sit next to him. And I'm already regretting the whole nipple thing. So I leave it, knowing there's enough of me out there for Mike to remember me by. For now.

As well as being a fervent social group online, there are real-life WLIG meet-ups, in which friendships are solidified, in-jokes created. I feast on the images of these geeks congregating in pubs, dissecting the dynamics. I am keen to get in on the action. Reading Festival is a major highlight of the WLIG year. Its members camp together and photos are uploaded to the forum afterwards. My best friends and I are going this year as a kind of send-off to our school years together. Plus, now I've been approved by one of the forum's most revered members, I've got a golden ticket to social acceptance; crowds will part when I enter the site. The queen has arrived.

In the weeks running up to the event, Mike and I exchange flirty emails and begin to talk on the house phone. Not so long ago it was my dream to have unfiltered access to such an idol, but I have now come to dread the calls. They're cutting into my essay-writing time and last for hours, but I can't say no. Although he is sensitive, extremely complimentary and ambitious, it is tiring work being the manic pixie dream girl for such extended periods of time. I have a list of revered cultural figures who I reference to get pulses flowing – 'Nigel Godrich' or 'Michel Gondry' for example – but most of all I ask plenty of questions. I ask what I should do with my future or if he has any advice about breaking into the music industry. It's a superpower, really, because while I am actually watching an episode of *The OC* with the sound on mute, I am also appearing assertive, and in return he is empowered by his tutoring role.

It's during these conversations that I also realize my high-octane relationship with Rory was not the norm. There's something perfunctory about my chats to Mike, as if I'm in a constant audition to prove I'm the most interesting person on earth; trading in information and cultural opinions rather than anything heartfelt, sincere or dramatic. I can convince myself that listing facts and enforcing mentorship is a worthy way to win someone's affection, but I miss the panic in the heart of primal attraction.

Our lengthy chats also involve careful planning so my parents don't intercept. Once again I've decided to enter an age-gap controversy by pursuing a 25-year-old while seventeen. Mike is comfortable with the dynamic as I appear pretty self-possessed, but I don't want him to be conscious of my lack of independence in the home. So I am hyper-vigilant when he calls. Sometimes my parents will walk in and I'll hang up the phone immediately, leaving Mike confused by the abrupt end.

Thankfully, I can pass this spontaneity off as being quirky and impulsive. The character I am going for is coy, quizzical, intellectual and random, and hanging up abruptly is just something a complex babe like that would do. And I suppose I am actually feeling quite complex at the moment, only not in a very horny way. The Microgynon still makes me sobby at night, I cry like a baby until I fall asleep, and I can't deny the fact I feel unattractive compared to the new girls at sixth form.

In my darkest moments I'm frustrated I can't just cut off chunks of my stomach with scissors or get a respectable quote for a minor liposuction session. Or a colonic. What I'd do for a colonic; to start over with my intestines from day dot again. Not that I'd mention any of this to Mike. As far as he's concerned, I'm a tiny fairy up a tree, listening to Jeff Buckley and giggling at the stars; a mere hallucination of a woman.

Reading Festival rears its head and I brace myself for the big meet. My best friends and I travel together on the train; I decide not to tell them about my plans to meet a man off the internet as they rightfully consider this excursion as a chance to spend time together before we each go off to different universities.

As soon as I step on site, I'm hit by the air: filled with the thick fug of festival musk; a dank flat stench like human manure, burning plastic, suspicious burgers and bongs. I feel like I've arrived in my spiritual home. The pounding music colliding from multiple stages gives me a sense of surging confidence and I immediately change out of my modest black t-shirt and jeans into a military-styled dress and a hat like the one Jamiroquai wears in the 'Space Cowboy' video. Emboldened by the bass rumbling from the Reel Big Fish set in the background, we go and explore. My swagger is soon punctured when a half-naked boy skids into me so fast he knocks my lunch into the air, and a group of sixteen-year-olds point and laugh at my jacket potato collapsing onto the contaminated mud.

Friday at the festival dissolves into carnage: sunburned faces shrieking, rowdy lads setting fire to tents, my stamina reducing each time I squat over the Portaloo, to the point that I eventually surrender and sit on the seat, absorbing the multi-textured liquids with hedonistic abandon. 'Whatever,' I mouth to myself as I hear shocking splats from the toilet next door. As the hours pass I grow more conscious that I could bump into the WLIG forum guys at any point and drink cider excessively to banish the nerves. I can't believe we are free to do whatever we want for three days but the limitlessness feels frightening when bustling alongside bigger boys with madder appetites for destruction. At my worst I am pushed and shoved and covered in a stranger's urine; at my best I am watching Morrissey play 'How Soon is Now' at sunset and feeling like a giant.

Saturday night is the night Mike and I plan to meet. At 10 p.m. I slink off from my friends and head over to Brown camp. It's the opposite end of the festival site from where we're camped, and the afternoon sun has dried the mud into a clay-like consistency that makes it impossible to wade through. The metal pathway is coming undone at the hinges; the security given up, the infrastructure of the festival falling apart.

On my two-hour trek there are endless high fives and free hugs forced on me by grotty groups of guys pumping out songs like Bran Van 3000's 'Drinking in L.A.' on tinny speaker systems. I keep passing the same people, the same landmarks. I am so lost, and yet still determined to get a glimpse of the man in the flesh.

Eventually I arrive at the right camp. I follow the landmarks and flags to see Mike's trilby on the horizon. Had it not been for the cider, I would have held back for a moment and observed, planned my entrance, and arrived elegantly, but instead I barge in with a garish 'Wheeeey!', ready to party, which receives a muted response from the WLIG crew, who are sat around a quiet speaker listening to the Pixies. It's anti-climactic in the way meeting anyone off the internet is – surly characters behind the keyboard tend to be timid and are often startled by real life. Mike remains true to form at least. He speaks as if he is always reading off a script, and while he's not radiating the ultra-sleek confidence that he does online, he welcomes me in with enough warmth to make me feel safe. Sitting in a circle, they debate the night's headliners; it feels great to be part of the forum's core, even if I'm not there by merit or force of personality, but because I might potentially have sex with one of them.

Mike hands me a bottle of vodka, which I drink neat. Another guy offers me a spliff, which I accept. This combination of the hot and cold, up and down, sends a warm wave of nausea into my body, gripping the sides of my brain, dragging it into my throat and pummelling it into the pit of my stomach. This is it then. I won't feel good again for five hours. I've finally made it to WLIG headquarters and I'm pulling a whitey.

For either ten or forty-five minutes I am quiet, praying the group can converse without me while it passes, and that nobody asks for my opinion. I am nodding and laughing, and hoping beyond all hope my reactions are appropriate for the current topic of conversation, which I cannot follow as my hearing has been muddled by the drugs and the sentences are hurtling from every corner of the campsite. Did the goths in the tent behind us just say that 'Bryan Ferry looks like the day Friday,' or was it Mike? Please, Lord, say it wasn't me, using my fingers pursed together as if my hand was a puppet. Unfortunately the nausea never passes; it only worsens with resistance. It will not cease unless I am in the foetal position on a cold bathroom floor eating toast.

The vodka bottle makes its way around the circle once more and Mike gestures it in my direction. When I shake my head and feign a smile, he touches my shoulder delicately and asks if I am OK. I shake my head again, certain now that my skin is green, and he helps me stand up by the arm as if I am an elderly witch. I then hide by the side of his two-person tent, and it's there, on arrival at his long-awaited love-making palace, that I squat on the floor and retch in the entrance for a few minutes before finally throwing up to completion. Somehow the hat stays on but to the detriment of its woollen tassels.

I hurtle into the next chapter of the night with an alarming loss of muscle tension. I am in Mike's tent, where he is spooning me. My belly is big and bloated so I undo my high-waisted jeans. The relief is magnificent but brief, as his hands cradle my tummy like a proud husband with his pregnant wife, and I am cogent enough to know they are now heading towards my pants, slowly but with intent, cold and soft fingertips searching for consent and losing patience. I think of the pants – covered in traces of other people's bodily fluids from the long days in communal loos, and I think of how disgusting this all is, that I don't want to be here, and of Pink's Top Hat in the 'Lady Marmalade' video, and that I wish I was lying in a tent next to Laura, and that I wish I didn't have vomit in my nostrils. After a succession of drowsy hand taps, he gives up and I pass out.

A few hours of blackout later, I wake to a blanket of dense heat on the floor of Mike's tent, surrounded by dead bugs, a water bottle full of urine or squash, and a box of Nature Valley crunchy bars. I peel my body off the floor, say goodbye to the pile of sick that sits outside in the morning sun, and begin the hike back to my campsite. My head is fuzzy and full of embarrassment, yet a new day has begun and I can tell by the strewn sanitary towels on the pathway home that I am not the only person who had a wild night out and regrets it. As I take in snapshots of frazzled conversations from people who've been up all night, or dedicated music fans planning their hourly band-watching schedule with precision, I kind of feel like I belong.

When I return to my friends, they are up and already having fun; all sorts of in-jokes from the night before are flying around – something to do with Paul Hamm, the word 'chode'. Everyone is having good clean innocent fun, apart from our friend Aiden, who took ecstasy for the first time and now looks as if he's committed a homicide. They ask where I've been and I can tell by their expressions – not laughing like I'd intended, but wincing in a sympathetic way, especially when I do an impression of Mike's hands creeping into my knickers – that what happened last night was actually quite sad. We head off to see Finnish rockers the Rasmus get pelted by bottles of piss, before hopping on a train back to our respective homes, whereby I avoid eye-contact with my mother for the next three days until the guilt has subsided.

★　★　★

Despite the vomit outside his tent, I am keen to meet up with Mike again. I feel a desperate urge to prove that I'm more than just a girl hurling in a bad hat. He's game too, so without thinking too deeply, I buy a one-way ticket to London and step on the train. When he greets me at his door, he is pillowy; feminine almost. We are both in our off-duty attire – Mike is without his trilby and wears a burnt orange hoodie made of t-shirt fabric, while I am dressed in flares and a strappy top on top of another strappy top and three layers of beaded neck-laces. I am given a cute cuddle in the doorway as if I am his pet, and he shows me into his apartment.

Mike was always secretive about his day job on the forum, but the exposed brickwork of his front room reveals a potentially large corporate wage that throws me off when I first walk in. It's a fanboy flat full of huge framed posters of artists, a manda-tory bubble-gum machine and a lot of light-wood IKEA furniture, including a coffee table with an abandoned packet of cheese and onion crisps on it. I considered a KitKat on the train too decadent ahead of a romantic union, but here he is killing time by eating a snack with the most fetid aftertaste possible. I compliment him on his spacious home and he thanks me while pouring a glass of Dr Pepper from a two-litre bottle. Mike says the schedule for the day is as follows: 'Tonight we'll go to a pub and then on to see the Thrills in Shoreditch. But,' he says with the roguish enthusiasm of a whimsical tour guide wearing a tiny silk scarf, 'before all of that, what could be fun is to turn all the lights off, shut the curtains and watch a horror film in bed.'

'Definitely, sounds good,' I reply with a vacant stare while mentally skyrocketing out of my body.

As predicted, we barely get past one drop of snot in the *Blair Witch Project* before his wafer-thin jumper and my jeans and necklaces are in a pile on the floor by the bed. I guess he has got a kind of gumption I respect, even though part of me hoped we might just go to Bella Pasta and the Natural History Museum, rather than make love to the sound of cracking twigs and crying women. I have spent a long time imagining what this moment would be like – or, rather, trying to fuck a trilby-wearing ghost down an alleyway – so I owe it to my former self to live out my fantasy in reality.

For the rest of the day we do a kind of newly-engaged-couple choreography that makes me nauseous: agonizingly long and meaningful stand-up cuddles and post-coital cups of tea in his kitchen, while rattling off an array of pre-prepared questions about recent album releases that I have been drafting for weeks but deliver with the breezy confidence of a preco-cious student wooing her lecturer on the last day of term. High on caffeine and Dr Pepper and scared that a silence might devolve into another bed-bound horror-movie session, I dare to show him my impression of a pterodactyl, which involves crouching on the floor and jutting my shoulder blades out like wings, while making a wiry squawking sound. I know straight away that it is too raw (much like the sick) and that it has punctured the honeymoon ambience. After a muted response from Mike that segues into some facts about *Jurassic Park*, he mentions that some of the local forum guys might come to visit us later, perhaps as a kind of threat to stop me from doing more gross stuff. This puts me on edge. I have not prepared enough questions for a panel situation and my stomach lurches at the possibility of having to win over his circle of loyal female friends, who will be wary of me, a reckless teen, and protective of Mike, an innocent adult male. I do not have the bandwidth to play the part of the stable future girlfriend rather than the one-off fling I absolutely intend this to be and wince every time his phone beeps at the prospect of their arrival.

Starving and drained of emotional sincerity, I prepare for a night out, one of the legendary nights out I've seen in the photos on the forum. Instead, we eat Dairylea Dunkers while standing outside a service station near the gig venue. It's the cheese and chive flavour my mum used to get for my packed lunch and I'm upset he hasn't considered that I've come all this way and might prefer a hot dinner. While at the gig I realize I hate the music; that I only know two songs and I am nodding along really fast as if I truly appreciate it, understand it, when I am actually just trying to process the day. I am seething, and resentful of all the creative ventures he's told me he'll pursue next year – the articles he'll write, the niche record labels he'll launch, the urban fantasy film he's written and will finish soon, the rushes of which are already looking really exciting. How happy-go-lucky and boyish he is while I am sad, hungry and running out of energy to be adorable.

The gig ends, there are no surprise visits from additional friends, and when I eventually leave the next day – with a sore neck from nodding and having faked sleep for six hours waiting for an acceptable hour of the morning to come around – he walks me to the local station, which is still quite a distance away from Liverpool Street, where I will get my train home. I feel a shameful sense that he wants me gone, too; that it was perhaps more fun for him when we were on the phone or on the internet; when it was a three-hour slot rather than twenty-four hours of slimy human interaction.

The tank is dry. I stand on the platform weak and unable to muster one more question about Evil Dead II or Jack White. I deduce that if I can't be prodigiously fit and I can't appear erudite then I will have to be excessively kind. 'Thank you, Mike, thank you so much,' I say with the sincerity of a woman on her deathbed to a nurse.

On the train home I vibrate with anger. Not at Mike, but at my obsequiousness and enthusiasm for enhancing his experience of the weekend. As if he weren't already deified by the forum and supported by a sneaky side-hustle in market trading. This is how he'll remember me now. A keen girl eternally grateful for her Dunker and dalliance with an indie gig hero.

I visit the forum that night with a sense of bloodthirsty vigour. Ignoring a new post about a Radiohead in-store, I enter the Newbie thread, type the words 'My name's Harriet and I wish I was Mike', delete it, and log out for good.

CHAPTER FOUR

Chriiieaaaaaash

It's not until Lewis walks into my brown bedroom in Bournemouth that I am conscious of how many images of Chris Martin's face there are on the walls. Chris on the cover of *Q Magazine*, Chris scratching his head on a French tour poster, Chris on the cover of the *NME*, Chris on a barren beach looking out to sea. No sooner had I been unleashed from the back of my parents' car on the day I left home for university than I had administered the little balls of Blu Tack for my poorly considered interior-design concept. Bournemouth, this is me – along with the 8-inch Jelly Belly figurine, the seven belts slung over a light fitting, and a framed photograph of my cat Kato drinking water from a bidet.

Lewis remains silent. My new friend holds a great power in saying very little in this moment. A quick 360-glance of the room and a raise of his eyebrows tells me all I need to know about my self-appointed status as the world's most dedicated rock chick. I'm realizing now, in the reflection of his startled eyes, in my aggressively low-slung bootcut jeans, that I am a parochial loser.

We go back downstairs where we lean on lentil-soup-coloured cabinets in the tiny kitchen and consume tea with semi-skimmed milk seven days past its expiry date. Lewis is telling me about what it's like to be on MySpace, a platform that showcases the talents of a new era of creatives as well as a load of 'scene kids and pricks with bad hair'. He is the drummer of the DIY group Help She Can't Swim, and via MySpace they've been building a fanbase, getting opportunities and achieving proper band-status milestones: travelling the UK with Dev Hynes's band Test Icicles, selling merch, doing photo-shoots. What do they sound like? 'Riot grrrl' and 'Mathrock'. 'Okay,' I say. He likes Mouldy Peaches, Cat Power and Deerhoof. I nod in fake recognition and silently inhale the smell of cheese wafting from my tea – while I don't know what any of these names mean, it's fun. Exciting. I'm learning something. Finally, I'm at uni!

I used to think I was an authority on music. As well as the forums, I was brought up in a home in which something was blasting out of a speaker in every room; a constant education in '50s rock 'n' roll, '60s pop, '70s soul, '80s new wave and whatever contemporary music had caught my dad's attention on the radio – there was zero prejudice, where you could hear the hour-long onslaught of Gavin Bryars and Tom Waits's 'Jesus' Blood Never Failed Me Yet' played back to back with Rachel Stevens's 'Some Girls'. I studied the *NME* as if it was cutting-edge contemporary literature and looked down at inhabitants of my small Essex town who were largely preoccupied with drum 'n' bass and classic rock. Lewis's short yet mind-expanding conversation with me has opened up a cavern of subcultures that I now need to know about. More subversive and complex, they thrive online; not just on MySpace but the pages of fledgling music website Pitchfork. It's 2004 and I am aware the Strokes have altered the course of music and fashion and the Arctic Monkeys and Franz Ferdinand are spearheading this thing called the New Rock Revolution. There's a lot of peacocking: backcombed hair, pointy shoes and pork-pie hats. Perhaps this might be to cover up the very literal, some might say naive, lyrical styles of the time, which includes descriptions of what people look like, where they live, what they're drinking and what their phone numbers are. Lewis finds all of that quite funny, and so do I, even though I've secretly never felt more alive than when raging alone in my room to the Kaiser Chiefs' 'Oh My God'.

Lewis is the coolest person I've ever met. He possesses the good looks of both Graham Coxon *and* Damon Albarn but is from a tiny town in the New Forest so is self-aware and sweet. He has the refined taste of someone who's grown up in a city but the softness and offbeat sense of humour of a country lad – the sort of quality that reminds me of my friends back home. Somewhere along the way I've convinced him I'm worth his time. Soon that might be coming undone, however, and my cultural ignorance isn't the only detail dragging my reputation into the gutter. There's also the issue of my housemates.

At some point during the application process, possibly on A-Level results day when I was out celebrating, a form was filled out by my mum and a box ticked stating I was an 'introvert' who would rather live in an eerie back alley of Bournemouth than with 96 per cent of the rest of students on campus. I can see how she arrived at that conclusion, because I did spend much of my childhood blushing any time

I was presented to anyone I'd not previously shared a bath with. Also, I can't really complain, as I was out strawpeedoing Blue WKDs when I should have been filling out important paperwork. Nevertheless, Mum really punk'd me there.

There's just three of us living in this semi-detached house, three bodies exploring an alien and often upsetting dynamic, our first experience of life beyond the familial bubble. Matthew from Bath has the bedroom downstairs. He is a lumbering farm boy with thick black hair, has the granite-hard confidence of a young Tory and is prone to leaving half-eaten tins of beef stew in the fridge that ultimately get nudged off balance and dribble onto the lid of my cottage cheese. If he thinks something is gross or unusual, he exhales: 'Chriiieaaaaaash' out of the corner of his mouth – maybe this is some bizarre West Country variation of 'Christ', but I daren't ask.

Matthew emits this sound often because he is perplexed by Raquel, our other housemate. She is a taciturn trainee nurse from Wales, who works long, gruelling hours, and we see very little of her. She is short and stout with curly hair and braces and scuttles in and out of the kitchen to avoid small talk. She is the shyest person I've ever met. Or perhaps she simply has nothing to say to this semi-threatening Clarkson-esque clown and the girl who sleeps within a Chris Martin shrine.

There's definitely a rogue energy bubbling under the surface, however. I know this because I am privy to her private ceremony of release. Once a month, between 2 a.m. and 3 a.m., I'll hear the boom of a Ministry of Sound compilation thumping through her bedroom walls. There's bumping and footsteps but no words: it's like she's bottled up weeks of tension and is now unleashing it in one burst. Alternatively, she could just be using the music to cover up the noise of her attacking a pillow with a photo of Matthew's face stapled onto it.

Raquel's freakout sessions are so infrequent that deep sleeper Matthew doesn't even notice the racket. It's where she comes from that appals him, her awkwardness affirming his dark belief that people from anywhere but Somerset are underdeveloped as a species. His bigotry in general is astounding. Some afternoons we'll watch children's daytime TV together and he'll shout things like 'Boys like that simply should not be on TV – scum!' at some seven-year-old boy from Wigan with a shaved head getting gunged. One night Matthew and his friend from home return from a big night out, run upstairs into my bedroom, switch on all the lights, tug off the duvet and laugh at me in my pyjamas, before shouting: 'Off! Off! Off!' and pumping their fists in the air. I laugh, scramble for the covers, and lock my bedroom door from thereon in.

Lewis is a man who is comfortable in himself and consistent in social situations; he reacts in the same way to Raquel and Matthew's odd presence in the house as he does to my bedroom: disconcerted but polite, and never nasty. After our tea he heads off to see his friend Ciaran who lives nearby, and I sit for a while digesting our conversation. Lewis and I haven't known each other for long – just two weeks. We first met in Consortium, one of the edgier clubs in the town centre, where he was surrounded by boys and girls with good hair, denim jackets and ripped skinny jeans. By comparison I believed that night that I was a little more glamorous.

After recently kicking off the parental stabilizers, I have been bolstered by a new kind of confidence. I am a blank slate, and I can be whoever I want to be. The combo of white rum and lime cordial and being liberated from my hometown has led to a unique approach to clubbing attire: part business casual and part vintage twee. The night I meet Lewis, I've donned a green-and-yellow A-line vintage skirt worn as a boob-tube dress, clinched by a pink belt and topped off with a pair of Robin Hood-styled suede black boots. There are lots of wooden bangles. The stacking of jewellery has never been my strong point; it requires a certain curated clutter that only the arty or rich can conceive of and yet I am in my Primark and multimedia-journalism era of experimentalism and giving it a go. My face meanwhile is covered in shoddily applied kohl eyeliner with glittery black eyeshadow. I've back-combed the sides of my hair, straightened my fringe and left the back to dry curly. Pale foundation – only on the nose.

In the venue, I knock back shots of sambuca, make liquorice roll-ups and talk a big talk about my dreams of becoming a music critic. I had Cool Doritos and sour cream and chive dip for dinner so it's likely my breath is bad, but thankfully I'm saved by the fact the whole place smells of cigarette smoke. On the night we met I was under the impression Lewis was bedazzled by my sophistication and independence. Knowing what I know about him now, perhaps he just found my normalcy and cluelessness endearing.

I don't get around to making a MySpace profile until I'm back home after my first term. When I do, I'm shocked at the vista that reveals itself to me. MySpace puts self-expression at the forefront; a window display of all your quirks and cultural interests. It's a destination for artistic people, attractive teens and twenty-somethings to hustle, socialize and potentially arrange sex; the possibilities feel endless; erotic, revolutionary. I go with the flow, accepting the friend request from MySpace founding member Tom, who is ironically the most creatively bereft and asexual man I've ever seen.

There's a whole style and language to adopt in order to prosper in MySpace, and it's the perfect tonic to the culture I witness in most Bournemouth nightclubs: terrifying blue and black hangars filled with threateningly alpha beefcake guys and ultra-glam girls. If MSN was all about conversation and connection, messageboards about gossip, humour and community, MySpace is the internet imagined by Rob from *High Fidelity*. How you look and what you listen to is who you are. With the right choice of song on your profile, quirky interests and punchy images, you can become adored not only in your micro-communities, but the world. An awkward emo girl from Hove hated by her peers at school can bewitch hundreds of kids in America with one overly exposed bathroom photo taken in front of a toothpaste-splattered mirror.

After adjusting to the shock of this new terrain, I search for Lewis's profile. It leaves me breathless. He is impressive in real life but has managed to translate his essence onto MySpace in a minimal and effortless way. He has a neatly curated selection of photos – scans of Polaroids and shambolic live shots of his band in which he wears vintage t-shirts to devastating effect. They're noticeably unlike the digital-camera pictures I've been taking of my new uni friends: in these photos we are red and shiny, standing in groups of eight, arms draped around each other and smiling too hard in ill-fitting tops. On MySpace, photography is considered and stark. There are a bold new breed of girls, often from cities like Brighton or Leeds, who have bowl haircuts and are armed with a frank type of flirtation. 'Fit,' reads a comment by one girl, Kim, who is always there, under his photos, in his comments.

Kim is from another planet all together. She has curvy, clean proportions that enable her to pull off a lot of bright Lycra leggings and leotards. I've never seen someone so photogenic, so blemish-free. A dainty little piercing sparkles from her flawless nose. The fringe is so impeccable I am convinced it is made of wood. She's really sarcastic and likes some of the extreme-noise guitar music that Lewis does. What's wrong with raging to the Kaisers? I keep clicking through more images, hoping I'll find the truthful one – the snapshot in which her pores and cellulite are exposed. I sigh with a private resignation when I realize that even her pores and cellulite are exquisite; a sign of her vitality and anti-establishment approach to beauty standards. I move on to the other fawning women cluttering Lewis's comments section. There's Kiera. Her profile is getting a lot of heat from boys in bands like the Horrors. She's different from Kim; her images are gothic – black and white and stylized – art. Her face is a lost little doll but there's a foreboding darkness behind her eyes which implies bohemian depths, like that she possibly owns crystals, and loves Tom Waits.

I dust myself off from the initial shock of the images before conceding that it's not completely out of the question that I can compete in this arena. I pick up my digital camera and flit through the photos I've taken recently. First thought is: face is always quite flushed. Whether I am eating a jacket potato in the canteen in spring or standing in a garden in November with a sparkler. There's one where I look presentable but you can see the gaps where my four teeth were taken out when I was twelve, my nose is oily and I'm standing with my course-mates, who are all dressed as cowboys, in a grotty student bar. My jeans are too low; I'm realizing this now. And the hair. It's not quite right. My photo archive offers nothing but I can try something new. I put some eye makeup on and do a shoot holding my iPod next to my face, praying Mum doesn't come in and ruin the momentum. I crank up the exposure and upload the best one. Not sure what I'm trying to say exactly – 'music, generally' – but it's better than any of the photos of me at Bar Med, amped up on vodka having stumbled away from a dancefloor pumping out the *Grease* megamix.

While the images of other women bring me spikes of angst, MySpace quickly becomes the way in which my brain derails thoughts of academic regret and failure, because straight out the gate I realize I've chosen the wrong course. I am too shy and childish for news journalism. It involves seeking out stories, chit-chatting with locals and cold-calling public figures to get interviews. I struggle to ring a GP to book a smear test, let alone corner a policeman to get the inside scoop about a fatal stabbing. Instead of learning how to be direct and decisive, I am much more comfortable resorting to avoidance and fibbing.

Nowhere is this more pronounced than in our video jour-nalism lessons. At the start of the autumn term, our tutor asks us to shoot a documentary, and I choose to explore the rising number of STIs among twenty-year-olds. Instead of visiting a local clinic to interview a doctor or a patient who'd be willing to speak on the record, I enlist the help of a guy from Yorkshire I vaguely know, who agrees to sit on Bournemouth beach and talk about his fictionalized and debilitating penis disease. Pat is the sort of guy who, in the most affectionate possible way, looks like a smell. He lollops around campus in a permanent, functional state of either drunk or stoned. With that in mind, it doesn't take much to lure him in. Two free beers later and he's looking out to sea melancholically while talking about how his 'agonizing genital crabs' have ruined his attempts to forge a meaningful relationship. He puts in a sublime performance, reminiscent of Matt Damon's breakdown in *Good Will Hunting* – if he were drunk and his pubes were covered in crabs.

My report into the rise of graffiti in Bournemouth was no better. After a lukewarm response to my STI documentary, I shoot for the stars and aim to be more courageous – managing to arrange a face-to-face interview with a local councillor. The big day comes but despite being armed with a print-out of a map, I find myself lost in the backstreets of Boscombe, the heroin capital of the UK and a forty-minute walk away from the huge shiny council offices in the centre of Bournemouth where I'm supposed to be. Devastated by my stupidity, I head back home to binge on Kim's profile – her face covered in immaculate neon makeup, her cheek squished against that of a model whose face must be chiselled from concrete. I visit the model's page, and his friend's page, and their band's page, and their fans' pages, and on and on until I am so numb with envy that I forget about my journalistic disappointment. The next day, to fill the void of substantial journalism, I shoot dramatic zoom shots of some of the locals tagging under bridges and on brick walls, and on top of the footage narrate sensationalist statements in my best sensationalist news anchor voice – lamenting this horrendous, community-wrecking crime/vehicle for local creatives. It's a complex debate.

Three years is a long time to feel miserable because you've misjudged your capabilities as a person. Instead of focusing on the long-term drag of finishing my degree, I take life minute by minute, a mental secondment to MySpace whenever I need it, which is chronically. I am enthralled by jealousy, a pernicious rapture that sits closely to pleasure in its spikes of adrenaline. I am half canvassing for style and cultural information to improve myself, and half desperate to discover a trivial detail that might make me feel in some way superior to Kim: a joke that lands badly, or an unflattering photo posted without approval by one of her friends. But Kim is flawless. She is out there living her life – she moves with the fashion and begins to visit London, where nu-rave and club culture is booming, a scene enhanced by party photography galleries such as DirtyDirtyDancing. Within these galleries I scan the hundreds of images of dazzling It-girls like Agyness Deyn, Uffie and Lovefoxxx until I find one of Kim, luminescent and adopting one of the prevalent poses of the time: tongue out, peace sign across the eye.

Lewis and I have remained in regular contact since those first weeks. We email every so often too, and our eyes meet on the crowded Consortium dancefloor every Tuesday. He is easy to be around, playful and perceptive. To receive one of his withering put-downs – and I receive them often – is the ultimate stamp of his approval. What he doesn't know, and could really have a field day with, is the depths of my MySpace addiction. He doesn't know that I know Kiera has faded out and Kim is taking the lead. I've ascertained by comments such as 'cool hanging with you' that they are visiting one another in their respective towns. In one envious self-improvement rage I go out and get my nose pierced like her, but the globule-like silver ball looks inelegant on my pink nose compared to the diamanté glimmering from Kim's immaculate brown skin. It slips out one night when I am asleep on a friend's living-room floor and I decide it is a sign to leave that dream behind.

Yet in spite of these many neuroses I have managed to explore some additional potential love interests. I put in the graft as soon as I make my way into university each day – rolling a cigarette and listening to David Bowie really loudly on my Discman so all the boys on the top deck can acknowledge that a highly evolved student has entered the bus. That kind of showboating continues throughout the day as I stroll around campus and ends in the evenings, at any of one Bournemouth's bars. At one rock club held at The Villa I meet a guy called Andy, who has shoulder-length hair, flares, long tight t-shirts, constantly erect nipples and a keyboard in his room. He plays self-composed modern classical pieces while I sit on his bed pretending to get emotional. We mostly meet up after the club night has ended. Frankly, I should be lucky anyone is interested in me after my performance at that place. Each time 'Are You Gonna Be My Girl?' by Jet comes on – which is three times a night – I point to my 'big black boots / and long brown hair', both of which are smattered in alcohol and sweat, and in that moment I believe I might just be Bournemouth's most intoxicating muse, rather than a pink sausage in a matted wig hurtling through puffs of dry ice.

Things fall apart with me and Andy because he gets really annoyed when I'm on my period and don't want to get naked. I have also met Gareth, who is a slight graphic designer from Bristol who likes *Spirited Away* and Squarepusher, but has a long-term girlfriend from back home. I convince Gareth that I like Studio Ghibli and industrial dance music too, and soon enough he calls it quits with his high-school sweetheart. Andy finds out about Gareth when there's a fire drill in the halls of residence, a huge block of flats they both live in. We're evacuated and Andy catches me hiding behind a bush in Gareth's t-shirt after not replying to his texts all night. His nipples double in size and he storms off, never to be seen again.

Life becomes slightly less socially turbulent towards the end of my second year, because I am tired and distracted. I've decided it's about time I lose the chip-and-dip weight. Dieting is now my hobby, inspired by celebrity stylist Rachel Zoe, a hyper-wealthy, high-functioning thin person inadvertently pioneering the aesthetic of an eight-year-old with an opioid addiction. It will take a lot of work without the personal trainers and mineral injections, but I am prepared to do anything, except quit alcohol or start to exercise.

My living situation has also improved. Long gone are the

backwater days of Raquel and Matthew; I now live in the centre of Bournemouth in a filthy flat above a chip shop and my new housemates include Emma and Becki: photogenic, sexy blondes who know how to do makeup and get followed around the aisles of Asda by perverts. I learn from them how to pout ironically and where to buy cheap versions of whatever is in fashion. Then there is the hair. It's hard to explain just how important the side parting is in 2005. My fringe is an enormous greasy swoop. Half of my head is a fringe.

Over on MySpace, I've deleted the iPod image – too on-the-nose – and replaced it with a close-up black-and-white self-portrait. I am hoping my expression is of someone who's been caught off-guard smiling at a compliment from across the room. To be captured unaware looking elegant is my ultimate ambition, but when I'm on a night out I'm still hurtling around like the aforementioned sausage in wig, so for now it'll have to be contrived.

Sadly there's not a lot incoming, compliment-wise. A bit of banter with my coursemates, but I'm not crossing streams; there's no interaction with anyone from, say, Sheffield. I've added a few additions to my profile to create a fuller picture of my personality. MySpace allows users to add a song to your profile; a theme tune of sorts. I choose the sassy, sarcastic 1980s new wave track 'I Know What Boys Like' by the Waitresses – a song I hear once on the radio and decide defines my entire life. My age is set to '99' and I've written a subversive blog about doing an Easter Egg hunt in my parents' garden. The overall profile is fine, slightly directionless, trying quite hard to be witty and sOmETiMeS UsInG ThIs fOnT. I'm not garnering the external validation of Lewis's girls. It's a real skill to articulate the best parts of your identity online, one that I will never grasp.

The truth is that my brain is myopic. Occupied by thoughts of small bodies. There are the bodies of women on MySpace: specifically, the many underage girls who emulate Edie Sedgwick, either by artful design or just having minute bodies and big eyes. (As a tribute to the famed Warhol muse, I cut all of my hair off in my second year, but that in turn creates further pressure – one imposed by fashion's lineage, or some innate psychological need for neat proportions, I don't know – to remain gamine-like: the shorter the hair, the smaller the body you require to make it work). There are also the waifish, childlike club kids on Dirty-DirtyDancing or The Cobrasnake – Cory Kennedy, Sky Ferreira, wired and tired, dehydrated but magnetic. The bodies that are forced into unflattering shapes, in cheap fabrics and with terrible haircuts on top, that are never quite good enough on *America's Next Top Model*. It's Kate Moss's sinewy body wading through Glastonbury in hot pants and Hunter wellington boots. Nicole Ritchie's brand-new small body, so abrupt in its reduction I wonder if she's had work done to her skeleton, and the bodies of the Olsen Twins, which haven't changed since they were kids. It's Perez Hilton's feverish dissection of 'size-zero' celebrity bodies and website Hot or Not's relentless ranking of bodies. I'm eating up all the photos on the internet but for lunch I have just a small ball of Lidl mozzarella and some tomatoes with whatever vinegar I can find. It sounds quite decadent, but I wash it all down with cheap laxative tea I get from a health food shop that wakes me up in the early hours with a knife-sharp twinge in my intestines.

It's so stupid that by my final year I'm the girlfriend of Lewis, a person who cares about my wellbeing and does this amazing angular dance while making fart noises, a lightning bolt in any room, and yet I am lost in this listless torpor. I am so self-involved and preoccupied by how I look, which is tedious for me but exhausting for him. I can go for days thinking only about my digestive system. After collapsing in a corridor, I see a free therapist via the university GP surgery, but she tells me my arms aren't thin enough for that of a woman with an eating disorder. It leads to a state of permanent confusion about my size, living off others' reactions to my body rather than the mirror's reflection. I am controlling, boring, irritable. Lewis says nothing negative about my appearance or insecurities, but he does worry when he notices my ribs have become a bit more pronounced, and assumes the role of quietly monitoring my proportional shifts. Within his concern I feel a sense of triumph; a pathetic cruelty to inflict your beloved with such pain and one I will always regret.

As well as the vortex of toxicity which exists on the internet, I'm also punishing myself for my lack of intellectual progress. I've found a warped pleasure in throwing up after every meal – a transcendent release from the claustrophobia of my academic deficit. I have been lagging behind since failing my first year and it's getting worse as the final months approach. The fewer nutrients my body receives the less enthusiasm I muster for catching up, and yet I am stuck in this cycle of needing quick temporary relief from my frustration. The lectures are about the intricacies of local government reporting and defamation rights, and my coursemates appear hyper-organized and compatible with this form of journalism. I just want to review Hot Chip for money and I don't have the guts to leave. Plus, university has its moments: I like living by the sea and still have a good time with Lewis and his friends. His band is doing well; I'm so proud to see him drumming on stage, and we go and see noisy shows in London and at festivals. It's a racket and I hate the music but I feel like I am part of something. As I stand in the audience, I compose my face in the hope Kim is there too, seeing me and Lewis together, knowing that I've won.

The final straight of my course has arrived, and with minimal time to alter my internal makeup, I decide to bend the curriculum to my interests – music and disordered eating – to whip up some enthusiasm. I start reviewing gigs and interviewing bands – even managing to snag an exclusive back-stage interview with the bassist from Elbow. For a magazine journalism module, I decide to lift the lid on 'pro ana' websites. These messageboards are at their peak: a kind of club or religion for people with eating disorders to share details of the quantity of food they've eaten that day in order to keep a record of their failures/accomplishments and to encourage others to keep going. Everyone has a goal weight, but they're based on arbitrary numbers plucked from thin air that become the booming mantras behind every daily decision, from standing to eat to running to work. Integrating myself into this online underbelly for my degree was ill-advised, admittedly, but I boldly decide to take it up a notch and throw in a detox diet too, for the sake of expanding my research. It's the one Beyoncé recently lost twenty pounds through: water, cayenne pepper, maple syrup and lemon juice. I can hear the rampant applause now, as I sink into a malnourished daydream about winning my Pulitzer.

I have a fortnightly meeting with my tutor about the project. As my fellow coursemates challenge local politicians and help the homeless, I explain I'll be pissing out chilli water and getting my BMI checked by an unregistered nutritionist. To my surprise, his response is not: 'It sounds like you are using this project as a veiled attempt to legitimize disordered eating. Please, for the sake of your future bone density – can you not?' Instead it's signed off and he asks how my dissertation is going.

'All fine, I've been looking at old *Melody Makers*,' I reply.

I'm studying feminism in the music press and want to explore whether or not language used to describe female musicians has changed since the '70s. Plus it's a great opportunity to stare at images of Patti Smith and wonder how she maintained her bone-thin physique *and* ability to push musical boundaries (answer: cigarettes).

Results day comes around and I've scraped a pass. The plan worked. But my body and brain are rattled and rinsed. I've been holding my breath for three years, absorbing eating-disorder messageboards and MySpace to sideline the stress, and now I can live. Once we've saved up enough money, Lewis and I plan to move to a house in London together, and we do just that, joined by two art students from Hull and a lovely Scottish man who holds a boom mic for a living. The hob is constantly left on, we get burgled, have parties and use sheets of newspaper instead of loo roll.

Lewis is a manager in a pub in central London and I've

started working at MTV as a paid runner. *The* MTV – my nirvana. A place where I will meet – and stay completely mute in front of – Kylie, Noel Fielding and Julian Barratt, Sean Kingston, Leona Lewis and Kelly Jones from the Stereophonics. It's a time where I become a reckless idiot, distracted by ambition and the new opportunities that are presenting themselves. On New Year's Eve I get so drunk that by the time Lewis has finally finished his shift at midnight, he has to say goodbye to his friends who've been waiting for him and take me home on the bus.

Soon we are both out all the time, without each other, slowly freewheeling into our respective futures. After eight months of cohabitation, the reality of our friendship has arrived and Lewis and I break up on a Sunday afternoon at home after going to Sainsbury's for a weekly shop. We continue to live with each other, in the same room and bed, for a few more months, until the lease runs out. One day he kicks off when one of our housemates rips up my *Hollyoaks* calendar in a strange drunken fury. Regardless of his excellent taste, Lew is loyal like that.

Years pass, the dust settles and we go back to being friends. It's impossible not to; I see Lewis everywhere: in pubs, cycling down Oxford street, at busy festivals. I run over to him instinctively, desperate to be privy to his thoughts, safe in his company. His band split up but he goes on to join more. He's got a girlfriend, who I've seen on his Facebook, and whose deep, cosmic beauty obliterates the girlish faces of those that came before her.

As for the infamous Kim, we do finally meet in the flesh, in an anti-climactic encounter in 2011. I'm seeing friends in a pub in east London and out of the corner of my eye I notice a wooden fringe on the horizon. She is working behind the bar, cleaning a pint glass and looking bored. Great skin, but did she peak during her MySpace era? Better than peaking at sixteen, I suppose. I go and order a drink and hope she'll double-take me, stunned by the aura of the girl with the iPod photo from 2005. As I tell her my order, she barely registers my existence. It's clear she's never seen my face before, or if she has, she's forgotten it.

Six years later, I am at an album launch party for a jazz musician. Florence Welch is here hugging people and there's free sushi. During a seven-minute sax solo I turn around to see how everyone else is surviving, and notice one of Lewis's best friends, Leon, at the bar. I head over and ask: how are you?

'Yeah, fine. Well, pretty awful,' he says, rubbing the back of his head. 'I'm guessing you heard about Lewis.'

I tell him no, and he explains that Lewis has an inoperable brain tumour.

The next day I compose, delete, compose a text to him and press send. Lewis replies to say he is in shock but along with his girlfriend they are trying everything to keep his body healthy alongside major treatment. And they do – for a year longer than any medical expert expected. He is in and out of hospitals and hospices, he gets married, his friends record charity singles, and he is sustained by sheer stubbornness and his social group's relentless presence and onslaught of love.

Lewis and I meet one last time. He is still smoking, like some devil-may-care rock star. He even drinks two pints of lager. A brain tumour intrinsically alters you, but there's an equanimity and originality to Lewis that remains intact: great in a t-shirt, savagely honest, soft and strange. I wish I could tell him how much remorse I feel for being so lethargic and urgently needing the loo for most of 2006, or that I hate that I spent so much time fawning over his credentials via a website rather than in real life. But we're on borrowed time and the unspoken profundity of the situation leaves no space for these kinds of self-serving confessionals.

I dream about Lewis all the time – in these dreams I see him on his bike in Bournemouth, kicking a football in the park. On the morning of 22 April 2021, I wake from one of these dreams and message to see how he's doing. A few hours later I get a response from his wife. 'Thank you for texting, womanly intuition,' she says. Lewis passed away this morning at home, being cuddled.

It's a startlingly bright spring day, as if someone's just turned every light on, and I walk outside to sit on the bench in my garden. I brace myself for tears but nothing happens. Instead I am stunned by a spiritual sensation. The whole sky is open and Lewis is everywhere. He is a bee. A cloud. The gentle breeze rustling the branches. He is a worm, the sun, and an aeroplane's chemtrails. Oh Chriiieaaaaaash, I realize. Lewis is everywhere. He knows what song I've just been listening to.

It is Lewis's funeral a month later. The street outside the church is packed with the most spectacularly good-looking group of mourners in well-fitting suits. Lewis's kind friends, small holes in their faces from their MySpace era of experimental piercing, are now all grown men and women, some with babies and baggage but still charmed by the same mischief and camaraderie epitomized by Lewis. In the crematorium they stand and perform songs he liked and afterwards we eat cheese twists in his honour and have quiet, sweet conversations with voices strained by the suppression of tears.

I look around at his friends and family, and think how lucky I am to be here. That Lewis ever wanted me here.

CHAPTER FIVE

Being A Dickhead's Cool

Striding through Camden side streets, discarded nitrous oxide canisters clinking majestically as we move our feet, my friend Luca and I shoot the breeze with a sprawling Saturday extending before us. I feel cool: last night we dabbled in a bit of depressive consumption by taking Night Nurse recreationally, in lieu of ketamine. We wanted to numb our disaffection but instead just got a headache and a pretty decent ten hours. Today, we are approaching drunk. I am bulletproof in a way that is so brilliant I know it'll crash and burn within the hour.

And it does, when we begin to walk towards a pub and I catch my reflection for the first time that day in a window, only to see both of my breasts staring back at me. Dressed in an American Apparel unisex thermochromic t-shirt, the intention was to be scuzzy and sexy – think Karen O or Debbie Harry – so I am wearing no bra but normal clothing.

I hadn't realized, however, that through multiple washes the shirt would become entirely sheer, and now my nipples and the actual outline of my breasts are casually displayed on the front of my person like a workplace lanyard. I feel if you're going to make that sartorial leap you've got to add a sprinkle of danger elsewhere – PVC something, smudged lipstick, or bleached hair with jet-black roots. As it stands I've got a gingham backpack, a sensible ponytail and tennis shoes.

I begin to have immediate flashbacks to the innocent grown adults I've interacted with today: the Italian dad in the cafe who served me my coffee, the elderly woman at the market stall who let me try on that green beret. Don't get me started on the kids holding their mothers' hands who I gave a saintly maternal smile to. I baulk at the thought of them being confronted by my indecent attire; that for the rest of the day I am *that* girl who's trotting around town on a Saturday morning with her tits on show.

'You can see my boobs,' I say out loud to myself and then to Luca. 'How come you didn't tell me?'

Luca shrugs. 'I thought it was just what you were doing.'

He kindly offers me his leather jacket, which looks stupid on me but is significantly less stupid than the accidental indecent exposure.

This moment is a wake-up call; a sign I have been carried away by the spirit of the time. Skanky, squat-party chic has taken over a generation and while I'm fine with the hedonism and unkempt elements of the 2009 era, walking around north London with my 'not even that big' breasts exposed is a step too far, both for me and the permanent spectral presence of my mother, who floats above me at all times.

To be fair, mistakes are easy to make when you have two minutes to get ready, live in a room with barely any daylight and have a friend who works in American Apparel. I bought the t-shirt in the sale and with a discount, and in addition to the clothes I also occasionally get titbits of information about the store's renowned clientele. At the time of purchase, my friend is traumatized from a changing-room incident in which he had to throw away a purple one-piece leotard he found scrunched up in the corner on the floor. A girl had covered its gusset in period blood while trying it on and decided to make a break for it. 'Poor thing,' I say. 'Poor me,' is his reply. It feels somehow emblematic of the era: something that starts out sexy and liberated, before turning uncomfortably messy, before eventually being defeated by shame.

I first came across adverts for American Apparel on the back pages of *Vice* magazine while studying at university. *Vice* was the counter-cultural bible I found stacked in bars and skate shops in Bournemouth, and the sight of the cover alone was like a bomb detonating in my mind. The Music Issue was illustrated by an image of a sweaty metal fan with a face like a hammerhead shark holding his middle finger up, and, of course, on the back page there was an advert for American Apparel. Unlike the artifice of the early 2000s bimbo era, American Apparel celebrated the Real Girl aesthetic – often using real porn stars with no makeup on – to sell their garments. Instead of the hard, sharp edges of Size Zero, all jutting clavicles and pointy hip bones, girls' bodies were overflowing, abundant: grabbable lumps and bumps in soft loungewear or sexy elasticated onesies. The creative direction was stark, young and corrupted: a pair of burgundy-striped retro soccer socks modelled on a nearly nude blonde college girl, the camera looming over her lusty, vacant face, as if the photographer is threatening her with a demand for a blow job once he's got the money shot. I'll take five pairs!

It makes sense that the popularity of American Apparel and *Vice* is erupting in conjunction. A decade later, both companies are accused of making their working environments degrading for women. But for now they are seen as hot – shaking up the industry, and frightening the stuffy old guard with their quasi-pornographic imagery and provocative tone.

Not only do I desire the American Apparel model's post-coital flush and the confidence to pull off jodhpurs, but I'd also love to be bold enough to submit my writing to *Vice*. Before moving to London it became a symbol of a liberated life outside of institutionalized education: I'd slap copies of it onto the desk during our magazine-writing tutorials as a decla-ration of my anarchic, untameable spirit, in a 'fuck you' to the rest of the students hoping to write for *Vogue*, *Men's Health* or *OK Magazine*. You can take your flan recipes and celebrity interviews and shove them up your . . . what would someone who works at *Vice* say? Fissure-laden, cum-seeping sphincter?

From this point on, the benchmark for modern journalism is all about taking the piss out of ugly and potentially vulner-able people, photos of dead rats in jars, sideways war reporting ('I Went Undercover in the World of Syrian Whorehouses', photos of six-year-olds with guns), images of prepubescent girls addicted to prescription drugs and reviews of albums that inevitably conclude with some kind of line about wanking off so hard it feels like you're blasting a bullet out of your cock.

Despite the fact that I know I'd get eaten alive in the offices for not being edgy enough – I've never heard of any of the artists they review and I have never taken acid at a funeral or during an abortion – I can still dream about being part of the clique; therefore when I do finally reach London it thrills me to discover that I am near their epicentre in east London's Shoreditch.

Fresh out of university, I'm desperate to go places, and desperate to please. I have a job as the editorial assistant at free music magazine *The Fly* – a role I believe I have secured because I am young and female, still a relative anomaly in music journalism in the noughties, despite the fact I'm middle class, boring and white. It also helps that I can have four alcoholic drinks at midday without coming back to the office screaming.

For the first two weeks of my job I am crippled by embarrassment, as I am convinced I am in love with funny and stunning deputy editor, JJ, who has a healthy black beard and symmetrical features. Fortunately I rapidly become romantically repulsed by him due to our instinctive sibling-like dynamic, and the fact that he sometimes belches at his desk. After that brief obligatory internal love affair, I get used to working in an office. It's a publication that you can find in beer-splattered piles in music venues across the UK. Because it's free, we're paranoid we are seen by the industry as cheap and throwaway. On the plus side, the lack of status does give us wriggle room to have fun; wasting a few hours of a Wednesday afternoon making 'comedy videos' in the building's basement that we'll never upload to the internet, or running away from the overbearing interns when we see them on the street on our lunch break. It's good, clean, innocent fun, yet I long for corruption.

My writing style attempts to replicate the macho *Vice* tone of the time: I am hyperbolic and swear relentlessly, but I also have vast gaps in my musical knowledge, which leaves me trawling through Thesaurus.com to pad out the word count. I yearn to be headhunted by the editors at *Vice*, to be this week's fresh young face of cutting-edge youth journalism, getting high with the Klaxons as we watch the rough cut of a new docu series about Bolivia's child labourers.

The Fly is based just three minutes from *Vice*'s offices, if you run fast enough. So I walk past its entrance on my way in to work really slowly, visit its black-and-white website on a daily basis, go for lunch in nearby cafes in the hope that I'll see what sort of sandwiches the staff eat, as well as visiting the two central pubs they all frequent on a nightly basis. Naturally, I never speak to them. But I don't need to. I can see, hear and smell them – and that's enough. I love to watch *Vice* staff move through life; and I'm reassured to find they are often just as intimidating in reality as they are online, like all groups of attractive teenagers are. I hear one of their interns talking to a friend outside the pub describing the polluted midnight air: 'It smells like the metallic tang of cocaine as it trickles down your throat,' she says in a morose drawl. She looks about thirteen.

I'll never be one of them because I'm not tough enough, but I am happy here – in my hipster-adjacent bubble. I study their clothing choices knowing I will probably end up wearing whatever they've got on now in six months' time once it's available in Topshop. I spend a lot of my evenings prepping for a DJ set I don't have for a *Vice* new-issue launch party that I'm not invited to on a huge laptop that gets so hot it burns my legs. I daydream about being the kind of girl who could pull off a moustache finger tattoo. Or Henry Holland stocking tights.

At the weekend I'll make my pilgrimage to London Fields. Like most of Hackney, it was traditionally home to a bustling working-class community, until the early 2000s, after which it was gradually gentrified by 'creatives'. In the place of the hardy Irish local boozer is now a pub called the Cat and Mutton, which sells huge organic scotch eggs and sees most of its patrons mingling and lounging outside on its benches and pavement, the stentorian noise of which you can hear from 100 metres away. It is impossible to decipher whether the shrieks are that of a malevolent fight or a good time.

As overland carriages race through its core, the hipster mafia congregate in their cut-off denim shorts and vintage floral dresses to its local park, armed with their disposable BBQs. Eating a lot of meat is one of the key traits of the time – charred sausages, steaks, burgers, dirty food and an unruly approach to cholesterol. The drink of choice is cans of Red Stripe, and the tobacco is Cutters Choice as it's cheap or American Spirit because the packet is nice. I wonder what it's like to spend all Saturday in a park; to greet people loudly, as if you did a blood sacrifice together the night before; to hold court with disgusting stories and opinions and roll around in the dirt as if at a perpetual mini-festival. Gently tanned after an afternoon in the blistering heat with no factor 50, they head off to a party to do drugs and stick-and-poke tattoos until they roll back into work on Monday morning.

When I share my infatuated thoughts to any friends or colleagues, I'm surprised to find not everyone has the same reverence for *Vice*. Perhaps it's because the website is on the rise, and that feels threatening. The gratuitous magazine content is no longer the preserve of people who've actively sought it out, and thanks to Twitter their articles are turning up on the timelines of people who'd rather not read about haemorrhoids before 9 a.m. Post-*Nathan Barley*, post the viral video 'Being a dickhead's cool', the word hipster is now a knee-jerk insult hurled at anyone who travels via bike, or has facial hair. It's not fair, really, because they're not all just thickos with cool clothes. Some of them are quite well read. Apart from *The Catcher in the Rye*, I've not read anything other than texts from friends in about three years, and even when I was reading *The Catcher in the Rye* all I was thinking about was texts.

I also suspect that most 'normal' people are turned off by *Vice*'s imposing sense of exclusivity. Personally, I don't mind it. Unattainability is always the heart of any youth movement worth following, and I quietly admire their unfriendly and exclusionary approach to fashion, humour, music and self-care. The goal is to treat your body as badly as possible and still look good while doing so. It's so hard to keep up, and believe me I was trying. A few months ago I ended up in hospital with too much acid in my stomach and can no longer eat lemon.

While the brand is generally regarded as a 'boys' club', I am significantly less interested in the men who populate *Vice*; whose hairy bums are always out, their mean opinions sacrosanct. A lot of them are funny but also basically bullies: I don't think they'd physically hurt you, but they'd definitely experiment with some form of psychological trauma. They often possess a brutal perspicacity that can cut you to the core. They are capable of pointing out your deepest, darkest insecurities, the ones that you work so hard to conceal, until you have to get the last bus home to spare yourself from publicly crying. Even as I write this I do so with fear, aware they may see it, track me down and point and laugh at me.

If they're not the snarky suburban lads, they're gnarly types with neck tats and chipped teeth who like metal and satanism but don't have the guts to make eye-contact with a woman. Or they're trust-fund guys who drink in east London now but are quietly planning their exit out of their slobbish cosplay by bagging a girl named India, who has a nice big head of blonde hair and a life-changing inheritance.

It's the *Vice* girls I'm more interested in. One of *Vice*'s greatest assets is their ability to headhunt and uncover unique talent – and at the moment they have a roster of genuinely grotty girls with a GSOH working for them. While the dominant voice is sarcastic and loutish, there are so many interesting women subverting the tone. Some have adopted the ladette approach, baring all for the sake of clicks and validation, whereas others are establishing completely original comic voices. I am the kind of person who wants to crowd-surf but is too scared they'll lose their bag. These girls, on the other hand, don't care about purses. They keep their money in their bras and their house keys up their bums. They write like wizards and look like It-girls. They've got all sorts of bodies and brains and come from different backgrounds;

so much so, I feel ashamed of my tragically conventional route into journalism.

Vice like their girls the American Apparel way: tough or young. Tough *and* young ideally. A lot of them are overtly sexual in a way that I find radical and completely terrifying. And when they're not writing about butt plugs or Xanax, they're blogging or uploading images onto Facebook. Despite its corporate aesthetic, Facebook has turned into a hipster goldmine. They go on there and upload eighty images a week of the parties and festivals they're attending, using random in-jokes such as 'Pete's Mouldy Condom' or 'Dog Dog Dog Dog Dog Dog' as album titles. Inside the albums is a plague of shutter shades and headbands, eyes spangled, surrounded by glitter; beautiful bodies lost deep within mind-rotting K-holes. I don't even need to go out any more to experience the *Vice* effect, I can just sit and wait for the Facebook dump.

It's the last few glorious years before Twitter properly takes over and everyone becomes more self-conscious, with sentences taken out of context before being shaped into a pitchfork with which to fight everyone with. It's also the early days of blogging, a form of personal documentation that still feels like a counter-cultural pastime, before the compulsive bakers and normal folk took over. Some *Vice* writers even have offshoot blogs where they can flex their creative muscle with even more abandon.

I first found Slutever's blog while at university and she's recently been hired by *Vice*. Her real name is Karley, an American writer who was raised in a Conservative Catholic family and now pens gut-spilling confessionals about her sexual exploits in an acerbic, detached type of tone. She'd sometimes come and visit her friends who studied at the arts institute in Bournemouth, a bunch of roguish indie boys with spindly legs, speaking in riddles and playing in a band called Hovel. I know one of its members, Alan. We speak sometimes at house parties and I often feel as if he's flirting with me, but he'll punctuate anything complimentary about me with a twist of the knife – a comment about what I'm wearing or a nasty reference to whoever I've come with. Still, it's good to experience a morsel of Karley's world, even though I can't imagine she'd tolerate such flagrant negging. After her trips to the coast, she'd head back to her London squat and write about her experiences – such as getting covered in a stranger's period blood in a toilet cubicle. Most days she's writing about her day-to-day interactions – sleeping with randoms, her love of 'rape' porn, tugging off her hospitalized boyfriend and interviewing her squatmates about dubious things they've done with their pets. The content is mind-bendingly gross but so gripping and gonzo I can't believe it's free to read. She's the real deal – an erotic adventurer and debauched hellraiser nestled among a cohort of posturing amateurs. While we never meet, I do interview her lovely boyfriend, who is in a popular indie band. We visit a funfair together for a feature and on the bus home he tells me that his girlfriend is a writer. 'She wants to do what you do,' he says. 'Maybe you guys should meet?' I don't have the guts to tell him I know everything about her already, and that I have modelled my recent life on her. Taking risks. Being reckless and feckless and behaving like a skank all for the sake of living life to the max. It's the first time I've ever been a really bad person. Humiliating myself or others or putting myself in vulnerable situations. This is my What Would Slutever Do? era – which is, in essence, absolutely anything.

Here are the lowlights:

- I try to write about my sexual experiences on a Tumblr blog that I plan to publish. I show a guy I am seeing, hoping he'll find it sexy, but he says it is 'actually pretty boring'.
- On the thirty-minute walk from the Tube station to my flat I pass a group of men outside a late-night supermarket. One of them asks me how I am, in a way that is creepy and insincere, but I decide to pull him up on it. 'Hi,' I reply, even though it's 2 a.m. He looks shocked that I'm standing still in front of him rather than yelling 'Leave me alone' like all the other girls have. Now we're face to face I realize he is tall and wiry with a faint trace of moustache hair. The chat is flirty, verging on bad ('You're so sexy! Tell me where you live'), and as we walk side by side for fifteen minutes towards my place I feel the rush of my first one-night stand. The liberation! The rush ends pretty fast as I realize the full gravity of taking home a complete stranger that I am more or less repulsed by, and I decide I should run. I begin a light jog; nothing too extreme. He speed-walks and catches up, both of us panting in the cold night air, neither of us addressing the sudden change in gear. 'Hey, slow down,' he says. He has no idea that I nearly signed up for a trial to run semi-professionally for Essex in 2000,

and that I'm about to move faster than I've ever moved in my life. Exhibiting final-lap-of-the-Olympic-relay levels of speed, I sprint all the way home, bolt the front door and crawl into bed alone.

- My housemates and I have a huge house party and a friend, Baz, who is the landlord of a pub in Shoreditch despite the fact he has never been a landlord, knows no landlords and is twenty-two, brings thirty people along with him. It's huge, it's thriving; I can't believe it's my house. I corner a guy I recognize from *Vice* for twenty minutes in the kitchen and boast to him that I am a music journalist while he looks completely unbothered, as if I've told him I sometimes eat bread. That goes badly, so I move away from him and instead become fixated by the front door: as we got burgled a few weeks prior, I'm very conscious of the fact that most people in attendance are not adhering to the usual rules of door safety. I start to wonder if maybe the thief has returned and that they're in here now, partying, using my loo. Just to make sure everyone knows the rules, I turn down the music and start shouting at the congregation that everyone must close the door – 'Pull it shut so it clicks' – on exiting the property. Nobody listens so I decamp to the hallway, where I become the gatekeeper of the front door, locking and unlocking it every time someone wants to come in or leave. I even adopt that cocky demeanour of a surly bouncer – 'H'okay, everyone, glad you had a good night, keep moving!' – only I'm wearing a vintage satin black top.

- A girl I know from work drinks too much tequila at a music festival and says she wants me to slap her around the face as hard as possible as some kind of punishment/pleasure dichotomy. After a few minutes of earnest persuasion, I agree to fulfil her wish and as Animal Collective's 'My Girls' plays in the distance I smack her across the cheek, in front of a semicircle of ten bewildered festival-goers unsure of whether to applaud or not.

- A group of friends heads to Shoreditch House for the launch party of a band's new album. I've never been in a private members' club before and am impressed at the soap options, free sweets and hand towels. When we get there my eyes are on stalks. It's the cream of the crop of socialites, musicians and models. Amy Winehouse is DJing and I'm trying not to stare at her but cannot resist taking in that bountiful hair. The It-girl of the moment is also freewheeling around the venue, and my friend has given her his wrap of cocaine – she said she'd be right back – but now it's been an hour and he's worried that it's gone. I'm feeling buoyed by the elite backdrop so I tell him I'll go and get it off her. As I step into the bathroom I see shadows and mumbles from the cubicle she's in, and stare at it for a moment, not knowing quite what to do. I knock gently on the door and say her name with a timid enthusiasm. She remains silent. I knock again, at the same time as three women stumble into the bathroom. She opens the door and I've no idea what to say, what lingo to use. 'Hello,' she looks at me blankly, incandescently. 'I think you've got my friend's thing.' She comes out a few moments later and hands me the drugs covertly. I try to make conversation but she thinks I am scum and leaves before the other girls in the loo realize what's happening. I return to my friends and hand over the drugs. Everyone cheers, and for twenty minutes I'm a legitimate noughties icon. Still hyped from my cocaine retrieval moment, I then go on to steal some makeup from behind the DJ booth at the private members' club. I excitedly show my friends what I've done on the bus home – that I've stolen Amy Winehouse's foundation for no reason at all. 'Why did you do that, Hat?' they say. No applause.

- I go to All Tomorrow's Parties – the ultimate muso-hipster festival held in the faded seaside resort of Camber Sands in Sussex. On its first night, a friend sells me pills that are largely cut with caffeine. Another friend has already had them and he says he's really, really awake; too awake. I take one, and then a second, and can't fall asleep for the next seventy-two hours. I am so weak that I am unable to help form the Human Pyramid – the ultimate festival formation of the hipster era and the only reason I went. In all the Facebook photos I look miserable.

- An impeccably neat model is supposed to meet me on Saturday night at Reading Festival. No camping for me this time; just get in, see a few bands, kiss a neat model then straight back home for a wash. I try to

pace myself throughout the day but the febrile energy
of Reading is such that it's impossible not to press the
self-implode button. Within hours of entering the site I
have inhaled two nitrous oxide balloons, followed by a
conversation with my late grandmother. By the time I
meet Sam eight hours later I am a smudge of my
former self – dazzled, permanently flushed and
wearing an XXL hiking jacket someone lent me as I
missed the last train home. In spite of such hindrances,
we continue to take the night by storm: I'm feeling
free and he watches as I squat and pee in a bush before
going backstage to hang out with fellow models and
musicians that Sam knows. We eventually end up on
stage in one of the big venues, alongside Florence and
the Machine, as she and her friends do karaoke along
to Annie Mac's DJ set. It's a form of extroversion I'm
struggling to participate in but as everyone else is
dancing like nobody's watching, and Sam has told me I
can stay in his hotel tonight, I smile and try my best.
My feet remain firmly on the spot and I move my
arms around gently, hands in fists, like a toddler having
a tantrum, unable to shake the fact that there are thousands of people just staring at us doing this. Maybe it's
a chemically induced paranoia but I swear the crowd
aren't even clapping or smiling; they're just looking.
Once that's over a group of us walk back into the
centre of Reading together. I assume we'll be in our
own respective rooms at first, only to realize that there
is only one room – and I will be sharing it with Sam as

well as Nick Grimshaw and his friend. When we arrive, Sam and I make a bed using towels as a mattress and our jackets as a blanket on the floor while Grimmy and his mate take the double bed. It's such a relief to be still and away from the noise of the festival, and for a moment it feels nice and cosy – until my acid reflux kicks in, suddenly and without remorse. I then burp relentlessly for hours, in this silent room with a Radio 1 DJ, a total stranger and the boy I fancy. When I wake up the next day I get up and get out of there before I can look anyone in the eye. The next time I see Sam is in a copy of *Grazia* magazine, two weeks later, stood at a party with his arm around the waist of Daisy Lowe. I am partly flattered that I am capable of pulling the same man as Daisy Lowe, but sad that his lasting memory of me is the belching girl sleeping on top of a towel.

- A mutual friend introduces me to one of the top editors at *Vice*. He says very little, in what is clearly a power move of sorts. So to try to impress him I ask if hypothetically he'd have sex with his best friend – a lesbian woman – in front of the roomful of people we are standing with, on a table in front of everyone, for a million pounds. He winces and asks: 'What?'

- I spend an evening in the basement of *Vice*-owned pub the Old Blue Last. At one point I sit on the lap of a forty-year-old man who's got gold teeth and a nine-year-old daughter. I eventually emerge to see some old friends who've been drinking upstairs. I am swearing a lot and cocky, not really that interested in what they have to say. 'You've changed, Harriet,' one of them states, despondently, before leaving me alone on the pavement. Two days later I visit a school friend for a few drinks and a catch-up. She texts afterwards to say my eyes seemed sad and that she had the number for a local AA should I want it.

It's around then that I call it quits on being a skanky wannabe cool slut and ease off my ambitions to live like an agent of chaos. I stop drinking for twelve months because of the agony of my stomach lining unexpectedly collapsing, an unfortunate by-product of attempting to keep up with a community of people who didn't know I exist. Quitting booze is tough at first; I eat a bag of Haribo Tangfastics every day and get three fillings. Going to gigs late at night is extremely taxing too. But after a while I get into running 10Ks and dabble in Shloer. I stop getting tagged in photos on Facebook but I no longer eat chips and mayonnaise from Dixy Chicken or drink Irn Bru for breakfast. Everyone else more or less cleans up their act too – big characters from the *Vice* boom have turned into macho chefs or brand consultants or creative directors with glossy and corporate Instagrams, far from the inebriated, uninhibited days of the hipster Facebook albums.

Not everyone sold out, though. On a Saturday afternoon in July 2016 I see Alan, the frontman of Hovel, at a festival scuttling towards me. He approaches, and after a bit of frantic small talk tells me that he's annoyed I didn't respond to a Facebook DM with a link to his song that he sent a few months ago. I say that I am sorry and he responds by inspecting my face, particularly the skin around my eyes, and gives me an eerie stare. 'Anyway, it's good to see you,' he says with a gleeful smile. 'Shame that you're not ageing so well.'

I am hurt in the moment but remember he is now alone in the perpetual dank squat of his mind while his peers are paying their mortgage by creating content and making mood boards for Adidas. I respect him in a way. For sticking to his guns. He's living out the *Vice* magazine dream – rock 'n' rolling well into his forties. Still snarky, edgy. A total, utter arsehole to the bitter end.

CHAPTER SIX

Shirt Day

Twenty-three years old, wearing black leggings and a baggy cricket jumper, I sit at the kitchen table enraptured as Jim riffs on the merits of wearing shirts. As much as I try to outrun my demons – the reality that I am a broke girl with a crap flat and a body that often malfunctions, or functions too abundantly – the truth keeps catching up with me. It's Sunday night – I've been at his since Friday, and as such my physical upkeep is getting slack. He doesn't yet know that my fringe gets greasy twelve hours after washing it; that every second here is a bloodthirsty battle between my pelvic floor and trapped wind; and that there is a bloodstain on his Egyptian cotton sheets upstairs. I try to park the intrusive thoughts for a moment to focus on what he is saying, because it is important. Whatever the mundane anecdote – favourite meal, significant childhood holiday or bowel movement – if it's coming from Jim's sweet lips, I'm all ears.

I've developed a delirious infatuation with this thirty-year-old A&R guy. It doesn't feel good – not a nurturing or peaceful kind of love – but it's funny how the body becomes inured to constant exhilaration and everything and everyone else who is normal and calm in the periphery becomes a drag as a result. Jim is the first man I've met that owns a chic small leather wallet that fits right in his jacket, knows how to tip, and also probably skateboards, or at the very least boogie-boards. The combination of his lived-in masculine sophistication and my adolescent insecurities have resulted in a relationship that frequently feels on the brink of combustion. I am desperate to keep him, so much so that I'm plagued with the same unhealthy fascination that an alcoholic investigator has for a notorious serial killer; I'd rifle through his bins if I could. Which I can.

There's a point in every man's life, says Jim, when they must upgrade from t-shirt to shirt. A sartorial surge into adulthood. Shirt Day arrived for him in his mid-twenties, when a friend came to visit him in London. Jim hadn't seen him in years and claims to have been rendered speechless as he watched this newly tailored acquaintance approach on the horizon. 'When did *all this* happen?' Jim gestured to his friend's shirt. 'Few months back. Wearing only shirts now. Moving up in the world.' The next day Jim felt so galvanized he bought a whole new wardrobe: five shirts, two blazers and some smart trainers. He's never looked back. 'Wow,' I audibly gasp before wondering what numbers make up his Blackberry pin and worrying when I last bleached my moustache.

Jim's refined style is intoxicating to me. His bedroom is totally white, minimal; barely a possession other than a big book of art or a pencil sharpener bought from a gallery. His sheets are cold and thick, like lying on a bed of fresh milk. It sets him apart from the rest of the student music-industry boys I normally hang out with, their mattresses on the floor among toilet rolls, ashtrays and other teenage trinkets like crisp packets, PlayStation controllers and suspicious tissues. Deep down I crave Jim's sparseness; his ability to look like a little smart man too. I'm not ready yet though; instead I go about in my cheap Alexa Chung costume: vintage floral mini-dresses with ripped tights and Primark ankle boots with slippery worn-down soles. The look is sobered up by a second-hand Barbour jacket, with a musty odour that makes me gag on the bus into work each morning.

Before Jim and I become an item, I often see him darting around all the major gigs and album launch parties, but never the sparsely attended, bleak ones. He clearly has quality control. I want to speak to him so desperately but he's always off to the next thing, never still – until one night in October. *The Fly's* editor Niall, JJ and I have been to a backslapping industry award show in which the same journalists win the same prizes every year as the rest of the room eyeroll while haphazardly holding four glasses of free wine. Loud men hold court – tedious anecdotes about press trips or bands they know the most about. Needless to say, it's the highlight of my year.

To console our egos, a PR called James invites a large group of journalists to a glamorous hotel bar over the road. 'Jim – you're coming too,' he shouts to the guy in the tiny blazer, who follows the crowd but remains fixated by his Blackberry.

When we get to the bar, six of us stand in a semi-circle, waiting for James to deliver us our booze as if we are toddlers waiting for a milky drink. Niall takes the edge off the awkwardness by doing impressions of some of the night's winners, but being so close to Jim makes my scalp feel cold and my reactions over-zealous. His eyes eventually rise from his phone and to my surprise he looks at me with the boldness of a man who's both fatigued by life and so desperate to act upon more of his intoxication before the buzz draws to a halt. As soon as James hands us our glasses, Jim breaks free from the semi-circle and asks if I want to check out the rest of the hotel. 'Yeah, OK,' I say.

For whatever reason, I'm completely unthreatened by this drunk stranger who is forcefully trying the handles on every door as we rumble down the hotel corridors together. He appears to me more like a child than a predator, and assuming the role of bossy chaperone gives me a sense of purpose and power that I've never felt before, certainly not for someone I regard as so desirable. That being said, if he were to shift gear and demand I break into a room and join him in the bath nude I'd probably comply. If he were to demand I block my family's phone numbers and kick a dog I'd comply. Thankfully he instead finds an empty gym in the hotel's basement. *A true gentleman*, I think to myself.

We naturally gravitate to the cross-trainers and begin to exercise. At first I struggle to ignore thoughts of the CCTV footage and our potential arrest, but am gradually lost in the thrill of using the expensive equipment and Jim's maverick approach to flirting. After a few minutes he hops off to use the loo and I catch my reflection in the huge fitness mirrors. Although I've stopped pedalling, my body keeps moving with the force of the speed I've built-up on the cross-trainer and I look like a maniac with my farmer's jacket and bright-red sweaty face. I decide to get off the machine and try to lower my temperature by pressing my cheeks against the cool surface of the pristine mirror-wall. A man in a black three-piece suit arrives wearing a security earpiece and tells us to leave immediately, and, sheepish from the circumstances, we say goodbye back in the bar having barely exchanged names. I get the night bus home alone; profoundly altered, glutes burning.

The next morning I arrive at my desk feeling nauseous and melancholy, as if last night was a magnificent dream that would escape my brain by lunch. My one encounter with Jim and I spent it so frantic and flushed. Two hours later it's a different story: as I try to focus on my conversation with Niall ('Saw you leave the bar with that guy – dunno if that's a good idea, Hat'), I am also writing the word 'Yes!' in an email to Jim, who has found my contact details and asked me on a date.

Armed with his full name, I do some minor snooping before we meet, but his social media presence is unpretentious, a little bit scattershot and with a character that's tricky to categorize. His Facebook profile pic is a blurry image of him looking busy on his Blackberry next to a plate of spring rolls. I am mostly impressed by his professional digital footprint, a trail of highbrow industry successes, a grown-up, prospering man, an intriguing contradiction when you consider the behaviour in the hotel. People have interviewed Jim about his work – and he speaks in authoritative, grand statements about the future of music and the artist he represents. I take a look at the images on my Facebook: I've been in a fairly feral state since joining *The Fly*, and have spent every weekend living in a tent at a festival, befriending different groups of people, occasionally blacking out or doing my impression of a pterodactyl. I ought to evoke some kind of adorable femininity to offset my tagged photos when we meet.

For that reason I've gone for the klutzy look – crouched down rummaging through my bag – when he approaches me at Kings Cross station. We walk arm in arm to a cosy wine bar and I am instantly swept away by his personality, both debonair and daft. He is bright, generous and kind. The chaotic man-child in the hotel corridor is gone. Or at least suppressed. A week later we are inseparable.

When word gets around that we are together, I am warned by more colleagues about Jim as a romantic prospect. They say we are mismatched and that he is reckless and will break my heart. All I have seen is a charming man with a limitless passion for fun and pleasure. Unlike most music industry bros, his friends are impressive, confident women, two of which he lives with in a house in north-west London. Bee and Sian spend their free time with the type of grungy socialites whose faces I normally pore over on the People and Parties pages of glossy women's magazines. They wear long-sleeve body-con mini dresses and party harder and with more style and composure than any hedonistic male musicians I've met. Bee and Sian are intimidating but totally accommodating; they confide in me about their complicated boyfriends, cook me food and, most thrillingly, tag me in their coveted Facebook albums. I am stunned and relieved to find they like me for my gentle qualities rather than the surface-level ones that I suspect initially interested Jim. There are exes and other women who I suspect are curious about Jim's love life, and every time we go out I pray for a pap image of us together. Once the photos are uploaded in the following days I feel both thrilled to be affiliated with them but concerned that the intensity of my eyes reveals the intensity of my singular constant intrusive thought: 'JIM! I AM OUT OF MY DEPTH BUT WILL YOU MARRY ME?!'

For the first three months we are together, Jim and I behave as if we are drunk tourists. I am living the romantic ideal I was promised in films – having rowdy weekend roasts and sitting in Regent's Park with picnics. The former is pricey and you get lethargic after three drinks, and the latter uncomfortable and problematic when it comes to needing the bathroom – but from the photos it looks as if I'm spinning throughout the city. I haven't updated my belongings since I left for university but Jim has provided some new additions that add some class to my existence – a pair of cherry-red Dr Martens and two tiny Le Creuset pans. That brief honeymoon period tricks me into believing I am moving into a new tier of existence, one in which I take on his slickness by affiliation and I am his youthful muse in return.

Jim's reputation remains troubling, but because I see only the sweet, childlike nature of our relationship I wonder if he is misunderstood. He appears to me as trapped between two worlds: a messy music-industry leader and an eccentric soul who dreams of being a wholesome grownup, baking and buying trinkets from Muji. Perhaps I have caught him on the ascent. It certainly feels like it. There is no sense of unfaithfulness or fickle moods. He spends his days networking; the type of guy who has back-to-back meetings in private members' clubs with pompous lawyers and label bosses. But he also has a taste for the absurd. We visit a beach and he brings home seven huge pebbles that he sleeps on without explanation for a week. If I were to pinpoint the moment I become truly infatuated with him, it would be the pebbles. My brain can't get enough of the novelty.

Other traits that I find attractive: he hates depressing restaurants and will happily move tables if a customer has a slightly annoying voice. He resents taking buses, so we get black cabs everywhere. I go along with all of this, splashing whatever cash I have on our high-octane lifestyle, pretending to be assertive too, but deep down all I really want is his company, alone and undistracted. I'm starting to worry it's all I'll ever want.

These are desperate times. Beyond being invested in someone who I am constantly warned will break my heart, I am in the midst of a distressing living situation. It's been six months since Lewis and I broke up and I have taken the first free room I can find on Facebook, posted by a pretty hipster girl called Sue. Also living in the house is Julia, a makeup artist with a pet chinchilla who goes jogging at 3 a.m., and a Canadian bartender called Lianne with a husky voice and leg tats. Those two are sweet, manageable. But Sue, the main girl, creates an atmosphere of alarm within me. Throughout my life there have been certain people who possess a cosmic control over my soul, rendering me unable to speak with any honesty or personality. I am so sad when I meet them, as I know I am about to sink into a period in which I will surrender to their every whim and command until the only option is to run away. It's not Sue's fault she is one of them. Perhaps in a past life I was her dog.

One morning I come downstairs to find that she is wearing my purple pencil skirt. She said she found it in my bedroom and liked the look of it. She says we should be able to share clothes – I can take whatever I want from her room, too. 'Totally!' I exclaim. Another night I return home from a gig bent over in agony with period cramps. She is in the living room partying with friends and I pop my head around the door to tell her I am going to take a quick bath as I am in so much pain. She says to leave the door unlocked as they'll probably all need to go to the loo at some point, and naturally I oblige. Nobody comes in, but for twenty minutes I lie naked in bubbles bracing myself for a gurning Shoreditch boy to stumble in and pass a stream of brown urine a metre from my head.

I am an aloof housemate: out most evenings and staying at Jim's at the weekend. On nights when a gig is cancelled or finished early I've taken to eating cheese sandwiches in Liverpool Street station on a bench with a mini bottle of wine so I don't have to go home. Sue wants to establish a tight-knit family spirit in the house, preferring group cooking and cleaning. I like to be alone and decompress at the end of a day and dread creating my unconventional dinners – for example, pasta, curry paste and avocado – in the communal kitchen. I appreciate Sue doesn't sound particularly malevolent, trying to create a free-flowing, sisterly ambience, but the good will is offset by the memory of an anecdote she told me in which as a child she chopped her cat's whiskers off with a pair of scissors.

With Christmas approaching and Liverpool Street station

increasingly cold at night, I make the rash decision to sign a contract on a new flat with a university friend from Bournemouth, assuming that I can find a new tenant and escape my current house contract with ease. In a stairwell at work I call Sue to say that I am leaving. Despite the fact I've known her for two months she is furious – 'we even went for a roast together in a pub!' – and tells me that my leaving will make her final year at university impossible to focus on. I am floored by guilt and arrange viewings of my room immediately, but chaotically. People arrive when Sue, Julia and Lianne aren't at home. Hopeful tenants are put off by my imploring expression, and the lack of other humans in the house rightfully spikes concern.

For three months I pay rent in two houses, using up the inheritance from three of my grandparents' deaths and all of my savings from working odd jobs in the summer before I moved to London. I become the girl who posts on Facebook about 'a lovely room going in E2' every other day in increasingly frantic tones. A mutual acquaintance claims Sue is renting my room out to friends for a few hundred pounds per month. It sounds too cruel to be true, but she once confessed she wiped Julia's toothbrush around the toilet bowl after they had a row, so anything is possible.

Meanwhile, Jim is a steady hand of assurance. While I can barely talk about anything apart from my living situation, such is my financial and emotional stress, I can get by on being relatively exotic because I am still new.

The relationship reaches its pinnacle when he takes me to Paris. For three days I'm a walking cliché: wearing heels during the day, in my vintage coat, drinking red wine, cycling along the Seine, visiting the Louvre, kissing on bridges. When we get back, his friends say he hasn't been this happy in years. I am overwhelmed by love and he affirms it by writing 'Everything all at once' on the back of a receipt for a bottle of wine from our first date in King's Cross, a memento that he leaves in my wallet for me to discover as I queue up for my Tesco meal deal the next day.

Such heights are unsustainable and, sure enough, as we hit month four the magic begins to wear off. For him, at least. I have found a mutual friend who is keen to live with Sue. Sue is quite nice once I've found a solution. Life is considerably better, but I am losing Jim's attention. He is bored and frustrated by me. I don't have a life outside his. Most of my friends in London are Lewis's, and I've realized most of Jim's are his ex-fiancées'. I think in meeting someone new he hoped to leapfrog into their world – to adopt a new brigade of pioneering creatives that he could cause havoc with and keep his escalating age lower by adjacency. But I'm nervous to introduce him to my friends in case they're not wild or industry enough, even though they are amazing to me.

If the process of falling in love with someone is an exercise in reappraising your brilliance in the eyes of another – a greatest-hits tour of your most endearing anecdotes, cutest body parts and charming quirks – the falling-out-of-love era is a shock art exhibition filled with snapshots of all your unsightly corporeality. With every slight undoing of my surface persona – a cool, young music journalist in a Barbour jacket – he becomes more and more disinterested. I am now aware that everything about me is rank. For example: in the midst of one heavy hangover, I apologize profusely for 'looking really ugly and gross'. He tells me to stop saying it, and I realize I am affirming what he already feels. I am constantly bleeding and twice leave used period-related paraphernalia in his bathroom sink that he goes on to find and dispose of, without mentioning. Even my writing is repulsive to him: I show him a feature I've been working on, an interview with the band the Temper Trap. Their music has secretly soundtracked our romance and I've written it from the heart. He tells me it's alright, but reads a bit like sixth form poetry. He hates sleeping at my new flat, which I empathize with. My room is positioned above a restaurant and the smell of cooking oil pours through my two tiny rectangular windows. The staff are up until the early hours clearing phlegm from their throats and playing booming electronic music. The room above me is inhabited by a guy learning acoustic guitar, which means I am the filling in a sandwich of Newton Faulkner and sinister techno. Reality has hit, and a girl with menstrual issues and who sleeps in hellish discord is less appealing than she was back in the hotel gym.

Now, when we drink together, he reverts back to the chaotic boy, slipping into a faraway place, totally unreachable. It is no longer roguish but frustrating and hurtful. I want to be on the same journey with him, not sat at the back waiting for him to fall off the table so I can take him home. I head off to meet him one evening but my phone runs out of battery. When I arrive at the house, at the party, nobody can hear the buzzer going, so I stand on the street watching him in the window having a fantastic time. I beg passers-by to let me use their phone so I can call him but I am crying and talking in such a frenzy that nobody trusts me. In the end I walk home. The next day, when he finds out what happened, I feel pathetic. A stronger woman wouldn't have reacted in such a hysterical way.

On the way back from one of his friends' birthday parties, a raucous night of paranoia, we get into an argument about something arbitrary that spirals into a bizarre tangent in which he tells me I am immature for being a vegetarian. 'Grow up, Harriet!' he shouts while storming off into the night, his tiny blazer fading into the distance. I agree. The next day I make a mackerel salad and gag on every last bite.

A week later, Jim takes me to the New Forest to cycle around some woods, to place the crumbling remains of our relationship into a new setting to see if there's anything left. I live in fear of an even slightly unusual bowel movement for the entire weekend and barely eat. I needn't be anally retentive; it's too late. It all feels forced and overly sentimental. We go on a silent bike ride through the woods; it is the first time I've cried while simultaneously experiencing the near-orgasmic sensation of descending a big hill.

We break up in a chain restaurant off Oxford Street a week later. Never has the arrival of a small plate of tempura carrot and a tiny dipping dish of sweet chilli sauce seemed so hopeless. I'm sensing that he wants me to stand up for myself, to have some little zero-tolerance monologue ready, but I don't want to tell him off. I don't want to be in this position at all.

Certain men in the creative industries claim to desire the laid-back, anything-goes girl, but often there's really just a baby boy inside who wants to get bollocked by their mum. If that's the case here, Jim has picked the wrong woman, because unfortunately I am a baby too.

The misery of adjusting to life without Jim bleeds out in every aspect of my day. I spend my evenings getting off night buses early so I can toddle around Hackney at midnight listening to music that reminds me of him. It's an oppressively melancholic period in indie music and while it feels as if the rest of the population are having sex to the xx and Beach House, I've taken to playing it while talking to myself loudly, asking the ether questions as if I can communicate with Jim from the dead. I write his name on my hand in biro so he's always with me. I spend a lot of time running around London when I should be walking, trying to burn off some of the distress. I don't even care about the loose pavement slabs that jolt when I step on them, the ones that leave my shoes and tights soaked with filthy city rain water.

The weekends are the worst, when I am not distracted by work and the brown noise of loneliness gets to me. On August bank holiday Monday, I go on a pilgrimage to the Tate Modern to find Jim's favourite painting: Francis Picabia's *The Handsome Pork-Butcher*, a satirical portrait of a man with many combs in his hair. It's not where it used to be; I run around the gallery rooms like a parent who's lost their child in a busy playground. Finally, I find it; I suppose I hoped he might be there. That I'd sidle up to him like in a mumblecore movie and we'd start to talk in wide-eyed wonder about Dadaism, leading into some kind of metaphor for complex love, our eyes gazing at the painting, two souls merging. We'd eventually hold hands and the film would end. I am weak and feeble when reality hits and it's just me and some tourists, sweating and alone.

I try to talk to friends about the gravity of my heartache but I'm finding there's an ego to the extremity of emotions that makes it unbearable to share. Every time a friend messages to ask if I am OK, to see if I want to go for a drink, my inner monologue steps in: *By all means go for a drink, but they simply won't understand. This is the first time anyone has experienced such devastating loss. Nobody gets us, what we were. He was mean. But there were good times too. Remember the little dough balls he got you a few times from the local Brazilian cafe? Or that pie he made you that was full of lentils? It's literally impossible for anyone to compre-hend the intensity of what it's like to lose a man like that, so better to suffer in solitary confinement and as humiliatingly as possible.*

Soon enough, Jim begins to miss me, no doubt in a familial way rather than romantic. But I'll take it. I am an accommo-dating person with a lot of patience, and I suspect he's been rejected by whichever woman accelerated the falling-out-of-love process with me. Tentatively we begin to see each other again, or rather we meet up at the end of our respective nights to fall into our melancholy union. It is dramatic and painful. I visit his house on a Saturday morning, after walking around the nearby streets for an hour waiting for him to text back. When I arrive in his bedroom, the crumpled bedsheets and the atmosphere of off-guard unease suggest another girl has just left. Bee and Sian now look at me sympathetically, as do the colleagues who once warned me about him.

Even though I know the multiple origins of his loss of love for me, our split has been framed as two twisted lovers who, for reasons beyond our will, are incompatible. This is a murky basis for a break-up and the lack of closure haunts me. He gives me a copy of Ayn Rand's *The Fountainhead* – a book I'd later discover is one of the few novels liked by Donald Trump and other right-wing hooligans – as if it will explain some of his internal conflict, but I can't bear to read it. I email and text him huge, sprawling messages constantly, believing he still loves me too. His initial responses are similarly wracked by sorrow but it begins to wane and can tell he's faking it. I take a punt and ask him if he would like to go for a coffee on 14 February, while playing dumb to the date's poignancy. To my morose horror, he is busy, and this is when my inevitable online mania begins.

Jim posts very little but is photographed often, and to watch his life unfurl without me is agony. Every day is a new potential heartache; I keep Facebook open on a tab at work, and monitor his new followers on Twitter. Bee uploads two photos of Jim smoking topless on a rooftop that ruin my weekend. Even the most straightforward images of him have the capacity to bludgeon my heart. I am maniacal and want to see everything: the blemishes on his face bloom and burst, stubble slowly shooting into an unruly beard, food in his teeth, snot up his nose. I am about to dedicate ten minutes to studying a new photo of Jim looking distant in a pub garden when I notice a comment from an unfamiliar name. Nathalia. She calls him by a nickname and pokes fun at his face in a way that only a new lover could. I immediately plunge into her photos. She is a vision – a woman who makes more sense, who makes me feel as if I am the intern who applied for a job way above my pay grade. Her feed is full of images of couture models and artsy magazine shoots – keen to promote her interest in quirky style, thin arms and sublime beauty as if it reflects back some of hers. She's got spiky teeth like a vampire, the style of an off-duty Victoria's Secret model, and a confident, all-girls'-school energy. Excess and glamour. Just the woman to set Jim straight.

Sure enough, Nathalia becomes real. One afternoon at work I email Jim to say I am going to see a band and wondered if he might be there, and if so perhaps we could leave with each other too? He replies to say he's going, but that he'll be there with a girl he's seeing. He hates to break the news to me on email, but he felt he ought to be honest. I should have known; he's dressing differently, more low-key and expensive compared to the high-street-smart man I first met. For the first forty-five seconds I can handle the fact he's moved on, but then I'm in the gutter. I call my sister, and she tells me gently that it's time to stop. It's good he's met someone new. We weren't meant to be.

Out of fury rather than want, I am thrust into my own transformative Shirt Day moment, when I ask *The Fly*'s IT desk to block his emails. It's time to enter a new phase, so I unfriend him and delete his number, writing it on a small piece of paper that I keep in my wallet, for emergencies. I then rip that into pieces, but still keep in my wallet for a year after. I date new men, but walking past landmarks or pubs Jim and I visited makes the temperature drop and ruins my mood and any potential. If I take someone back to my stinking, noisy room, I've started to put on a DVD of Chris Morris's terrifying sketch show *Jam*, as if warning them via sketches about dead babies and sexual abuse that I am dark and broken.

In the years that follow, the sadness dissipates but a new form of anger rears its head. I bump into one sweet girl on a night out who asks if I am Harriet, Jim's ex. She says she is seeing him at the moment but she doesn't know whether or not to trust him. I tell her maybe, who knows, and, to my surprise, utter the words: 'Next time you see him, tell him I want to kick his head in.' This sentiment continues when I bump into one of Jim's colleagues at a pub. We have a polite chat and I ask if he still shares the office with Jim. 'Because', I say with red-wine lip liner and wolf-like eyes, 'if you do, tell him I want to kick his head in.' I don't know where this catch-phrase has come from. Maybe a physical fight is the only way to rid myself of the hangover of unresolved emotions. Maybe I'm trying to shift his focus away from my reputation as a snivelling desperate loser into a fearsome brute.

In the following years we are no longer in touch, nor do I want to be. I walk past him having a meeting near the location of the Oxford Street split and note that the blazer has been replaced by an athleisure jacket. It's good to know he's still evolving. I certainly have. Or at least I believed so. I am scrolling Twitter one morning when I see that Tshepo, my friend and an esteemed music writer, has tweeted about a new band she likes, one that Jim has been doing A&R for. In a moment of abrupt bitterness, a real emotional blast from the past, I reply to her tweet saying that they 'sound like Reef'. As soon as I press send, I am horrified at my pettiness. Carried away by the thrill of the moment, I've also included the band in the tweet, so they've seen it. Jim has seen it too. His name arrives in my inbox and for a second I am flattered that he's managed to track down my new email address. 'A bit harsh,' he says. I write back to say that I actually like Reef. The conversation ends. I never expected the 'Place Your Hands' 1990s Somerset funksters to put the final nail in the coffin of this particular relationship, but, then, life is full of surprise and wonder.

Jim's since become a father and has left London, but that's enough information for me. The last time I looked at his Instagram I felt so exposed, as if he was looking right back at me. Now his social media is something I remain totally in fear of finding. I no longer love him and he was no monster; our relationship was but a harsh lesson in temperamental incompatibility. Yet there was an extremity to my heartbreak that I'd rather not recall while fumbling around the internet. To see his name alone takes me back to that unfortunate year with frightening velocity. To see his face reminds me of his brain inside his skull and the sacred space in his memory I hold. Forever decaying as the girl in the grotty regions of her twenties – eating the dead flesh off a mackerel, asking for a casual coffee on Valentine's Day, the used sanitary products in the sink and threats of physical violence. Too gnarly for someone who wanted glamour. The shame, the shame. The shame of giving too much and loving too hard. Jim was wrong in many ways. But on my sixth form poetry? So very right.

CHAPTER SEVEN

(It's Totally Fine to Check In On Your Ex)

This one applies only to the easy exes. If, like in the case of the aforementioned Jim, the sight of their 2D face brings back emotions akin to a stress dream in which you're singing Ellie Goulding's 'Starry Eyed' in the middle of a German exam while wearing only eyeshadow, please do not revisit the past.

However, should their memory hold no physically harmful symptoms, then there's nothing to be afraid of. Because there is truly nothing quite like it. The first hit of discovering an ex-lover's Spotify profile. That electric sensation of candid, uncurated exposure. I'm crouching in the cupboard in their bedroom, they're fresh out of the shower and I am *alive*.

Most internet users are savvy when it comes to the availability of their digital information, with the relevant privacy controls turned on where necessary. But in streaming platforms there remains a gap in the door, a sliver of light – a forgotten porthole into their intimate lives. There's MixCloud and Soundcloud, but the real dirt – the raw truth – lives on Spotify. As I feel the 3 p.m. drag of an afternoon slump, I devolve into my inner worm, wriggling into a blanket with a tasty apple, the name of a former boyfriend from ten years ago, a big old search bar and: bliss.

Once inside, a whole vista of vulnerabilities is revealed: heart-clutched expectations, furrowed brows and whispered thoughts. The abandoned 'Bday' playlist with just one track in it ('Blurred Lines'); the Recently Played artists that deliver a plethora of potential daydreams (Morcheeba, 50 Cent); the Running playlists, the Cooking playlists and, my ultimate kick, the covertly titled Sex playlists ('Late late nights', 'Nice chill time').

Anyone who has ever hesitated before using the search function of social media as a new partner sits beside them will know that the act of looking up an ex is forbidden. It is considered illegal to harbour curiosity for those we have formerly shared intimate moments with. And I do understand why, when a 11.25 p.m. Facebook DM could unexpectedly unlock a hit of nostalgia that threatens to wreck your entire life. If you are, however, coming into this in a relatively stable place and not on a mission to self-destruct, why deny yourself the simple pleasure of honouring love lost? Perhaps we should be kinder to ourselves. For me, it is a fulfilling and wholly natural impulse. The act of cyber-stalking your ex can offer an immediate rush of satisfaction more wholly pleasurable than the act of sex with the ex itself. It is an emotional safari, a slow-moving exploration into the following:

Peace

The ultimate sign of resolved, content emotions is the ability to look an ex dead in the eyes and know that everything turned out as it should have. I don't have romantic thoughts or unfulfilled fantasies about my past lovers. We are but old friends; creatures who cared for one another until we evolved into something else. Their profiles, social media, streaming, or otherwise, provide portals into another life I could have been part of. The holidays in Palm Springs with the constant diner stop-offs that would have made me constipated, the ratty dogs I'd reluctantly mother, the overprotective sisters I'd struggle to trust, the inspirational Brian Eno interviews on YouTube I'd pretend to appreciate. I cherish the life I have without them and am happy they are happy too. And by 'looking them dead in the eyes' I of course mean 'browsing through sixteen photos of cabbage and spade selfies taken on their new allotment alongside a ruddy-faced new fiancée'.

Total fear

For our own protection we need to keep them under surveillance. Exes know too much. They've witnessed you at your very worst ('I hate how my legs look in skinny jeans and I don't want to go to your fucking birthday drinks!!', the time that bit of nose hair fell onto your lip mid-argument) and your best (the first three weeks, that one cup of tea with the right amount of milk in). It is horrifying that they are able to walk around with that – a hard drive full of prime archived content and under no contractual obligation to keep any of it concealed. Horrifying. *Never* stop knowing where they live.

Safety

It's important to get a good look at their new partner. To

affirm your unflinching suspicion that they secretly always wanted to date the type of human who could host a supper club at the drop of a hat – lanterns, pomegranates, charred aubergine and all. But mostly it's vital to know who to run from should you see them in the wild. Realistically – would you win in a fight? You might need to, because they probably hate you. In their house you are now forever referred to as 'that nightmare, emotionally volatile, actually quite nasty and boring ex-girlfriend whose little toes look like dead grubs'. Well at least I'm not an alcoholic, bitch!!!

A desire to feel something, *anything*, after a difficult commute

Bored? Numb? Trick your brain into recreationally falling back in love with an ex by playing 'Something' by the Beatles while looking at a Facebook profile photo taken of them in Crete, 2011, when they still vaguely reminded you of Dev Patel. A guaranteed three seconds of self-induced somethingness.

Affection

At the core of this deranged impulse is true affection. It's a legitimate desire to wonder what your old friend is doing, to see if they are alright. To check that they are alive and well and still finger-blasting women to Lonestar's 'Amazed'. So, if you are ever struck by doubt before taking a sneaky stroll down memory lane, remember that it's fine. Everything is totally fine.

CHAPTER EIGHT

Career Opportunities

It's 2019 and I am watching the BRIT Awards out of one eye, while the other eye is taking in a slo-mo Instagram video of macaroni cheese coming out of the oven. Matty Healy, frontman of the critically acclaimed and incredibly popular pop band the 1975, has kissed his girlfriend, hugged his manager and has now taken to stage to accept the band's BRIT Award for Best Group. Dressed in a suit and looking serious, he begins to read a few lines from a recent viral article about misogyny in the music industry. 'A friend of ours said this and I thought we should all think about it . . .', Matty says with the veneration of Matthew McConaughey reciting the Bible as he reads the quotes from the inspirational call to arms. My eye is still on the cheese until I hear him say the name of the author of the article – Laura, my long-time colleague, peer and . . . nemesis? No, that's too sinister. Rival? Too reciprocal. I'm not sure how best to define my decade-long parasocial relationship with a young indomitable music journalist whose talent is far greater than my own. All I know is that in this moment I am completely overwhelmed with rancour. It hits me with such force I've no option but to tweet her to say well done, rather than what I'm really thinking: 'It should have been me. Why was it not me?'

My inability to process Laura's triumphs dates back to 2007, while working at *The Fly*. One morning I am minding my own business, writing 250 words of copy for an advertorial upselling a sponsored show – 'Like live music? Like vodka? You'll love this gig' – when Niall chucks a copy of the *NME* onto my desk. It's open on a review of my favourite band. He says I should check it out. It's written by a new girl who's 'really young' and 'really good'. 'That's cool!' I say in a sisterly tone. Inside: I hate her.

I convince my face to remain expressionless and take a look at the *NME*. It's the lead review. 600 words. Her sentences zip along, full of cleverly observed context and curious phrasing. The last line hits me like a bullet: 'Bow at the feet of pop's new Picassos.' An art reference? I didn't realize Mary Beard moonlit as a music critic but, fine.

As bitterness sours my insides, I become conscious that behind my swivel chair is a drawing of a really long, haggard penis snaking into the mouth of a sad, withered head – one that I drew in biro and stuck on my wall a few weeks ago. It's next to an orange razor hanging from a piece of string and a tissue with some sunflower seeds sellotaped onto it. Here, anything goes, including my below-par journalism.

Into our filthy little kitchen I go to make myself a concilia-tory sweet instant coffee. Reading the review has brought up a lot of negative emotions. This girl is barely out of her teens and is as cerebral and insightful as a fifty-year-old philosophy professor. I am in a nurturing environment among colleagues who acknowledge my inexperience constructively and kindly, but given the direct nature of digital journalism, I am frequently finding damning external feedback for my writing. I am haunted by one comment, left under an online track-by-track review of the new Bombay Bicycle Club album, which states: 'This is one of the worst things I've ever read on the internet.' My ego is fragile and I don't have enough self-esteem in the tank to take another line about my turgid prose.

Much like my twisted infatuation with *Vice*, anyone writing at the *NME* immediately becomes an emblem of tantalizing success. Despite the depths of my love for my colleagues at *The Fly*, climbing the ladder is a preoccupation of mine. I yearn to work for a more stable and mainstream publication. *The Fly* is constantly threatened with closure by the company who owns us and we are regularly reminded we are the black sheep of the 'integrated live music and artist services business'. It has created an atmosphere of rebelliousness and extraordinary insecurity that often manifests itself in cock drawings stuck on the wall.

Graphic phallus illustrations aside, we create quite a decent product each month. We can't pay most of the writers and there are no sub-editors – pedantic magazine staff employed to monitor grammar, spelling and the fine details – so some mistakes fly under the radar. The week before I join, the words for last month's cover feature are printed alongside the photos for this month's cover. A Franz Ferdinand interview is illustrated by a photo shoot of the Kaiser Chiefs. A massive error, but an easy mistake to make when 90 per cent of bands of the period are white men dressed in tight waist-coats and winkle-pickers who look like they're in an ongoing battle with iron deficiency.

While it sounds as if we are working on a joke fanzine, we are also technically the biggest music magazine in the country, with over 100K readers. Also, thanks to our tenacious and charming editor Niall's excellent relationships with PRs and managers, we are given access to artists and events that blow my mind on a weekly basis. I spend most nights with the same people at the Barfly in Camden – it's a bit like *Cheers* but everyone's on coke and most of the corners smell of TCP. I love it there because it's also the first stop for all the new buzz bands on their UK tours, and I get exclusive access to its back-stage area and viewing nooks. The job provides no pension scheme, but I do get to stand on a small rickety staircase to see the Drums.

It feels as if I've snuck into the industry during its last hurrah – right before record labels stop ploughing money into getting music press – so I can live quite a glamorous life from Monday to Friday. Rubbing shoulders with We Are Scientists on a Wednesday night in the K West hotel or hanging out with the Levi's' marketing team at a sponsored event in Soho. Going to a Santigold album playback and drinking warm white wine at 11 a.m. I get to travel to Iceland for folk music and Finland for heavy metal – but most importantly I get to eat. Beyond buying bottles of Pepto-Bismol, London rent sucks up all my wages. I am over my overdraft. For the majority of 2008 to 2010, I have half a tin of kidney beans and some questionably damp hummus in the fridge. They don't realize it at the time – or maybe some of them do, depending on the speed with which I eat the pizza – but the free lunches given to me by the generous people working for PR companies and labels are literally keeping me alive.

Music journalism is the ideal job for someone who's just left university; nocturnal and fuelled by free booze, it's relentlessly sociable and overstimulating – three gigs a night. I'd classify it as quantity over quality, mostly. I wish I could recount some stories of the boundary-pushing shows I've reported from but it's a culturally void era, and a boom time for mediocre artists. A lot of alternative music is cold, apolitical and nihilistic and sounds like it should be blasted from the tinny speakers of a MacBook – blogpop, witch house, the rise of EDM. Unknown writers are blogging relentlessly and as a result there's an influx in flash-in-the-pan hype tracks flooding my postbox. I've no choice but to keep up.

Print journalists are feeling the looming spectre of bloggers – their websites are a faster form of communication and consumption. Magazines are in a precarious position; sales are dwindling and some are folding. But their writers still have huge egos. And as Real Critics it's our responsibility to contribute to a more thorough type of music writing. Rather than professing whatever synth pop duo is doing the rounds on the blogs that week as the new Kraftwerk, we wait and see the bands perform live – find out for sure if they stand a chance of forming some kind of long-term career. I learn all the right phrases to say during the show and use them with authority even if I don't always understand the meaning: 'A bit bassy',

'Krautrock', 'Lynchian', and – my favourite – a sarcastic 'Yeh!!!! Wooooo!' with a clap if there's an awkward silence as the guitarist takes too long tuning up. Oh, also, 'tuning up'.

I respect authority and the office routine, but I still struggle to get my body into work by 10.50 a.m. after a big night watching the buzz bands. When I arrive it's just a matter of waiting for stupid things to happen. We occupy a corner of an open-plan office and blast out whatever promo CDs have arrived in the post. I am not jaded yet; very open to persuasion and mostly agree with whatever Niall says.

Being so amenable doesn't exactly get you a name as a music critic, however, and after a while I realize that in order to stand out I ought to experiment with being a massive one-star bitch. I first introduce this persona when I write an album review for indie / electro band Does It Offend You, Yeah? which concludes with the sentence: 'It's either shit indie, or shit electro, yeah?' It's the first time I've been cheeky in my writing and I am feeling like I'm on the cusp of a new chapter in my career. Harriet Gibsone: the truth-seeker whistle-blower holding entitled, millionaire musicians to account.

A week after the issue is released, I get a direct message on Facebook from a name I vaguely recognize. It's one of the band members with a message that completely punctures my dream of being the new Julie Burchill (circa 1977). He is hurt by what I've said about his record – a body of work on which he bared his soul – and asks why I thought it was OK to write something like this. It's a great question; one that chills me to the core. I scroll through his Facebook photos to see a selection of photos of a young man who looks caught in the crossfire of youth and hedonism, but fragile too. I cannot cope with the brutal feedback I get from my blogs – the ones that reaffirm every dark thought I've ever had about my capabilities – and yet this pains me even more. I know all about the lineage of music journalists being rude about artists then attacked in response – Nick Cave beating up Jack Barron or Johnny Cigarettes getting threatened by Keith Allen and Liam Gallagher. It was all part of the wild spirit of rock 'n' roll reportage and it made for great copy. This new digital gateway between the artist and journalist has wrecked it all. I'd take a macho kick to the nuts over a haunting 2.34 a.m. Facebook message any day.

In my downtime from slagging vulnerable men off, I am filming DIY sessions in our car park, which we've rebranded as a 'courtyard'. I upsold my multimedia journalism credentials when applying for my job, and JJ and Niall are under the impression I can launch a video channel and boost web traffic, when actually I have little experience beyond my series of cutting-edge university documentaries.

We have been inspired by Blogotheque and SBTV – successful YouTube channels that capture the raw, unvarnished talent of new and established artists. Nobody at *The Fly* seems to mind that I don't know how to do lighting or use a boom mic. Sometimes the bands (the Rakes, Badly Drawn Boy) are horrified and I have to convince them to go ahead with the performance, essentially telling them: 'Don't worry, it's meant to be shit! That's our USP!'

As my writing is still quite wobbly, I pour all of my energy into booking musicians to play these sets – and, remarkably, it pays off. Sometimes we run competitions where fans can win tickets to watch a session being filmed. I manage to snag pre-mega-fame Ed Sheeran, Alt-J, Ellie Goulding and the Kooks, all of which are a success. But sometimes, when the act is slightly less high-profile, only about two people enter the competition. I can always guarantee one person will show up: a strange, silent guy who looks like a grey toilet brush and keeps his belongings in a plastic bag. On the bad competition days, I have to run around the building and see if any of the 150 or so staff occupying the rest of it will support *The Fly* and pretend to be competition winners so the talent and management team don't clock that nobody has entered apart from the toilet brush guy. It's a tricky negotiation, as while I am appreciative that some of the people from the office have agreed to stand in a cold car park on their lunch break, they barely hide their lack of enthusiasm and often forget to get into the headspace of a buzzing competition winner. It must be incredibly confusing for the artist to play to an audience of sixteen 'fans' who are all either eating sandwiches, chain-smoking or chatting among themselves. The worst incident comes when a Mercury Prize-winning artist who's received an inexplicably low number of entrants (translation: toilet brush) arrives to play on a miserable November afternoon. She is expecting an effusive and interactive crowd of devotees – and launches into a sing-along to the chorus of a song from her new album. Nobody knows the words and nobody sings, due to the fact that a large proportion of the audience have their mouths full, or because they work in HR and stopped listening to music in 1998. We scrap the first take and try again. Take two: I float out of my body and sing so passionately I hope to mimic the volume of many. In the playback of the video, which goes online shortly after, and will have been circulated across her entire label and management team, all you can hear is my matronly voice speak-rapping lyrics about inner-city strife.

I should have known it would be a disaster to get the rest of the building on board. The company that owns *The Fly* also employs band managers as well as gig, festival and club promoters. It takes a special kind of person to work in this industry. A lotta guys who don't know how to interact with women. Misfits, hedonists, chancers and pricks. There's a former cage fighter. A guy called Vegas who wears wooden shoes. An intensely jolly dad who is said to expense calls to phone sex lines. Cubic Alan with the foot fetish. About eight seriously posh people who hate music unless it's a funky house remix. The Kitchen Gremlin. A guy who used to be in a ridiculous rock-synth fusion band in the '80s. One of the original Shoreditch hipsters from the '90s. Their respective ventures – night clubs, bars and festivals – are all thriving. The environment is freewheeling and furiously unprofessional. There are no social boundaries. People are microwaving fish at 4 p.m. There are no bonuses or guarantees of a job next year, but on a Friday we get free pizza.

In spite of the unorthodoxy I am completely at ease in this environment and singing a lot. Niall says my voice is so weak it makes him feel physically sick. Ben, the newest member of the team, likes to have control of the stereo, and gets experimental, plugging the AUX cord into his laptop and playing Frank Ocean's *nostalgia, ULTRA* at the same time as a BBC News bulletin.

It's all been fun and games, even during the dark bits where we're hauled into meetings to be told we're on thin ice. But this Laura girl has made me question my trajectory. I do have bigger ambitions than *The Fly*, but I don't know how to leave; where to go. I pathetically text a guy at the *NME* every few months to ask if there's any available jobs and he says he'll keep an eye out. Deep down I'm worried I'm not good enough. That I'm neither a renegade rock 'n' roll rebel who's as anarchic as the artist, or a contemporary internet wizard who understands SEO. Laura leans towards the latter – she has a popular Twitter account where she talks passionately about the music she loves and engages with the responses. Even though she is young, she is serious and intellectual; every feature she writes makes an impact, creates a cultural happening. It's so different from my boisterous, blokey entry to the scene – I write like a tragic lager lout when everyone else is sobering up. And I've got no brand. Laura's printed words and tweeted words have coalesced into a destination for 24/7 music-related wisdom.

This is all part of a new pressure I'm feeling. To contribute to the Twitter debate, to further my career. The early 2010s are a transient time on the platform. It's not yet riddled by division and trolls, and is more or less motivated by normal people wanting a laugh on their coffee break at work or dual-screening at home. There's been a power grab on the platform, and the journalists have won. They start convivial conversations and viral word games (Beatles songs as fish: 'Day Kipper' etc.). They are editors, columnists and broadcasters and their friends, some of which are original and witty, but are spawning mind-numbing replicants who've co-opted their identikit sense of humour; either arch or outraged. There's a formula and twee cadence to the tweeted one-liners, and while I hate them, and hate it, I want in. It appears to be the only way to ascend my lowly status in this industry, and to get onto the 30 Under 30 list that arrives in a music industry magazine each year and crushes me with my omission each time, even though all I've ever really done is Q&As with a few wonky pop trios who wear their guitars far too high up on their torsos.

On the nights the online elite live-tweet *X Factor*, I try to join in, but my voice is a meek squeak in the digital cacophony. When I'm firing on all cylinders I get, on average, one Favourite per well-timed tweet. When I am not trying to join in with the topical back and forth, I go off-course and do some observational material: 'An earwig crawled out of my honey jar. Coffee tastes of pincers and bronze medals. Day ruined. Life over.' No likes. Neither amusing enough nor relatable. I experiment with something silly and media-inclusive: 'If we had a journalist battle I wonder who would win? I'd do well, using a bayonet & my incredible inner strength.' Zero engagement. I refresh the page and see that some freelancer for a broadsheet has tweeted about David Cameron being a 'cunting cockwomble' and it's racking up fifty RTs by the hour. One night I am at a Grimes gig and spot one of the major players in the Twitter clique. I stop her to tell her how much I like her writing and, as a few male friends pass me, I wave goodbye. She raises her eyebrow and responds drolly: 'I bet you know all the boys.' I do; she's right; and I take her ribbing as an invitation into her inner circle.

As I get onto the night bus home, I send her a public tweet about fringes that she doesn't respond to.

I am faring no better with breaking into celebrity inner circles either. I'm a scared, terrible interviewer. My first for *The Fly* is with experimental indie group Yeasayer – the music press love them as they aren't dressed in little indie-boy suits but they're the sort of boorish Brooklyn hipsters who might wear ponchos and want to talk about Nietzsche or ayahuasca. 'So what's with the name?' I ask cheekily, like Paula Yates without the charm or attitude. The frontman looks at me for a quizzical moment, and responds: 'Well, do you know the phrase naysayer?' I say no. He gets his phone out, calls his manager to order a Nando's and answers the rest of my questions using only disdainful grunts.

I also fall too hard and too regularly for the artists I am exposed to. In many ways it is faintly creepy and vaguely unprofessional. I am not acknowledging a good hook or poetic lyrics – I am having an emotional epiphany during a melancholic chord change that suggests the guitarist and I should be platonically or romantically linked immediately. As such, I've legitimized my time spent ploughing into a musician's personal social media accounts, now all for the purpose of research. Can I formulate any printable questions about the frontman's mother's new husband and how much he looks like her son? No. But it does give me a secret glimpse into his unspoken neuroses. In that his mum fancies him, and that must be hard. Alternatively, if it's not hard, and he likes it, maybe I should dress like his mum for the interview.

One of the first such bands is Friendly Fires, to whom I

am desperately dedicated. It's too much. I am often on my own at their shows and excessively emotional. I'm not sure why their tropical pop resonates so much when this kind of hysteria is reserved for more earnest artists or stadium pop stars, but they're shaking my world. They have a song called 'Jump In The Pool' which is transcendent; when I listen to it I feel like I am showering in holy water. The music, combined with the confetti, dancing and tin drum outro, moves me so profoundly I have to hide my breakdown while within the shimmying crowds.

Then Niall asks if I'd like to interview them in New York. My chance to shine; to charm them into dedicating their future Glastonbury headline performance to 'a special little lady who changed our lives! Harriet – we love you.'

I've never been to New York before and when I arrive I am so chronically jetlagged that I can't eat anything. I head straight to the interview and, star-struck beyond all belief, order half a Cantaloupe melon with cottage cheese from the diner. I prod at it occasionally to project an air of ease with what I've ordered but inside I feel as if I am swimming in honey and might be sick. I ask them the big, hard-hitting questions: if they are nervous about playing in America; how they found writing the album. Stuff worth flying across the Atlantic for.

That night, the PR invites me to see them live and to hang out backstage. It's humid so I'm wearing awful brown wicker sandals from Primark and a very short pink animal-print dress I got from Oxfam. I am quite drunk and confused by the end of the show, but manage to suppress my tears and head back to congratulate my guys. After telling them how good the gig was, I mainly nail their rider and stare at them from afar while they interact. The next day I wake up in the pink dress and full of regret upon realizing that I had stolen frontman Ed's expensive sunglasses and two bottles of spirits from their rider, as a memento. It's then I'm also hit by memories of looking out at the skyline from my hotel room while wearing Ed's Ray-Bans and listening to 'Empire State of Mind' with my iPod volume cranked up to the max. I text the PR to confess and she says 'haha' but agrees I should probably give it all back immediately. We're all heading to see MGMT play in an abandoned swimming pool later in Brooklyn so I can do it then.

Inspired by the Big Apple and needing a confidence boost, I go into a thrift store and purchase a completely new personality on my way to the show; for a few dollars I get denim hot pants and a grey trilby hat, which I get changed into immediately. As I arrive at the venue I spot the band, and, choosing to ignore the bassist's quiet yet stunned comment about my 'big new hat', I hand Ed a bag with his belongings in it. He is very gracious, agreeing it was a drunken night. But it was an undeniably weird move, and naturally there's a cloud of confusion hanging over me and my intentions for the rest of the day. What happens next doesn't help. During MGMT's performance, someone who knows the band shows up, sees the trilby and, assuming I must be down to party, hands me a metal cigarette filled with weed. I take one toke and fall into a slow-motion tornado for the next four hours. We go for lunch in an agonizingly chic restaurant and the woman at the record label gets us cold red wine. They all opt for pasta while I order myself more melon and cheese –

this time watermelon and feta. I just need salt and water. I say absolutely nothing. Every time I put my wine glass on the table it makes a total racket and I delay taking sips, but I'm so thirsty, and unable to find an opportunity to ask the drummer to pass me the communal water, or to figure out if the conversation has paused or if they're mid-flow still. I'm desperate for a wee but the thought of navigating my body around this minimalist nightmare of a restaurant inhabited by artists, actors, moths, my late grandad, a supply teacher from Year 9, six pairs of scissors and the ghost of George Harrison fills me with dread.

Eventually it's time to go home, back to where I belong: in my crap flat, writing up my big scoop and frying rancid kidney beans to a crisp.

After the New York trip, I do see the band again, at events and festivals. I'm sure we bonded slightly over our brief experience in the Big Apple but simply by proximity rather than any deep connection. Nevertheless, I add them all on Facebook; they accept but the conversation stops there. I've always been amazed by journalists who manage to hit it off with celebrities – interviews that evolve into mutually appreciative, long-term relationships. I can't think of anything more discombobulating than sustaining that unspoken power imbalance for a prolonged period of time. The pressure to justify your role as an interesting and enlightening newcomer to the sacred inner circle when you're up against their remarkable and interesting creative peers, and Diplo. Holding in all that adoration, that sycophancy, when it would be far more relaxing and sexually fulfilling to stay at home writing fanfic about their Oedipus complex.

It's hard to leave *The Fly*. It's particularly hard because I don't get offered any other jobs. But eventually, after eight years, and a crushing phase in which I feel obliged to go on a series of dinner dates with an editor at a magazine in order to pitch my ideas, I decide it's time for a radical rebrand. I buy a fur-collared coat and apply for a features-writing role at a women's magazine. I put my heart and soul into the application by building a private Tumblr profile that I send to its editor, Kate. On the profile, I replicate the pastel-colour tones of the magazine, dripping in a sickly millennial pink, and fill it with pretty images of girls with lush hair, big hats and knee socks, chunky boots, massive scarves, Suzi Bubble, Swedish street-style bloggers and an About Me section that includes the phrase 'a passion for fashion'. The Tumblr works and I get an interview. Conscious of my lack of experience in women's publishing, I plan to dazzle and distract with my outfit, and on the day I meet Kate wear a navy pinafore dress that I get in the Big Topshop sale.

Once in Kate's big glass office I sit neatly on the edge of a fuchsia pouffe; a maid spouting hyperbole like a football player in a post-match interview. Phrases and words I'd never repeat in any other context: 'I truly believe I can do this role to the best of my abilities,' I declare, bottling out of eye-contact and staring at Kate's fringe instead. Something about 'taking it to the next level'. Then: 'Ten years' time? If I'm honest I wouldn't mind sitting in your seat, if that's not too bold!' Ambitious, sure, but I know when to have fun too. We're having a laugh! Are we having a laugh?

While Kate riffs about bloggers with iPads on the front row, my mind idly wanders to a mid-game assessment. How is this going? Time to stop twiddling the dead skin-flap on your thumb. And the words you're saying – are you absolutely sure we are still collectively, as a society in 2012, repeating the generic job interview script about perfectionism and team players? And what happens if you do get the job? You'll have to see Kate on a daily basis; befriend someone who has seen you on your knees, crawling around so craven and corporate and lying about your skills. She'll suss you out pretty soon. And she's looking at you now.

'I'm really interested in working on the app. I wondered how integral that will be to the role?'

Nice. Time to tap out for another two minutes and watch Kate take centre stage. She is good. Confident. A peppy slick blonde with sparkling blue eyes, professional and fun. All the best editors are mini-celebrities in their own right; a magnetic charm, natural minglers and skilled at convincing people to do stuff they don't want to do.

I suddenly become aware it is silent again.

'I love apps,' I say as my bra strap slowly slips down my arm.

Two days later I get a call to say I've got the job. My first instinct is to say no. No! 'No, thank you, Kate. Instead I'd like to live with my parents in Essex. I do not have the capacity to leave my friends at *The Fly* and to perform at this level of app-based enthusiasm for ten hours a day.'

But I say yes, and that I am over the moon. Because I do want this life, and the entrance into professionalism it brings.

★   ★   ★

Within hours of arriving at my new desk in central London, I realize that moving from *The Fly* to a teen women's magazine is the equivalent of being raised by wolves in a wood then dumped on the Met Gala red carpet. The pace is fast, all very above-board, and in order to stay on top of the flow of work I barely have time for a lunch break; also I'm struggling to keep up with small talk about the royal baby while waiting for the microwave in the kitchen.

It's a consumption-based society here. As well as all its staff milling across the open-plan office floor holding Pret coffees – a *Devil Wears Prada*-inspired symbol of focus, efficiency and frivolously spent cash – there is always free stuff arriving from PR companies who want us to tweet about their brand. The cupcakes are the worst: huge boxes of them, covered in brightly coloured thick icing that bypasses a sugar high and goes straight to white-knuckle breakdown and gritted teeth. I'm hooked on the buzz and the only one who's guaranteed to take a cake. I will take anything free, actually – green lip liner, orange eyeshadow, a rubber necklace or a tiara promoting a new range of fake tan. Whatever turns up on the free table is fingered speculatively for a few minutes and shoved in my bag, never to be used again. Freeloading isn't the chicest personality trait so I'm trying to take it easy by reducing my enthusiasm and inspecting the options on my way back from the toilet rather than sprinting over as soon as the fleet of crap arrives.

Five months into the role, five months of treading water while bingeing on red velvet cakes sent to promote Frankie from the Saturdays' new line of pop socks, I get an important email. The subject line is 'Fancy some work?' and it is from an editor at *The Guardian*, who says I've been recommended by a few PRs and he wants to know if I'll do some shifts covering music news. I say yes absolutely, take one last electric-blue eyeliner pen from the freebie table, google 'How to write news' and 'Wikileaks' and hand in my resignation.

When I get to the vast glass tank of an office in King's Cross, I am struck by the seriousness of the job. No more pissing about. People are grown-up, well educated, wearing suits or shirts. There are no cage fighters or loud singing; the level of conversation is exclusively professional. If free stuff arrives we have to declare it to someone at HR. There is no stereo to play music; there are many meetings and my mistakes have bigger repercussions – I'm learning how to become a journalist in real time in front of one of the most belittling comment sections on the internet.

In terms of bonding, I do try out some kooky personality stuff with some of the younger colleagues, but it's not getting the big laughs it would have at *The Fly*. I start replying to emails with stock professional chit-chat such as 'nice to e-meet you'. And the feeling of imposter syndrome grows by the day, as I realize how little I actually know about Bob Dylan, and that I hate the harmonica, so I decide to make myself indispensable by working excessively hard and saying yes to every opportunity. I learn how to do pre-meeting small talk like an adult ('I love that jumper. Very Scandi noir!') and get a little byline photo too. For the shoot, which takes place in a cupboard, I wear a green top that makes my neck look as thin as a pencil. My face is bright and cheerful. I've physically made it, even if my brain hasn't caught up yet.

Laura's doing well too. She's the star writer at the *NME* and has thousands of followers on Twitter. Part of a new wave of journalists who are always online, always responsive. Laura is a clear-minded feminist who always has the right hot take on any newsworthy music event. If something big happens – a cultural controversy or celebration – I'll check her Twitter to see what the correct response is. She's actually inspiring me to be a little bolder with my online voice. 'I am sick and tired of men discussing which member of Warpaint they'd most want to have sex with!' I tweet one afternoon. It gets three likes; I'm blown away. For the rest of the day I walk around as if every man in London is thinking: 'That's that girl who posted the Warpaint thing – she's not afraid to say what she thinks. Let's stay out of her way.'

Two months into my trial period at *The Guardian* I get a full-time contract – the biggest rush of validation I have ever experienced. I can afford Wasabi at lunch and new clothes; fabric softener and insoles. I no longer need to prove myself in social situations; the mere suggestion that I am paid by the publishing behemoth allows me to remain completely mute at dinner parties.

That's not to say I am complacent, however. It's 2013 and I'm far from an anomaly. Laura's only getting more powerful within the industry and I can't help thinking she will take my job at some point. So I whip myself into a frenzy, trying harder, my speciality being speed-typing. I can write up a story, find and crop an image, and upload it onto the internet in seven minutes, which is handy given I feel the only way to prosper here is to pump as much content into the ether as possible.

On my breaks I'll sometimes punish myself by looking at the Twitter elite's current topic of conversation. They're still going strong but I've given up trying to muscle my way in. Having a job at *The Guardian* hasn't helped me make any inroads on Twitter. A couple of decent follow-backs but we aren't chatting. I just watch them instead: squabbles, some falling out of favour, others usurping, crawling, chewing, chatting, snickering, burping; persistent noise and frenzied motion; a desperate struggle to shout the loudest. The climate is more politicized than before, however. Men have started to put 'feminist' in their Twitter bios and pop feminism is the dominant force behind every online debate, from Miley Cyrus's 'We Can't Stop' to Robin Thicke's 'Blurred Lines'. The traffic on the music website is huge.

Eventually I get a new job at *The Guardian* as an editor on the pop culture magazine. It is fantastic to be off the 24/7 grind of online editing; no celebrity death can take over my weekend. It does, however, mean my job on the music desk will be advertised, and this is the moment I have been dreading. Laura will replace me.

Which she does; or, rather, completely revolutionizes what my job could be. She is prolific, secures interviews with the world's biggest pop stars, writes viral opinion pieces and reviews, and is so popular among young female music writers that interns apply to work on the music desk purely to get closer to her. I am amazed at how carefree and breezy around her I am at the *Guardian* teapoint, chatting as if I haven't been terrified of her eclipsing my career for the best part of a decade. I actually really like her.

Still, every time she publishes some new work I get lost in entire scenarios in my head in which the top bosses at *The Guardian* hold emergency meetings about how Laura is surpassing the talent of any other music journalist who's come before – and it's come to their realization what a total mistake Harriet's time on the music desk was by comparison. Then I imagine being in her inbox, and the *New York Times* editors who are begging her to quit her job and join their team, with an average yearly wage of $300,000. And the fan letters from students and musicians and probably even politicians, who are considering discussing her recent article about Robyn in the House of Commons. It's a form of madness. But her reputation is venerated; she is so good, I wouldn't be shocked if it all came true.

What makes her different from me is that she is brave. I am sent a single rape threat on Twitter after writing a blog sticking up for Courtney Love, and another one after a snarky review of Eminem, and it's put me off expressing my opinions online for life. It doesn't stop Laura. She keeps going. Not only is she driven and encyclopaedic, but she engages with the readers in the comments under her articles, which is part of the job that I simply cannot stomach. I can see how many comments there are under the pieces I've written but I daren't look at what they're saying. Everyone else does, though. I bump into another music writer at a pub who I never felt liked me much, and he asks how I am getting on at *The Guardian*. 'I hope you're OK,' he says. He's seen the comments under my articles. 'They can be so nasty, can't they?'

Instead of reading them myself, I spend a lot of time imagining every possible criticism the commenters might leave underneath: bad writer, doesn't know enough about the subject, boring, lazy. I stay silent and pray my articles go unnoticed, ashamed as soon as they're out in the world. After so many years of desiring a life as a music journalist, I am beginning to realize that I am not built for this industry; or at least its new iteration. I have nothing to say; I have no desire to start the conversation, let alone sustain it all hours of the day.

The 2019 BRIT Awards are truly the final nail in the coffin. For the first few seconds after Matty Healy says her name out loud in front of the nation, I am in disbelief. It's like one of my daydreams, and I am struck by the same sensation of jealousy that I had the first time I saw her byline in the *NME*. But it quickly disperses. What is there to hold onto, to compete with? I haven't done what she's done, nor could if I tried. Where once was naive passion and conviction for writing about music is fear and cynicism. Laura is steely-eyed in the face of push-back or negative attention, born with a faith in her own thoughts, the type that leads countries and ends wars.

A year later Laura quits Twitter; she writes a piece about how its constant presence in her life fed into a sense of self-hatred and paranoia. I am both shocked and comforted by her revelations. She's a social media micro-celebrity who has prioritized health above validation. I quickly find myself missing her on there – there's no easy access to the right answer any more; I'll have to think of it myself. At work we sometimes chat on

Instant messenger; she is easy to confide in, and I feel bad for the way I've resented and deified her. 'What's it like to have left social media?' I ask. She says it is incredible. A revelation. How bold to know you can still thrive without visiting a little website filled with people's names and opinions all day long.

It's spring 2020 when I decide to leave *The Guardian*. My editor suggests Laura would be great to cover my role. I say I think it's a fantastic idea, preparing to once again participate in my secret humiliation as she excels in every area I've failed at. Can't do anything to stop it. I'm pretty sure that until the day I die Laura will arrive and do whatever I've just been doing but just so much better. Instead of being bitter, I vow to celebrate her talent, not weaponize it. I will praise her intelligence, safe in the knowledge that we are different creatures on different paths, suppressing desires to draw penises versus securing world-exclusive interviews with Taylor Swift. It's time to appreciate the ambition, stop this barbaric comparison. Let her go.

Yes, I think. This is progress. *This* is feminism. I inhale deeply, profoundly, considering what a mature woman I've become, how much I have grown. 'Plus,' says a voice at the back of my head, 'music journalism's dead anyway.'

CHAPTER NINE

The Subtle Art of Alexa Chung

Alexa Chung once said on a fashion podcast: 'If you study an image for long enough, you take on those attributes by osmosis.' With that in mind, I've been staring at a photo of her in a preppy smock dress off and on for two hours today – on the bus, in the loo, then peering at it on Google in my pocket like a lucky stone. In the best possible way, she looks like a marzipan baby-doll triangle princess. When I try on my interpretation of the outfit later that day, all I see is a shapeless satin sack that grips to every lump and crevice on my body, like a tea-towel draped over a bowl of grapes.

At this point in my life I have scrutinized every single image of Alexa Chung uploaded onto the internet. I follow her progress like a music fan would their favourite band; each new photo a new song, a new season, the mood of the moment. She gives a little but never enough: I want to know if she drinks cow's milk. What form of contraceptive she uses. How her endometriosis has affected her life and if she has a good relationship with her mother. If she considers the success of modern influencers shallow, and if she's ever considered Botox.

If we were to meet, I would diminish to a shadow. I am the finger puppet on the pinky tip of her grand marble statue. It is hard to imagine her acting timidly – her voice lost to the loud chatter of a party as she asks a guest if their journey was OK, once, twice, three times, until they finally hear it, and answer back dispassionately. When she talks, everyone listens. Because as well as being both funny and clever – the sort of person who's inexplicably good at poker, darts and bowling, and has literary quotes and references appropriate for every occasion – Alexa has been blessed with extraordinary beauty.

Her style is undefinable and delights in inconsistency. Clothes fit her so well, whereas they – dungarees – so often feel as if they are wearing me. Preppy, shabby, cool, she shape-shifts from poised street style to reluctant A-lister; dishevelled bed-head to silky Hollywood tresses; battered Converse to sexy Prada boots, PVC and Peter Pan collars. She's at her zenith on the go and off-guard – with a coffee or cigarette, the wind in her hair as she strides through the city to a ballet class; lanky limbs, short shorts and high-quality faded t-shirts that look like they're made of fine, very fine lambswool. She keeps things simple underneath: I once heard her say that she wears sensible white pants. This information entered my cerebral cortex, nudged out the file marked 'How To Convert a Decimal', and has stuck around ever since. So now I do too, because Alexa understands that more is less – as long as you've also done barre every day for two months and have a body as smooth as a balloon animal.

There's a regular stream of content on her own social media

and YouTube channel, but the real gems are on Facebook account Alexa Chung Unofficial, which is updated daily with new paparazzi shots, interviews and photoshoots. I have yet to find one picture in which she looks even slightly ragged or dirty. There are no red-carpet misfires or double-chin pap shots. Sometimes I am hit by a wave of melancholy when I consider how much time it must take for the Alexa Chung Unofficial Admin to maintain the page – the calls she didn't make to her frail grandma, the coffee breaks she missed while surreptitiously scanning copies of *Vogue* Japan on the work printer – but we're in this mess together.

I don't know what dark arts Alexa learned at Peter Symonds College, but she's successfully duped me into thinking this level of rich eclecticism and sophistication is obtainable. I keep buying new clothes, expecting them to catapult me into another tier of stylishness, and cannot come to terms with the fact there are insurmountable physical differences between us. God bless me and the patent pumps and the seersucker midi dresses that I've purchased over the years, praying they might make me as whip-smart and charming as her.

I'll never forget the first time I saw her bounce on screen with *Popworld* co-star Alex Zane, a moment that ushered in a new era of snarky adolescent presenting that wore thin within about six months, but set a new bar of beauty for women all over the UK. A former catalogue model and pony fanatic from rural Britain, Alexa skipped uni to go on a road trip with a photographer and quickly fell in with a culturally cool crowd in London – the booming indie scene of the mid-'00s. There she announced herself as the arbiter of androgynous elegance – a tomboy bombshell, with flushed pink cheeks and a mischievous smile. An alpha woman among a cohort of silly boys in bands. Always, *always* chic – even when playing an acoustic guitar in the gutters outside the Old Blue Last. She is one of the last true It-girls before the social media aesthetic distorted the beauty standard – the green-juice girlies whose faces are too tweaked and taut to possess long-term iconoclasm. Sure, Alexa probably gets vitamin C injections in her bum and goes for the occasional hike, but she has a rebellious spirit. No matter how much she smokes and parties, her genetic code is written to determine her forever-luminescence. No matter how unachievable her body type or personal style, there's a thrown-together effortlessness to her aesthetic that scams me into thinking that this time I might just pull it off too.

Today I'm looking to her for a specific kind of inspiration. I urgently need at least a semblance of her nonchalance, bravado and seductive powers as *The Guardian* have sent me to the penthouse suite of St Pancras Renaissance Hotel London to meet with the Arctic Monkeys frontman Alex Turner, otherwise known as Alexa's ex-boyfriend. I listen to their new album on repeat while choosing what to wear; wondering which songs are about Alexa and whether I could even say her name in front of him.

If our brains are made up of a committee of characters – some kind, some cruel – over the years I've come to acknowledge that the role of my most critical voice is played by Alexa. The version of Alexa that resides in my head is scathing; mean, bitchy and ultimately correct. For one frenetic hour, dresses and skirts are picked out and chucked on the floor, nothing fits the way it does on her, how it should on me. 'You're frumpy!' 'Too boxy!' she shouts huskily from my bed, a glass of whisky balanced on her chest, one arm arched around her head lazily. I dare to go bolder. 'Very "Dirrrty"-era Christina Aguilera!' The mounds of fabric pile up on the floor and my body temperature rises so I reluctantly resolve that I'll go safe, nothing too ambitious. Something from Cos maybe; better to look like a navy laptop case than a try-hard.

On the day, I am disorientated. Alex and the Arctic Monkeys' drummer, Matt Helders, are two men notoriously resistant to snappy, compliant quotes, and I'm on my last burst of adrenaline before we even shake hands. Cortisol hijacks my body the minute my editor asks me to do the job, pumps through my veins consistently the week before the interview, and rattles my bones three days after the camera stops rolling. It's coursing through me during the interview too – a maniacal surge as I slowly realize it's not going to plan. The reality is that my interviewees are bored and unresponsive to most questions. A more experienced journalist would come down heavy and hard, expertly ushering them away from insolence. I instead persist with nice sweet giggles and smiles. I'm no threat, lads; I'm actually a tiny six-year-old. Love me?

It doesn't help that Alex keeps punctuating his sentences by saying my name in a soporific Sheffield-cum-California drawl. At first I was stunned by this, a classic method of persuasion. To hear one's name said by a celebrity is deeply moving. But when it is accompanied by indifference it becomes clear the name calling is more a polite affectation rather than out of genuine affection. It doesn't help that he won't take off his sunglasses – I don't even ask, but my eyes implore him to do so. There's a fundamental barrier between us, no chance of genuine intimacy.

When this type of altercation happens in print you can write around the awkwardness, but when it's on camera – as this is – the consequences are far greater. I'm totally exposed for what I am. I'm new to interviewing on screen and the sensation of control slipping away from me in front of two cameras, a boom mic, and what will soon be *The Guardian*'s discerning audience, is brutal.

When I finally watch the footage back, the Alexa in my head winces. They've done a good job at editing the silences out but on screen I look fragile and buttoned-up, like an elderly royal at a charity summer do. The camera is at an unflattering angle in which my pasty white legs are centre stage. I'm growing my hair out from a heinous pixie crop; it's bushy, unkempt and in a side parting which reveals a sliver too much of my forehead. Alexa says, 'It's a bit like a toupee,' and I agree. I am appalled at my default gestures – how unable I am to control my hand movements; my flagrant attempt to calm down my nervous system by pinching my fingers and tapping my thumbs. My body exudes desperation and panic, whereas Alexa is louche and groovy, sarcastic. The overall ambience is: granny gone rogue. 'No wonder Alex kept his sunglasses on,' adds Alexa, while sketching a wilting flower onto the back of a napkin.

Later I'm hurt to discover that a video goes viral of Alex 'flirting' with ITV's Susanna Reid, who, I've noted, is wearing a denim jacket rather than her usual formal wrap dress for the interview that shoots a few hours after mine. There are sparks flying, and he's not wearing sunglasses, either. 'Cheer up, mate, I'm sure he liked you too,' says Alexa. 'Or at least you reminded him of me, albeit a version of me with osteoporosis and wearing a Tena Lady.'

Beyond the look, Alexa's career is one that I have tried to emulate for much of my own life. Often this ambition turns into a deluded form of one-sided competition.

Before Alexa came into my life and really ignited my ambition, I had already dipped my toes into the cut-throat world of showbiz. Aged nine, I auditioned for the lead role in my primary school's Victorian Music Hall and got it – wowing crowds as the former silent shy girl who could now sing *My Fair Lady*'s 'Wouldn't It Be Loverly' with the cockney panache of Hepburn in her pomp. Soon after that, my mum, who worked as the education officer in a museum, managed to get me a fleeting appearance on ITV News in the '90s during which I dressed as a Tudor schoolgirl and stroked a saffron petal in a package about the heritage of Saffron Walden. I thought I did a pretty good job at turning up and looking like an ancient child. But it turns out this did not prepare me for talking on camera, a merciless experience in which anyone without unyielding levels of confidence appears vulnerable and unpleasant; walking, talking raw nerve; a photo of flaccid genitals with the flash on. Alexa has mastered the art of making it look easy: dry, acerbic and unflinching. She laughs but never too much, and never to appease a guest.

I don't think it was too ambitious to try to become a presenter. I smile a lot, which is one of the basic requirements. And I'd dabbled in modelling back in my late teens while at university. My debut shoot took place for the Bournemouth student magazine: the theme was 'autumn', and my housemate Becki did my hair and makeup; we kept it low-key with smokey eyes and a choppy straightened bob. I laughed my head off in a tweed jacket by a tree and was over the moon with the images. So much so, I emailed the best few to a modelling agent in London, who never replied.

The second opportunity promised a more mainstream audience: a local culture and listings magazine called *Big In Bournemouth*. I'd been doing work experience there for two weeks and volunteered to step in on a shoot when the model couldn't make it. The editor sent me to a shopping centre to get my makeup done at the Bobbi Brown counter. I told the makeup artist I wanted a 'Sophie Ellis-Bextor, minimal look', to which the young man said, 'Sure,' before smearing thick layers of orange gunk onto my white skin. I kept thinking that at some point it would come together and I would look like a pale doll, and the tan shades would dissolve into porcelain. But the moment never came, and as the shoot was running early, I was turfed onto the street before he had time to do any eye makeup. My face was essentially a slice of burger cheese with eye sockets and nostrils.

When I stepped into the set, I caught the editor recoiling subtly and the room went quiet for long enough for me to overhear the words 'What have they done to her face?' said out of the side of someone's mouth. The stylist handed me some clothes, all of which were tiny. 'Sorry, we thought you were a bit smaller,' said the editor, giving me a wink and a cheeky nudge, one that was gratefully received by my eating disorder.

Luckily, they had a plan. As the jeans didn't do up, I posed with my back towards the camera, looking over my shoulder. I channelled all of the hours of *America's Next Top Model* I'd seen and managed to smize my way out of an uncomfortable situation.

To my relief, the shoot was signed off and the magazine printed. In the right hands, the back-to-the-camera pose could have evoked a flirty sensuality, but instead I'm giving child walking home from school imploring a group of bullies to stop throwing chips at her head. Appalled, even though I was right there in the room, I banished the copy to a box under my bed along with the deranged letters from Rory and a select few notable condom wrappers.

Resigned to the fact that my modelling days are over, I turn to journalism, a career that offers endless opportunities to show off and find validation. I've been following Chung's career for a few years at this stage and have noted that she often hints at how she harbours a desire to be taken more seriously, to be more than a pretty face, to become a fashion journalist. I bask in a fleeting sense of superiority when discovering this, but after reading a number of her articles in *Vogue* I realize she can write as well as she does everything else, and fall down to my knees, begging for mercy.

My one-sided duel with Chung rattles on: the plan now is to do a couple of videos for *The Guardian*, get an agent who can fix me with a full-time career doing talking heads on documentaries like Paul Morley or Ringo Starr, before inevitably at some point graduating to my own talk show.

Around the time of my Arctic Monkeys shoot, I am invited to appear on a BBC show about new music, and believe this is my chance. I go in my casual Alexa get-up – jumper and jeans, with a shaved leg; they ask me questions and I feel confident; the right words arrive at the right time and the producers give me encouraging feedback. A career waxing lyrical about Top 10 best Britpop bangers awaits me. I tell my family and friends to watch the broadcast. Twenty-three minutes into the 25-minute show, the brutality of being edited out hits me.

Such is my desire to win, I dust myself off and continue to accept all offers to go on camera. For whatever reason, I am robust, perhaps naive. While working at *The Guardian* I am tasked with interviewing famous people at Glastonbury for three days. Me and my friend Tshepo, who is filming me for the weekend, trudge around the vast site and interview the likes of Elbow and St Vincent. I ask Matty Healy from the 1975 if he likes Michael Jackson ('Yes') and ask Clean Bandit if they mind the rain ('Yes'). The next year the editor decides against me doing video interviews and I probe no further. I am fairly happy with my work on the BRIT Awards red carpet – smart/casual Alexa in chunky heels and a pencil skirt – but regret asking John Newman very quietly what his middle name is, and that I am chewing on an imaginary piece of gum throughout. That night I get a selfie with Noel Gallagher and follow Paulo Nutini around the afterparty. I am in a dream.

It's also the era of vlogging, so *The Guardian*, hoping to create viral videos about hard-hitting subjects, have commissioned me to write a script about double standards in the music industry. As is the style of the time, the edit includes wacky cuts to stock photo images and zany sound FX. I've been directed to do zealous pointing hand gestures. As soon as I start speaking, my voice becomes an exaggerated version of my Essex accent, and my tone is embarrassingly angry, my eyes startled. The response is very positive, half a million views, even if I come away from it with a new paranoia about my wiry neck.

In the days afterwards, I'm rushed with attention and praise on my Twitter – euphoria; Tshepo even tells me that her friend at a talent agency has seen it and thought it was OK. It's certainly given me a bit of clout at *The Guardian*. A man I've never met before but who I often see walking around the building holding his laptop open asks me to chair a panel about the future of rock 'n' roll. It's an hour and a half, and the audience have spent money on tickets. I do rehearse a bit, but spend more time worrying about what top to wear, heading to Zara on Oxford Street at lunch to panic-buy a dress, or maybe a white shirt. I do my shopping blissfully unaware that my last flicker of youthful, breezy confidence is about to get snuffed out.

In the green room, before the show begins, I sit with the panellists – a critic, two musicians, someone at a record label and a radio host. We sit about eating snacks as the chattering hum of the audience begins to fill the venue and I finally feel as if I am part of an elite crowd of big thinkers about to spar it out and set the world to rights. The critic – witty, sharp, sometimes cantankerous – asks what the panel is 'actually about', as the title is vague. It's a legitimate question: 'the future of rock 'n' roll' could refer to the genre, the spirit or the music industry in general. I say I'm not sure and he replies: 'Well, you'd better figure it out quickly as we're on in a second.' At this point I realize it's too late; the new shirt I bought is not going to be enough to carry me through. I walk on stage and the crowd of 100 people clap. The room goes silent and I am handed a microphone. I dawns on me I've never held a microphone before and take a moment to look at it. Heavier than I expected. 'Like a gun,' says Alexa, who is now side of stage, heckling me while simultaneously texting Christopher Kane to arrange a fitting.

Time is now sludge. My mouth is claggy and I attempt to open a bottle of water at the same time as holding the mic, wedging it between my legs, cranking open the plastic lid and ignoring a torrent of water that splashes across my knees. 'Hi, everyone,' I say before I take a glug from the bottle, all eyes on me, every elongated minute of silence a wasted 50p for them. I make eye contact with a man on the front row who is wearing a black leather trilby and looks a bit like D'Angelo, except really disdainful.

It's time to bring out the panellists. I impulsively give the critic who I am now scared of the most clout by prefacing his introduction with 'And, most importantly . . .', which is a jarring place to start. Throughout the ninety-minute conversation I communicate like an AI Chatbot – scattergun questions, my mind barely registering the answers save a few basic themes. My strands of thought are slack; there's no coherent narrative. I'm free-form, saying 'politics', 'streaming' and 'major labels' with enough dramatic emphasis to hope that something sticks. This reminds me of when I got accepted into the school concert band but I found the parts too hard to play, so I would mime it on the clarinet, which was fine for a while but then they made me do a solo and I tried to mime that too: instead of a blast of Bizet's *Carmen* it was little clicks of the keys and the puff of silent air coming out of an instrument. 'What *do* you guys think of Ed Sheeran?' I shriek into the abyss.

Gruff Rhys from the Super Furry Animals talks about festivals and I can't comprehend a word he is saying. I keep making eye contact with the man in the trilby for reassurance but his eyes have glazed over. He looks as if he is thinking: *Should I stop off at Itsu for a vegetable fusion gyoza to eat on the train, or have leftover mushroom risotto when I'm home instead? And why does this woman on stage with a wet knee look like she's going to cry?*

Towards the end of the panel the radio host intervenes and cuts into my question to the record label guy: 'Sorry, can I stop you there, Harriet,' he says, almost furious. 'I'd actually rather hear from one of the musicians what they think about Spotify . . .' 'Absolutely!' is my reply. I've now lost so much authority that someone else is taking the lead. In the weeks and years that pass, the sound of his genteel voice on the radio continues to give me flashbacks, and is my cue to slag him off for twenty seconds before turning the radio off entirely.

Once the show is over I go into the dressing room, grab my bag and get out before I unravel in front of everyone. On the street outside I bump into the critic and radio host, who tell me I did great – parental reassurance that makes me fond of them even though they are clearly liars. Shaken up by my stupidity and inability to perform on demand, I end up having a panic attack in Piccadilly Circus, loud crying and spit streaming from my mouth as I crouch on the floor and vow to avoid anything so bold ever again. It's over. My moment in the sun is over.

It's right there and then I decide to block Alexa on Instagram. I can no longer see her rarefied updates every day from the Met Gala red carpet or with a bouquet of tulips at a busy Sunday market. I have put myself out there, repeatedly, so publicly, demanded to be seen, and have finally received the message that I do not possess the requisite charm to hold a room in my hand. I cannot outsmart the lads, the ladies – anyone – when presented with a microphone, silence and a stage. I can be amusing to a small, very specific group of friends in a confined space, but get me on a stage in an unscripted situation and I am frankly unstable. No amount of vintage-inspired tea dresses can change that. This block is a bleak and reluctant acceptance that I do not have the effort-lessness that allows for a fluid experience of life. To be loved and earn a living for smiling is not my fate. I need a short grieving period to get over this devastating news, and to possibly call my mum and ask her some more questions about what it was like for her dad to work in a navy submarine during the war.

This liberation from my online fixation would be emancipating were it not for the algorithms offering me a string of other Parisian-themed babes to dodge during my mid-morning social media slump. The other issue is that I've transferred all my obsession for her onto Alex Turner and his new partners. At first it feels like a huge 'fuck you' to Alexa, to get back at the fact that I'm not as good as her at presenting, as if staring at his new girlfriend could in some way give me the upper hand. But then I am swamped by the same nostalgia that a cohort of thousands of other freaks on the internet are also lost in: a world in which Alexa and Alex live on for ever.

In reality, I know that Alexa is not floored by heartache a decade or so after her split from Alex Turner. I know she has moved on with numerous studs – models, actors, musicians (I am physically unable to discuss the image of Alexa and Chris Martin in a restaurant together in New York). Yet there was something so pure about her relationship with Alex Turner. It's the one context in which she appears tender and vulnerable, rather than just aloof.

There are Tumblr profiles, messageboard threads and entire social media accounts dedicated to the former couple's ephemeral tryst. Fans of Alexa and Alex share images of the love letter he wrote to her on the back of a napkin, a cherished symbol of fairy-tale indie romance. Fans repost archive images from their relationship, icons of the naughts-era, smiling and uncynically sweet, on the brink of super-fame, walking around Glastonbury, kissing on the street. It was a big love. 'We fall asleep with our arms round each other,' she told one interviewer at the time. 'He's really little and so am I, so no one gets a dead arm. Sometimes we wake up in the same position. It's the best thing ever.'

Down my Alex Turner rabbit hole, I discover gossip websites lavishing in his new cartoonish LA rockstar lifestyle: papped at airports with a pristine actor-cum-influencer type with long valley-girl hair: his new girlfriend Arielle. It both bruises me and fills me with a dark glee, as I'm reminded of a passage from Alexa's debut book, *It*: 'Boys say they don't mind how you get your hair done,' she writes. 'But then they leave you for someone with really great standard girl hair and the next thing you know you're alone with a masculine crop crying into your granola.'

I've seen her hair. I've studied the shots. There's not one in which she has a masculine crop – unless she's referring to a brief Mick Jagger shaggy bob, which doesn't really count because she looked like a rock star. But herein lies the key to Alexa's popularity beyond celestial looks: self-deprecation. Hoodwinking her audience into thinking she is flawed and chaotic, just as susceptible to heartache and humiliation as the rest of us. Using her alleged inadequacies to puncture the veneer of superiority and manipulate the public into investing in her. It's a classic trait of a good old-fashioned people-pleaser, fearful of the displeasure of others, willing to throw oneself under the bus in a plea for connection, approval and love.

Alexa coughs and stubs her cigarette out on my forehead. 'Maybe we do have one thing in common after all.'

CHAPTER TEN

Dead Cat Strategy

On Tuesday at 11.30 a.m. in an otherwise empty Pret A Manger, I order my regular. It's the early days of the company's questionable free coffee era: a no-charge policy for its most charming customers. As such, I am feeling the heat of potential scrutiny. So conscious of the constant stream of fakery its staff must encounter in the craven quest for an on-the-house latte, I've decided to give them a break and double down on a bad attitude instead. I assume the sullen expression and no-eye-contact demeanour of a banker on a comedown as I hiss the words: 'Strong soy mocha, please.'

'Anything else?' the barista replies. I waggle a packet of dried kale flakes miserably. 'Just these crisps.'

Suddenly, the hairs on my back prickle. Someone is watching me. A man in a teal Harrington jacket and battered '90s Nike running trainers. Sidling up to the counter, he arrives as a bundle of twitchy energy encased in a lanky body, a sweet, neat face covered in a beard speckled with brown, ginger and greys, and a tiny, almost triangular nose. A scribble drawn by a genius.

We wait for our drinks, holding our breath. The coffee-making barista snaps at the order-taking barista, in a savage exchange that helps to puncture some of the pressure building between me and this stranger, both paralysed by the thrill of potential attraction.

I leave the Pret, only to feel the burn of his eyes on me again, the sound of his shoes rushing to catch up.

'That got a bit tense, didn't it,' says the stranger softly, as his run segues into a walk.

It is a rare treat to be chased by a man in London who is neither a potential rapist nor alerting me to the fact that my 'payment hasn't gone through', and, carried away by the novelty, I tumble haphazardly into a chat about the overall Pret experience. Our sentences overlap; words upon words in a nervous tussle: I have entered altruistic-angel mode and defend the barista's right to take her time frothing my milk, while he asks me what I ordered and where I am heading to. When I gesture towards the big glass building in front of us, I assume he'll be impressed by my job at *The Guardian*, but to my surprise he says, 'Me too.'

As we take the escalator into the offices, he asks me questions about what I am working on, if I enjoy it. I feel suspended in mid-air while talking to him; like a new pathway has opened up in my brain, one of ease and peace. I tell him I am working on the Culture section, and prepare to engage in some intelligent back and forth about Samantha Morton or Kamila Shamsie, but instead he replies: 'Crikey, poor you.'

This scurrilousness and kindness is a heady mixture. His swagger and self-effacing demeanour. I assume he must be a designer – the type of guy who could name a New Order B-side. Respectfully, most news reporters look like they stan

Simon Rattle, or once lost it at a Toploader Onka's Big Moka anniversary gig.

That Sunday I buy the paper and flick through the news. There it is. That tiny nose, a headshot next to a headline about detainees at an immigration centre facing sexual abuse. I delete the imagined footage of him sipping his coffee while adjusting fonts from my mind, and start the fantasy of our philanthropic lives together afresh. Sunday mornings spent volunteering at a Guide Dogs sanctuary, growing our own courgettes, eating both the body of the vegetable and its flowers, while laughing at Steve Bell's searing take on this week's scandal with the monarchy. It's boring but it's bliss.

Back at my desk on Monday, Mark re-enters my orbit, with his sprite-like energy and melodic Cumbrian accent set to double-speed. He chats playfully with a colleague in my eyeline. Adrenalized, I ask my friend Tim who he is.

'That's Mark. Don't know much about him. He used to go out with Margot.'

What a stab to the chest. What a name. Couldn't she be called something a bit less beguiling, like Fiona?

I head to the loo with my phone and fire up the Twitter app to try to find *Margot*. Her name repeats in my head like the last line of a poem or a curse.

There's not much to ascertain from Mark's feed – links to harrowing stories about government corruption and other global injustices, in other words nothing interesting or of any value at all. He is incredibly offline in general – not on Facebook or Instagram, and there's only one photo of him on Google, in which he is wearing a boxy suit and shaking hands with a balding man. I search for Margot in his followers list, excited by the thrill of the potential chase. Yet there is only one. And it is her.

The oddest part is that I know Margot. That's too strong maybe; we've crossed paths digitally. I emailed her a year ago when I was a freelance journalist and she worked at a lifestyle magazine. My pitch to her was a first-person piece about Zooey Deschanel and the affinity I feel for her, being a fellow quirky girl. The subject line was probably something like The Joy of Kook. Margot knows my truth.

Now that I've established there was a break-up, I need to know how serious it was. There is nothing more appealing to me than a man in his early forties who's slightly broken. That added punch of vulnerability denting the middle-aged stability. I just need a few more snippets of information – ideally a photo of them together, an exchange on Valentine's Day – and I can decide how much baggage we might be dealing with. There can definitely be *too much* unaddressed melancholy – I once asked one of my exes what his favourite object in his house was and he said, without skipping a beat: 'the painting above my bed that Anna did'.

All day I long to finish my work so I can get on with my research; every task and meeting a petty inconvenience until I am alone and scoffing down Margot content. As soon as I sink into the scratchy warm fabric of the 55 bus seat, I focus, with laser-like precision, on her Twitter profile, my pulse surging, pupils fully dilated. A naked man could get on and yell my name, PIN code and graphic details from my recurring Hulk Hogan sex dream, and I'd barely twitch.

Margot is impressive – funny and smart – but she's not giving anything personal away. Pop trivia, politics and other zeitgeisty tittle-tattle. She's clever and eclectic, her brand is high/low culture. I head back further and further and further. Now I am reading her thoughts from three years ago, my wrist aching slightly with the repeated strain of the scroll. I eventually get to 2010 and there it is: Mark's name. She has quoted him professing his love of 1990s indie band Cast. In fact, the joke is the extent to which he loves Cast, the sort of devotion normally directed at a seminal, cultural disruptor rather than a mediocre (sincerest apologies to John Power) indie band. The fact he is willing to die on that hill not only suggests Mark is deeply unpretentious but also very self-aware. I now fancy him even more. Great couple. What went wrong?

I dig deeper. His skill for misplaced hyperbole continues – to things he's eaten, and places he's been. Strange turns of phrases. He's flippant and silly, a surprising trait for someone with such a serious job. She was proud of him, as I would be too.

A few weeks later there's a work party. I see Mark on my way out of the office by the tea point. My skin prickles as stress sweat leaves it.

'Oh, hello,' he says in a fluster. 'You heading off to the do?'

'Yes indeed . . .' I pause.

'I haven't seen one of those since '93,' he says, referring to my orange-lined parka coat. I bought it brand new from Topshop, after a harrowing attempt at eBay left me with one very large, dirty version that looked like it came straight from the set of a Shane Meadows film.

'I really like indie – what can I say?'

I internally wince.

A lumbering senior writer I've only ever stared at from afar interrupts our developing frisson to talk to Mark. I'd hate for him to think I am the type to outstay my welcome, so wave bye and head off to the party.

The venue for tonight is a warehouse lit with theatrical blue floor lamps. Moody house music plays and there are circus entertainers on stilts. Despite all the journalists and sub-editors eating mini burgers, the atmosphere is sexy, and I feel embarrassed to be in this coat and in this space. All night Mark and I manage to steal quick happy glances at one another, and exchange succinct updates on our respective nights. At one point he hands me a neon-pink iPad case he won in a raffle and I keep it in my bag. We never speak of it again.

It's time to get the night bus home. We spill out onto the street and I find Mark so I can say goodbye. In a bid to keep me talking a little longer he asks me what good new music he should listen to. I tell him about an artist and watch as he inexplicably types their name into his iPhone Contacts and presses 'save'. I'm not sure why insubordinate usage of technology has sealed the deal for me but it's fair to say I am beguiled.

The next night we end up in the same bar after work. I have a hangover and with two large white wines on top of that peaky feeling, I am loose-lipped and bombastic.

'What is the best kiss you've ever had?' I ask the small group of colleagues I am stood with, including Mark.

In an attempt to impress him as a raconteur, I describe my most cultured kiss, which took place inside a huge, pitch-black art installation at the Tate Modern. The others offer anecdotes ranging from 'on a bench in the mid-noughties' to 'with a stunning girl in Sweden'. Mark won't answer. I get the sense he isn't a fan of showboating, which I do admire, as frustrating as it is.

Around forty minutes later I take him to a corner of the bar and pragmatically explain that while I don't know much about him, I'd be keen to fall in love. He agrees. We still haven't touched yet. It's moving at a remarkable pace but I am reassured in his total willingness to let me take the lead and make all the moves, because he has none. Unless you consider the iPad case an erotic gesture, which I now do.

We arrange to meet at his place in two days so we can spend some time with each other properly, away from the gaze of the staff of a broadsheet newspaper. He texts me his address the night before, so naturally I search for his house on Google Maps, Street View, dragging the yellow man onto the road, legs astride, and taking in my future home. It's a beautiful townhouse in Hackney, with six steps leading up to a shiny red front door. It'll be tricky to get the buggy and weekly shop up there, but ultimately good for the upper thighs.

This rich and urbane exterior confirms what I was fearing, however. He is a grown-up man: probably bilingual, with some really good thoughts on architecture, and able to casually rustle up seafood linguine. I feel out of my depth and a bit scared.

'This alright for you?' asks the cab driver as we pull up to a shabby little house across the road.

'Thank you . . . I think it's that one over there?' I point hopefully at Linguine Townhouse.

'Nope, this is 101.'

He is right, I am wrong, and into the shabby little house I go.

The interior of Mark's home is, quite frankly, shocking. The living room is empty apart from a beaten-up cream leather sofa, the other barren rooms a hangover from his break-up.

Suddenly a blind, emaciated tabby cat called Shyboy moves across the floor erratically like tumbleweed. The room smells like a lavender Air Wick plug-in, but with a sharp shock of acidic bodily excretion floating underneath. In the kitchen, on top of the microwave, is a chopping board covered in the remnants of pink Smartie-like pills for the cat, which have been crushed by a spoon and have splintered off into different directions. A corner of the carpet upstairs is covered in some of Shyboy's liquid crap, with a single sheet of *The Times* on top of the worst-offending stains.

Suffice to say, I move in the next day and agree to marry him a year later.

Mark has unconditional love for Shyboy. His entire home is a stage for an ailing feline to bow out disgracefully, and while it's incredibly gross, I can get on board with it. It's testament to what a deeply loving and loyal man Mark is, caring and gentle and giving you space to be you, regardless of whether you're projectile-vomiting Sheeba on an hourly basis or evacuating lumps of hair from your gullet on the stairs at 5 a.m.

Over the next few months, in which Mark and I fall hopelessly in love, I am the most secure I have ever felt. He's unmoved by my surface details – the usual wild anecdotes and snobby cultural references I throw into conversation to seduce other men. There is no linguine or chat about architecture. He seems only really interested in remorselessly ribbing me or empathizing deeply about both my big and trivial concerns. I am struck by all those wasted years without him, a sorrow that we hadn't met when we were ten.

I am even dressing like I did when I was a little girl: thick tights and unflattering dresses. I wet myself with laughter on a few occasions and he doesn't care; it instead becomes a victory – the marker of a good day. He never misses a call and establishes himself as a person who is reliable and available. We have a riot whenever we can, whether it's walking to the local shop to get crisps or on a train to see my family.

The first time he meets my parents we go along to a Martin Creed exhibition on the Southbank. My dad is unflappable in the face of X-rated content and inside the show is a room in which a video is projected onto a large wall: footage of a small woman in dainty patent heels squatting while she defecates onto the floor. Runtime: approx. ten minutes.

Dad sits on the bench and watches until the bitter, spluttering end, completely emotionless as if it was a *One Show* segment about electric cars. My mum and I giggle and grimace. Mark, an eternal ally, joins Dad in his earnestness. Later that day Mum whispers to me, some might say sinisterly: *He is one of us.*

We are having the time of our lives. And yet, there is something wrong. Before he gets back from work every night, I use that precious alone time – ten minutes to an hour – to torture myself. I am morbidly curious about Margot. I want to know how she navigates life: is she funny-haha-funny or just sarcastic with good taste? How long did she spend in the shower? Did she hate the bug-eyed clownishness of the ten-second countdown before midnight on New Year's Eve too? I need to know it all, to crack the riddle, and to answer the key question: am I better than her?

Mark couldn't be more clear about their relationship's end. There is no lingering weirdness. It's over, and he's OK. Nevertheless, she's confronting me with everything I'm not: mysterious and chic; brave with her colour palette. We don't look anything alike; she's yogic with wavy baby-pink hair and golden skin. I saw a photo of her once, drinking a pint. I truly realize why this incredible man wanted to be with her. The thought gives me a sad ache but I still want more.

As a fellow journalist, she has also written about herself, and I'm careful not to binge, rationing articles as if they'll run out. There are features about her eclectic hair choices, her insecurities and past romances. One through line is that she really likes eating protein, but not in a disordered-eating way. More Parisian – eggs and steak for a long lunch. When I hear Mark's key in the lock I speedily delete my search history, my fingers well trained, in pilot mode. I'd hate for him to ask for my phone to check the weather and find the words 'Margot sex' – in case she's ever written about sex – typed out in my Google.

I am gripped by fascination. God forbid I ever have to meet her. God forbid she gets a job at the same newspaper as me, on the same floor, with a desk ten metres away from mine.

She looks the same as she does in the small stills online; there was no filter or farce. Here she is. In reality. Tapping away at her keyboard. Talking to colleagues. Working! As if it's not the biggest moment in the history of humankind that I too am sat ten metres away. Absurd, really. I wish I could pause time and have a better look. Calculate her face's parameters. I feel a little weak. The type of weak you get when you meet the love of your life. Or, in this instance, the love of your life's ex-girlfriend.

At lunch, I go for a walk with Mark and tell him the news that I now work within a stone's throw of his ex. I say I'm a grown-up and it's not a problem. He tells me that it's alright to feel strange and to let him know if I feel insecure about anything.

I can't tell if it's insecurity that's nagging away at me or something more nuanced. Such is her lure that I often wonder whether I am myself attracted to her. I can hear her voice if I listen closely. She talks quietly so you really have to strain. I try not to, but every time she walks past, her cosmic kimono billowing as she goes, I picture them together. Cycling on holiday, or lazing around in our home. Laughing, intimacy, romance and friendship, the twisted, gorgeous horror.

It is only a matter of time until we are face to face, forced to interact. I dread that inevitable first conversation, so to get ahead of the curve I allot the last part of my journey into work to practising potential conversation starters.

'I'm Harriet! How's you?'

'Work, haha! You good, Margot?'

'Nice bracelet! Thailand, 2009?'

My brain sifts through layers of nervousness – at the top of the pile is my paranoia that she already knows that I've been incessantly looking. Since the mid-'00s – when a friend down-loaded software for MySpace which enabled her to discover who was viewing her profile most frequently, and she discovered her boyfriend was visiting her page twenty to thirty times per day, and so she broke up with him – my fear of being exposed as a creep has been agonizing ever since. I'd hate for Margot to see the data and for all of our mutual friends at work to ostracise me. So I limit the checking of her Twitter and Instagram to once a day. Ten minutes. A bit more if I'm hungover. Constantly wary, in case my thumbs whack a Like button from a picture of her up a tree at a festival in June last year.

Eventually, Shyboy's puke starts to have blood in it, so we have him put down. Mark is devastated. Margot is too: it was her family's cat originally and Mark breaks the news to her via email. She probably thinks that this was all my doing. But who wants to live like Shyboy? For weeks he had moved through the world like a glitch. Just a brittle tail, quivering and leaking lurid fluids. He couldn't even meow, instead just emit-ting the occasional dusty croak. But, yeah, essentially I suppose it is true I was the one who suggested we kill him.

Slowly we move on from the loss, and buy furniture, two more sofas. We get rid of the cream one. I find parts of her life in the house: hairbands, photos, birthday cards. I read the affectionate ways in which Mark referred to her, and she to him. I put it all in the bin.

Back in the office, we manage to avoid each other, which is ridiculous really, when you consider the short distance. One afternoon I need to talk to someone in her department about Miley Cyrus and cultural appropriation, so I walk over there, a metre from her desk. I manage to execute the chat with her colleague efficiently but internally I am begging to be acknowledged as a serious woman who is definitely not kooky.

A few more weeks pass and eventually we speak. At a party in a basement in Soho, where I don't know many people. I have an iffy hangover from some pub red wine the night before, and no amount of food, sleep or psychological coaching is able to regulate how wonky I feel. The sight of her hair alone makes me terrified. Eventually she approaches me. It feels as if the whole room has stopped to watch. 'Will you quit looking at all of my social media, you horrible little bitch,' are the words I brace myself for.

Instead I am presented with a cool, cheerful smile.

'Hello, I thought I should come and say hi . . .' she begins quietly. The conversation continues, undramatically, but the red-wine hangover adds a layer of intensity to every twist and turn. I'm just a moist, pink lump opening and closing my mouth. I worry this is my first and last chance to be at my best, but I'm barely there, phoning in the anecdotes, whatever's easiest, just peripheral noises and exaggerated expressions. She talks about acupuncture and I tell her I downloaded the Headspace app. I can't remember who is meant to have the power. Is it her, for having had a rich, seven-year history with Mark, or is it me, with our present love and probable future? It's impossible to focus on the conversation with all this psychological chatter going on. The general sense is that she is immaculate, but we will never be best friends. My curiosity about her life has created an uneven playing field, and true friendship cannot thrive in deceit.

Now we have met, my creeping does feel like a bit of a betrayal, to her and to Mark. But I have a hard time accepting that all of this is actually bad. Is it taboo or just a normal, necessary neurosis? If jealousy is an erotic wrath, then maybe it is a compliment to both Mark and Margot's allure that I am so overcome by the sensation.

I think back to the other exes of exes or amazing and threatening girls who've cluttered my search history over the years. Nathalia. Kim. Kiera. I respect them, to this day. They interest me, exotic creatures who will forever remain enigmatic in the corners of my mind. They're kind of like film stars, only film stars who've shagged my boyfriends.

There is something about Mark – his modesty and security, his tolerance for everything, his empathy always – which leads me to believe I could actually tell him about my purgatory state with his ex. On a drizzly evening at home, I pluck up the courage to break the spell – explain what I've been doing when he's not there. I'm incredibly nervous. There's no going back once he knows what I know, what I am. And yet, he remains unperturbed – happy, even, that I've been so honest.

He lets me take the stage for my tragic one-woman show: I tell him about the sad ache – how looking at her online makes me unsettled, but I am addicted. I love him and while I don't want to invade his privacy or pry too extensively, the internet has enabled me to take on my own solitary investigative quest: exploring his ex-girlfriend's profile to find out the type of woman who could make such a spectacular man happy for so many years. To see if I might be able to do the same.

I tell him that I learned a lot about him via her, and in recognizing how cool she is, it reinforced how cool I already thought he was. Maybe, teasing your brain with such jealous thoughts actually adds a sexy layer of electricity to your life. After all, what is joy without a little pain? What's a lazy Sunday afternoon with a lover without a little snoop at their childhood sweetheart's Pinterest while they've popped to the loo?

Like Shyboy's excrement, he lets me do my business, uninhibited and unashamed. This is love.

'Have you ever googled my ex?' I eventually ask.

'No, I've never really thought about it before,' he shrugs.

Weird! Too busy helping asylum seekers, I guess. But still. Weird.

The only problem is, once a taboo is exposed, it becomes less forbidden and no fun. In the weeks that follow, I take a look at her Twitter but barely feel a twinge. I google her name, out of a motor memory, but find nothing of any use. The sensation is fading. I have a look at some old classics from the genre, just to try to stoke up some drama. It doesn't work. Not even Kim with the wooden fringe can stir the dormant beast within.

In owning and outing my tendencies, I am feeling less of that familiar toxic thrill I am so accustomed to. I am on the cusp of something healthy, something great.

But what do I do now? In the moments between work and socializing? I gamble across the internet, searching for something, someone, I am not sure what. My fingers are leaden with a lack of direction. I find this contentment unnerving.

CHAPTER ELEVEN

A Rush of Blood to The Head

Following a brief fling with an electric-blue plastic chair in the local library, my true childhood sexual awakening was Bart Simpson's vocal performance on *The Simpsons'* debut album, *The Simpsons Sing the Blues*. I already admired the caustic wit and disobedience he flaunted in the cartoon, but hearing his mischief and moments of vulnerability translated into music elevated his status from yellow kid next door to pure bad-boy rock star with hidden romantic depths. That voice, that hair. Who could resist?

I'd listen to the tape continuously, in the same way I'd rewatch old episodes of *Red Dwarf* I'd recorded off the TV to feel closer to the gorgeous dreadlocked space slacker, Lister. As I got older, however, my celebrity crushes accelerated as the internet became an immediately accessible keyhole into their lives. In 2007, my most treasured online space was a messageboard filled with candid black-and-white photos of indie TV presenter Alex Zane drinking in a pub with fellow host Emma Willis, several of which I printed out and kept in a box under my bed. I fancied brooding Kelly Jones from the Stereophonics so chronically that I made a fanzine out of photos of him I'd found on Ask Jeeves.

I did the same thing with images of Coldplay's Chris Martin. It was the old Chris Martin, the gangly one with lamb-like ringlets, huge spots near his mouth and saggy clothes. I didn't know the old one would turn into the new one, but the fact that I've been horny for both iterations for over two decades simply affirms what I've always known: we were meant to be.

Chris doesn't post much on social media. There are boundaries between us, but there are also numerous Instagram fan accounts that exist to fill the void. I allow myself a once-a-month pass to go on the *Daily Mail* website, where I can catch up with his holidays, see how his body is looking and check on how his relationship with cold-hearted nepotism-benefactor Dakota Johnson is progressing. While I have never met Chris, I have been in the same vicinity as him on many occasions, at Coldplay gigs. I relish the moments before the band come on stage, knowing that if I feel nervous, he probably does too. The fact we are both breathing in the same air, even if that air is 98 per cent beer burps, remains exhilarating. There have been two metres of distance between us at a 500-seater venue and hundreds of metres in the worst seats at a stadium, but sharing his quasi-proximity always feels the same: like ecstasy.

The first time I see Chris in real life is in 2001 at the V Festival in Chelmsford. I wear a padded bra, green body warmer, and ragged flares held up by an aeroplane-seatbelt-styled belt trying to strike the balance between practical and feminine that I think Chris might like when considering the photos of his pre-fame girlfriend and his upbringing in Devon. Along with Laura and a friend called Vic, we arrive at the stage five hours before the band's set begins to get a decent space at the front. I avoid liquids to prevent urination and eat an entire pack of oat snack bars to maintain my energy. We are forced to watch a dreary set from Embrace and a moody one from Faithless, during which the audience gets rowdy, my body is pressed against the metal barrier and I feel thrust into a new universe of adult hedonism. Coldplay eventually enter the stage to a robotic voice, a homage to Radiohead's technophobia-era. 'Now you must go crazy, because we are ready for the band to play,' says the voice. And crazy I go. I rock out like I've never rocked out before (I've never rocked out before). When Chris walks on in his gastropub-waiter-styled baggy black shirt and trousers, for the first time I truly understand Beatlemania. My knees buckle and I emit a primal wail that I have no ability to suppress. It feels as if a parasite is attempting to leave my body via my throat. I wasn't ready for this level of helplessness.

The way I feel about Chris is best described as a toxic turbo crush. I feel ill and limp when I think about his face, and I have an aching, animal instinct to be near him. I've watched enough interviews with him on YouTube to know that he's game for a laugh. Despite the sometimes oppressive sentimentality of Coldplay's music, rarely does he give a journalist a serious answer. As well as being cheeky and contrarian, he is also an athletic eccentric with a God complex – the dream frontman. Obviously I am bowled over by some of his sartorial choices, but the neon-splattered t-shirts and enormous high-top trainers all contribute to the fact that Chris moves through life as his uninhibited and authentic self.

Mark is aware of how I feel about Chris. I get it all out of the way in the infatuation stage of courting, along with unloading any additional mental defects worth flagging up. Graciously, he kindly agrees that Chris can be the sole name on my celebrity 'free pass' list. Which sounded like a good idea at the time, but the more I've dwelled on it, and I've really, seriously, frequently, vigorously dwelled on it, having sex with Chris Martin might just ruin my life.

Chris and I have mutual acquaintances in the media so it's not completely unrealistic that we might one day meet. Probably at an after-party at an award show. By some stroke of luck, I'd be feeling on top of my game. A friend would introduce us, knowing full well I'll be starstruck but trusting me to keep my cool. He's fresh off stage and in a classic Rat Pack suit, jacket slung over his shoulder, tie loose around his neck. I am in a dowdy dress I got in the Toast sale but am two free champagnes in and feeling enlivened by the showbiz atmosphere and Jamie Cullum playing the double bass in the background.

'Has anyone ever told you that you look like Texas' Sharleen Spiteri?' he'd ask, his gummy grin even more sexy and devilish in real life than I'd anticipated.

'Has anyone ever told you, you look like Chris Martin from Coldplay?' He likes the confidence, the back and forth, the central vein in our respective foreheads rising to the surface.

There's an awkward silence, so I panic and ask one of my default questions: 'So what do you think you might have for breakfast tomorrow?'

He is suddenly solemn, his stare seductive and direct. 'Meet me in the disabled loos.'

I'm startled by his provocative demand, and before I even have time to agree, he bounds off into the swarm of bodies that block his way to the bathroom, a patch of sweat splayed on his back the shape of India. He is larger than the other celebrities at the party, more physically cumbersome, a big wet dog running riot in a chic city skyline bar. Stanley Tucci and wife Felicity Blunt attempt to catch his eye for a chat but he's a man on a mission. Before he gets to the toilet door his attention briefly turns to Billie Eilish. He's doing the earnest double-hand shake to show his appreciation for Gen Z's cultural output and complimenting her on her artistry.

As I watch him wrap up his conversation with Eilish, I wonder if I should let my husband know in advance that I'm going to cash in my freebie. 'About to fuck Chris Martin! Hope all cool!' I type. A sign-off for this sordid affair was agreed many years ago, so I decide against the text and act on impulse instead.

I arrive at the toilet door and decide to kick things off with a joke, knocking loudly so he can hear me above Cullum's rendition of 'Uptown Funk'. 'Excuse me, sir, it's come to my attention that you're in the disabled loo and actually able-bodied . . .'

Chris opens the door and drags me in, planting a heavy, super-wet kiss on my mouth. He flips me around to face the basin and the mirror. He is smiling demonically. I'm wearing tights but I sense he's used to stockings and suspenders. I turn around and say: 'Let me slip these off first.'

'OK, OK – sorry,' he replies bashfully, taking a step back.

At this point I notice the toilet is blocked and has a soiled piece of tissue stuck near the seat. I wouldn't be surprised if Chris went before I came in. He is just so comfortable everywhere he is.

He's noticed me looking at the loo. 'That wasn't me, by the way.'

'No, I know,' – I'm taking off my shoes so I can take off my tights – 'If you did I wouldn't care anyway. Sincerely, that sort of thing doesn't bother me. Poo.'

Awkward pause while I take off the second shoe. 'So long as you wipe.'

I stand up and reposition myself by the sink, facing the mirror, dutiful and polite. I can see the moment's gone, and the sensual spirit has left us for another couple.

'You know what, maybe we should head back into the party,' Chris says. 'Shall we do this properly another time?'

'Yes, totally,' I say, crushed. 'I was thinking the same.'

I am full of shame. Will I ever get this chance again?

Chris heads back into the party first. I follow after him, and notice Amal Clooney giving me a withering look as I exit the toilet.

It occurs to me that I should have at least asked for Chris's number before he left my grasp. By now he's seamlessly slipped into a small circle of industry bigwigs at the bar and is already holding court. I feel as if the decent thing would be to let Mark know what's just happened; perhaps he'll find my misfortune funny and it can be a story for a future dinner party.

I sidle up to a large plant to avert Amal's sobering stare, and dial Mark's number. It goes straight to answerphone. He must have run out of battery.

The night goes on, I keep drinking, having fun – one eye fixed on Chris, who I've noticed has changed into four layers of t-shirts and has been whispering into the ears of Jameela Jamil, Hayley Baldwin and Jodie Comer. He looks my way occasionally and I laugh hysterically at whoever I am standing with as if to prove how capable I am of carrying myself in a room full of celebrities. 'What's so funny about the long, slow death of my Australian labradoodle?' Olivia Coleman barks.

Just before midnight the party is winding down and I check my phone to see ten missed calls from an unknown number. It rings again so I answer. It's the hospital. There's been a bike accident. My husband Mark is dead.

My knees buckle and I collapse to the floor, for ten seconds or an hour; I've no idea. When I come around, it's Chris's face I see; kneeling above my body, giving me the kiss of life.

'Harriet, can you hear me?'

He tells the crowd of people huddled around us to give me some space, helping my limp body to its feet before ushering me into a dimly lit private room guarded by a bouncer.

'So what's the deal? Is it something that happened earlier?'

I tell Chris everything; how the love of my life has been killed and how I am now a widow. He holds my hand, ingesting the information calmly, just how I need him to.

'I've got a car coming in twenty minutes. Come with me. I'll take care of you, OK?'

I nod, sick with sorrow. The car journey through the city feels so surreal; Chris respectfully tells the driver to turn off the radio and he holds my hand as we rush through the anarchic night-time traffic, amber and white city lights blinking back at me menacingly.

We arrive at a five-storey townhouse in west London where I'm shown his daughter Apple's room – she's in Miami for the next year, so it's all mine if I want it. He says I can stay here for weeks, months, whatever I need. And so I do; the palatial beauty of the house gives me space to grieve. Severely depressed, I barely leave the bed most days. Chris is on and off tour, but calls every day to check in on me, sometimes sending a Deliveroo driver to drop off my favourite tofu curry.

When he's back in London there's a tension in the air, as if we are both suppressing our elation to see each other. I play him songs he's never heard and we unwind with a glass of wine to Elizabeth Day's *How to Fail* podcast as we top and tail on the sofa. In spite of this unaddressed attraction we have for one another, he always sleeps in his own room. He does like to take a bath with the bathroom door open, however, belting out Simply Red's greatest hits as he soaks those bulging post-tour limbs.

It's Christmas Eve, eleven months after Mark's tragic death. Chris says I am welcome to spend the festive period with him in the townhouse; a few friends will be popping over. It's low-key but might take my mind off my first Christmas as a widow. I agree, and to my surprise we consummate our love a few hours later. It's very fast and not altogether pleasant. The next morning I realize that the tryst was imaginary – the combination of a visceral night terror and thrush.

Christmas morning is perfect. We go for a 10K, watch repeats of *Sunday Brunch* I've recorded for him while he's been on tour, and drink mimosas and matcha tea. At midday there's a knock at the door. I get that sinking feeling, disappointed that someone is puncturing our blissful love bubble. I hear a roar at the door: old, rowdy pals excited to see their A-list friend. He's invited the neighbours too, and the energy shifts immediately as he abandons me to focus on being host and entertainer. I rush around making drinks and snacks as if I am his housewife, knowing I'm no way as charming or as good at hospitality as the multiple Hollywood starlets he's been with before. There's another knock at the door. Everyone's eyes light up. 'That must be our special guest!' beams Chris. I'm struck by a sense of dread as I hear a melodic, clipped Californian accent from the person who is stepping through the door. It's Gwyneth. I can smell her before I see her – burnt oak and satsumas – and once in the room, she is surrounded by celestial light. 'Harriet, I've heard all about you!' She moves close and takes both my hands. 'I am so sorry for your loss.'

'Thank you,' my lip wobbles, and my eyes fill up with tears. Too much ugly emotion too soon. Gwyneth – 1, Harriet – 0.

She also comes armed with gifts – outrageously generous with luxury creams, CBD oils and crystals from Goop. There's even some water-based lubricant and a 'silicone massager' that she doesn't seem embarrassed by. After winning my heart, she turns to the rest of the room, widens her eyes and declares that she needs a stiff drink; everyone falls about laughing. I say 'me too' and mimic glugging a tube of mayonnaise I've picked up from the table, a grotesque impression that lasts five seconds too long. One neighbour shouts 'Woah – go Harriet!' condescendingly, and the conversation quickly moves on.

As the day hits its natural post-lunch lull, we gather around the piano for a singsong of festive classics and contemporary pop hits. I miss Mark and his raspy, high-pitched singing style, and the fact he would be repulsed by the performative concept of singing around a piano. I don't know the words to all of the songs and my voice is very poor, while it appears to me that everyone else has had some kind of vocal training and can harmonize. I've taken to miming the lyrics until Chris puts me on the spot and says, 'Over to you, Harriet' towards the end of Beyoncé's 'Halo'. 'I can see your halo,' I croak with a timbre akin to gravel and dust. Chris can see I am shy and stops for a moment to break the merriment. 'Can I play you all a new thing I've been working on?' The room whoops and cheers, before he launches into a song about a lonely girl with 'tired eyes' who's wracked with grief but beautiful underneath – 'My dark sweet angel / Please don't fly tonight.' During the last line he looks up from the piano to make eye contact with me. It's so intense I can barely breathe.

The night rolls around and friends begin to head back to their respective homes. Gwyneth has made the last few standing some aromatic negronis; I marvel at her ability to navigate appropriate adult conversation punctuated by salacious, hilarious gossip. On the way back from the bathroom I bump into her on the landing. She asks if I am still sleeping in Apple's room and I say yes. She says her daughter will be back in a month or two, and is interested to know how long I might want to stay here for. 'It goes without saying you are welcome for as long as you'd like,' but at the same time, she adds formidably, 'I'd really appreciate some kind of clarity.' Is Gwyneth jealous? Have I done something wrong? I panic and tell her I'll be moving into my own place next week, thank her so much for being so patient and head back into the group game of Uno feeling hollow and empty.

Once the final guests have left I begin clearing up, tears rolling down my cheeks as I scrub pans and scour glasses. Chris loves to kick back with a hot chocolate before bed, so I begin my nightly ritual of warming some milk up in the microwave for him. He enters the kitchen barefoot in his brand-new burgundy dressing gown, tufts of dark-blonde chest hair poking out like sensual shrubbery – never not the most stunning man on earth. He tells me to leave the mess and to come and sit with him for a while.

'Is everything alright? Was it the song? Or is it your dead husband?'

'I loved the song. And yeah, I do miss Mark. But, Chris, I think I've got to go. I can't stay here any more. It's not my home.'

'What do you mean? This is your home. I am your home.'

'Chris . . . I can't.'

I stand up to leave; he stands too, his flannel dressing gown loosening and exposing his greasy bulky torso and skimpy pants. We stand face to face, and I place my hand on his chest.

'Your heart,' I say, shocked by its propulsions.

'It's your heart,' he replies, placing his hand on top of mine, locking in the love.

We collapse into a kiss. The kiss of all kisses. A year of anticipation dissolving into sweet, saliva-based synchronicity. It feels as if we are two dolphins entwined, our soft silky lips frolicking beside one another. The microwave bings, we giggle nervously and he leads me upstairs for one of the top five greatest nights of my life.

At 5 a.m. I awake from the most blissful sleep. I marvel at the man who lies next to me: a specimen of pure beauty, creativity and masculinity. I quietly pack my bag: my clothes, toiletries and mementos from the past year; postcards from Chris and the vibrator from Gwyneth. It's time to leave, confront reality and start again. I don't know where I am going but I know I'll be alright. I step out of the west London townhouse, my head held high as I admire the swallows gliding in the peacefully pink sky above. I soak it in, not realizing that this is the last sight I'll ever see. As I step into the road a white Toyota Prius speeds towards me and knocks my body into the air, breaking every bone and killing me instantly. The wheels screech on the tarmac as the driver escapes into the hazy morning light, leaving an unmistakable aroma of burnt oak and satsumas in its wake.

As I float up to heaven, Mark is there to greet me at its gates.

'Hey, babe, great to see you. I'm so glad you got to fulfil your fantasy before you died. But just so you know . . . that was Chris's poo on the toilet seat. And he *barely* wiped.'

We collapse into laughter and stride into the sunset arm in arm, for ever.

'What are you working on?' Mark says, peering over my shoulder as he walks into the kitchen.

'Nothing. Emails,' I reply, slamming my laptop shut.

I suppose from his perspective one small bonus of being

married to someone who insists on maintaining such intense, vivid parasocial relationships is that it totally eliminates the desire to pursue a celebrity affair in reality. Been there, done that, got the silicone massager.

CHAPTER TWELVE

William

I lose half a stone in the five months before my wedding to Mark. Hanging in my wardrobe is the dress – a pink and purple floral gown from the 1930s. My findings from Bridal Instagram – #bridesofinstagram, #indiebrides, #vintagebride – have conclusively revealed that I should appear as if there is no visible human body underneath the fabric; just the soul of a new wife and virgin haunting the shoulders of a delicate crêpe prism. To achieve this, I do twenty-minute daily HIIT workouts and go on the 5:2 diet, five days of eating normal food, two days of 500 calories. It's hard to concentrate on work when in an extreme calorie deficit, and colleagues wince at the sound of sloppy gut-friendly yoghurts and crunchy seaweed crackers being desperately consumed in an otherwise silent office. 'A deal's a deal,' I say to myself in between bites. 'Even if everyone hates you for it.'

The fastidious rituals work. Half a stone isn't a particularly newsworthy amount of weight to lose but it's a shock to the system and a significant physical shift that I later quietly attribute to kick-starting what happens next: a soul-quaking health condition that turns me from a prospering young woman to miserable husk.

Before the darkness descends, the wedding day takes place and is marvellous. I'm a true indie bride, frolicking in a field with a large purple flower in my hair. My mum loses her voice but brings down the house with her speech written on *Love Actually*-styled cards. The reception is in a tent in a field so food comes from a truck, some relatives go hungry and friends are free to dance until dawn. There's a sprawling, chaotic atmosphere when it gets dark that threatens the ethereal ambience of the dress. I think Mark and I were supposed to have a moment of sentimentality – just the two of us – but we're so excited to have everyone we love in one place that we don't really speak for the rest of the night. That's OK. To see him at the end of the night spinning around a tent dressed in someone's tiny pink fascinator reassures me of my decision to commit to this man for life.

The morning after, I am the first person back in the tent again to tidy up. I eat handfuls of leftover warm, sweaty cheese and chocolate cake that's been sitting out overnight as if I were newly released from a basement kidnapping. My body fizzes with gratitude and abundance. Then it's back to business as usual. Just a thirty-something professional living a quiet life.

We go on our honeymoon. However, I start to feel tired; there's pain in unusual places and I'm unable to sleep without worrying hysterically about trivialities at work. I look really cross in all the photos; my brow furrowed and a cold sore on my lip. We go on a catamaran and a man who works on it makes me stand up and dance with him in front of the other boat people; I try but find it so difficult that I begin to cry. I've lost my sense of humour and am not as supple and free as I expected I'd be as a new wife in Mauritius, which is not to say I'd be bodyrolling to the Black Eyed Peas' 'I Gotta Feeling' otherwise, but there's definitely something dragging me down.

When Christmas comes around, my emotions are sunken; a numbness that is drawing me into existentialism. The busy buzz of the office reduces to eerie quiet as people head back home for the holidays. It's a particularly dark month, 2016's December, and it feels as if we have entered a new era of brutality. I'm consumed by news of Brexit, Trump, and the inescapable image of a three-year-old Syrian boy's body lying face down on a beach. At first I feel justified by my engulfing misery; I am even quietly proud of my extreme societal empathy. But the irregularity of it hits me at unusual intervals. At times I feel possessed.

On 18 December I go to a friend's birthday party in a Chinese restaurant that doubles up as a karaoke bar. The room is decorated in red and gold, with lanterns and fairy lights illuminating plates of sticky meats and vegetables. Cheap red wine is flowing and people are loud and merry. There's a girl there, with nice soft hair and hazy eyes, breezing through the night; she appears to me as a Chloe, Sophie or Ruby – someone whose parents have a house in the country, and who knows how to shell a crab. I feel very uptight by comparison, stressed out about the masses of edible flesh in front of me and worried I've got nothing to say to anyone. I also have a pre-existing layer of total contempt for karaoke underlying everything. I don't get it. What's the joke? Bad singing? Or, even more desperate, good singing? I swear to God this girl is looking at Mark.

'Do you know her?' I ask, gesturing in her direction. He doesn't. But people lie. Perhaps I've married a liar. I head off to the pink loos and sit in a cubicle, silently screaming as if I'm Wendy from *The Shining*, my eyes bulging with a berserk level of devastation.

I look in the mirror with both hands on the basin before heading back into the karaoke room. I am somewhat startled by my extreme reaction; I've not felt such visceral jealousy since I was fifteen. The night's barely begun but I ask Mark if we can go home. I just can't cope with this level of socializing when whatever emotional turbulence I'm battling is so close to the surface.

When we get home I ask him about the girl again, desperate for him to satiate my paranoia. Are you sure you hadn't met her before? Did you used to date her? I don't mind; you can tell me. She was pretty, wasn't she? Prettier than me. And happier.

The melodrama continues at work, in the toilet cubicles after failing to proofread a live review. What am I doing? Who *really* cares about the Killers? I'm at it again in my parents' loo on Christmas Day, shortly after fake-laughing through my heavy despair. We're having a nice time but, Mum and Dad, shouldn't we address the fact that at some stage you're both going to die?

It's my birthday. I go to a comedy night in a church and cry in the pews because the jokes are good but I'm unable to access joy. I have lost my cogent thought processes; my head has no expanse, no words or ideas. I am constantly desperate for sugar, pain relief, alcohol or anything to help me escape my burnt-out brain. I am beginning to lose the ability to speak in coherent sentences at work. Meetings are daily and impromptu and I've been rendered completely unable to think on my feet. I tug strands of information from my mind but find nothing at the end of it, just dithering riddles and rambles.

For New Year's Eve, Mark and I go to visit my friend Anna in some arty gentrified quarters of seaside town Margate, where everyone I meet is incredibly high. I don't know if this is just a pink-boiler-suit-wearing, bohemian-Margate type of trait, or a genuine desperation to escape the heavy rain and nastiness of 2016. Either way, it's full throttle from the moment we get off the train. George Michael died a week ago, so at 1 a.m. Anna, I and a few others dance in a circle along to 'Club Tropicana' in someone's empty scuzzy living room. That image seems a bit tragic on its own, but when you consider that the woman shout-singing 'You can sun tan!' the loudest is full of her own private, inexplicable desolation, it's even worse.

2017 crawls into view. I take myself to the doctors and tell the GP that I can't stop the way I am feeling, and please can you have a look inside and tell me what it is? He asks me if I would consider using antidepressants. My instinct tells me to persist without them, that there is something else attacking my body and mind.

I haven't had my periods in a while. A year, in fact. I attributed that to wedding weight-loss and general menstrual inconsistency. I am also sweating, all the time – aggressive sweating, sharp, violent perspiration that feels like a spank across the skin and a slow melting of the face. It happens throughout the night, and during the day at work when I have to do anything moderately stressful such as speaking in a meeting, making small talk with the intern (apparently 'Where do you live?' is *not* appropriate) or asking for holiday leave. I keep visiting the GP, asking for other investigations, praying they'll persist and not palm me off as a time-waster. I pee inside a huge container on and off for twenty-four hours. I get blood tests. I reinstall the Headspace app and before bed scribble down my darkest thoughts so they're not with me throughout the night. But mostly I google, and the results are definitive. If it's not cervical cancer, schizophrenia, dementia or a really, really long stroke, it is likely I am going through the menopause.

One day on my trudge into work, I see a man waiting at my bus stop. His hair – it's dark red; his clothes are familiar. Understated but expensive. Pays attention to modern trends but self-contained and professional. I feel a sensation, as if I've worked with him in some capacity, as if we're about to have a chat. He looks like he has a job at a record label or a magazine. I sidle up beside him as he stares into space. My clean, bright perfume is strong and I wonder if he can smell it, hoping it might trigger a memory. He glances at me momentarily, shocked by my closeness to him rather than the warm recognition I was expecting. The bus arrives and we get on after each other. I stay near him and take a closer look. Probably early thirties. Formerly in a band? Wedding ring. A faraway stare, bordering on the gormless. He notices me looking so I double down, adjust my gaze slightly to the right of his head so it looks as if I am daydreaming. Who are you and why aren't you looking at me?

I get off the bus, leaving him behind and feeling hurt. I wonder what has happened. Maybe I am unrecognizable. I am far from what I was in August 2016, let alone the years before that, my glossy young hair now limp, and plump skin dry and sunken. It's six months after the wedding and I've stopped having showers. My greasy hair is scraped up in a bun and I have a grey uniform: one pair of faded black jeans that accommodate my bloated stomach – a drop in oestrogen is thought to increase abdominal fat in menopausal women; a big charcoal jumper that lives on the floor and inside it a white t-shirt, encased as if it were a hostage, the armpits getting more stained by the day. No makeup, maybe a blob of moisturiser if I can manage it. My nails are yellow, flaking, the skin around them bloody. My hands are a repellent five-legged spider gripping on to the yellow bus poles. If this distant man knew me before, it was a version unmuddied by insidious hormones; a me with better hands, better hair, and better BO.

Another curious symptom: the anger I feel on most days is like being on steroids; a masculine desire to headbutt anyone who walks too slowly or stands down the wrong side of the escalator. I try to exercise to release some of this tension but my muscles ache so much I start taking the lift into work rather than the stairs. I take a day off and head to a local sauna underneath a gym that sometimes smells of cigarettes. It's just me on my own for the first part, and with every drop of sweat I feel as if I am expunging whatever freakish toxins have taken over my body. Then, two men turn up. One keeps making angry phone calls – in the sauna, in the chillout room. Then he starts talking to me. 'Where've you come from?' he asks, and I reply politely, even though I know it's wrong to be conversing with a topless rage-filled bloke in a dark, hot room. After a few minutes of courteous and stressful chat, I move on to another hot room but realize that a small string bracelet my mum got me for Christmas has fallen off somewhere so I am forced to return to the two men. I tell them what's happened and they make a valiant effort to help me, but really entrap me in a series of other benign personal questions that I must answer while stood up in the centre of a dark room, dripping sweat from my nose, in a tankini. I can't seem to cut a break and it's starting to infuriate me. Once I've left, I sit and fantasize about what I could do to them in the dark sauna – army self-defence methods I could use; a grip of the neck that could paralyse them for life. It's one way to spend an afternoon.

In the middle of autumn 2017, in an endocrinologist's office in central London, I'm finally given a definitive diagnosis. I have spoken to so many doctors that I'm not expecting progress, yet on this unremarkable day in this bright white room a hormone expert with a corpse-like demeanour clinically informs me that I have the ovarian supply of a fifty-two-year-old. My anger almost immediately dissipates and is replaced by a dizziness and confusion that lasts for months. There's nothing that makes you feel less like the Fittest Girl in Year 11 than knowing all your eggs are dead.

It turns out no amount of face masks or laxative tea can reverse this condition, or can halt the speed with which I am internally and externally decaying. Perhaps it is a punishment, a revenge from within for treating my capable and strong body with such disdain and entitlement for so many years. The big emotions, the migraines, sweating, spikes of anger, weight gain, lethargy, aching joints, heart palpitations, stuttering, night terrors, insomnia, memory loss, loss of libido and confidence: they're all symptoms of Premature Ovarian Insufficiency. It used to be called Premature Ovarian Failure, which I prefer, as it sounds more dramatic and finite, rather than just lazy. He says that spontaneous POI affects 1 per cent of women before the age of forty, and that it could be attributed to an underactive thyroid, which I have. I will be on hormone replacement therapy until my fifties to protect my heart and bones, which are now at risk from my low level of oestrogen. I'd love to ask if it's because I propped my molten-hot laptop on my womb for too long, but I nod and ask him to write it all down on a piece of paper that I then shove in my bag and never look at again.

When I leave the hospital, I call my sister immediately, who is driving her two boys home from school. I am on speaker-phone.

'Hat! How did it go?' Libby asks.

'Not great, not great,' I reply. 'I mean at least we got to the bottom of it. I've got a thing which is like the early menopause.'

'What does that mean?'

I tell her it explains all the strange feelings I've had, but I've got less than a 5 per cent chance of conceiving naturally. I wasn't quite ready to be talking about children, even though I'd always vaguely wanted to be a mum. Now I've been told I'll need to do IVF – well, actually I'll need to use someone else's eggs in order to do IVF because I don't have any – the potential absence of a baby, the complex process of fighting for it, feels like grief. I don't know how it works, but we need to start soon as it'll probably take ages. I shout above the crowds of tourists.

There's a brief moment of silence while her brain does the maths.

'Can you use my eggs? You can use my eggs?'

And like that the deal is done.

When I get home, Mark is shattered by the news, before immediately being uplifted by Libby's solution. There is a straightforward plan and appointments are made. In the weeks and months that follow we are moving forward with the baby, tests, scans, lots of highly technical chats about blastocysts, but in the downtime I am all-consumed by my ineffectual body. Haggard. Sexless. Unable to procreate without medical intervention. I google POI and – affronted by the words 'dry vagina' and how prominent they are on the search results – decide to refer to it from now on as the early menopause. I can't really believe it. I have spent so much of my life willing on a form of adulthood and womanliness – my habit of dating older men, my constant struggle to achieve an air of sophistication and worldliness – but somehow these aspirations have manifested by me just skipping directly straight to the bad bit of later womanhood, where you've got all the mania of puberty but in an aching, withered body rather than an abundant one to facilitate it.

I begin to assume a new identity built from cruel archetypes. Older, leatherier, drier, colder. I try to distract myself online but everywhere I look is a fetishized pregnancy body: Instagram is filled with photos of women's bumps being kissed by their happy fiances in front of mock-Tudor fireplaces at Christmas. Bumps accentuated in floral wrap dresses at gaudy cupcake-filled parties. Blossoming tummies and juicy boobs in Demi Moore-styled photoshoots. I'm muting people who've just had babies, and a few other people who've just had good years in general. Sometimes I have to actively restrain myself from writing sledgehammer comments like 'I can't have children' or 'I'm infertile' under other people's happy family posts.

My algorithm, meanwhile, has detected a vague spike in fertility-related searches, but hasn't listened closely enough to the crucial details. Every YouTube ad is for breastfeeding vitamins, high-tech nappies or Clearblue pregnancy tests. Actually, Google, I'd mainly like some therapy. And a photo of my eerie empty uterus. What exactly is going on in there?

The sensation of isolation is intensified by the man I see at the bus stop. Every day. He is there. Taunting me with my non-existence. Most days, I stand as close to him as I can without it pushing the boundaries of legality. Sometimes I turn up my music as loud as it'll go, or spend too long searching for a credible song with my screen in his eyeline to try to catch his attention. If I could just hear a single word from a conversation, I could trace it back to a theme, a cultural tribe, and find him on the internet. I get nothing: he stands motionless every day. He doesn't even listen to music, simply scowling at emails on his phone. He seemed quite together when we first stood next to each other but now I realize he carries an ambience of depression wherever he goes.

There are some mornings when he's not there. On those days I am glad to be relieved of my duties. I find myself attempting to show him my straight teeth and cheekbones by subtly distorting my face while reading or responding to the people around me, in the hope that he might see it's me. The only time he does acknowledge me is on a Monday morning – a woman calls another woman a 'fucking bitch' for not getting out the way and I am stood right next to her. Being a witness to such a minor aggression makes the busy bus heave with embarrassment, and seconds later we all sink into our phones.

Soon I begin to see him everywhere, off the bus and out of context. Perhaps he has gone through a divorce; I would assume so by the saggy tote bag he carries. I consider giving him a cheerful, non-threatening smile to kickstart the conversation but he doesn't seem like much of a smiler. Although he does look fairly jovial one Friday night – walking up my street with a white carrier bag full of Budweiser beers. Six beers on a Friday night. What does it all mean? It's been another crap week of feeling thick and ugly at work and this small morsel of information is meaningful to me. I wish I could speak to Mark about it – see what he could decode from the beers in a bag. But I don't have the mental capacity to share this secret with him; nor do I have the words to do it all justice. It would all seem so unhinged when you combine it with my list of other recent traits: agonizing discomfort during sex, lying in a cold bath crying of an evening, and saying, 'I'm going to punch the fucking TV screen' during disagreements. I start sleeping on the sofa downstairs but we live on a busy road and I spend a lot of the night staring at the front door, half-dreaming that a predator has broken in and is lying on top of me. This is the first thing I tell Mark when he comes downstairs in the morning. I am also telling Mark that I want to move back in with my parents and become a dinner lady.

I should be making a nest, paddle-boarding or checking my ovulation schedule on an app, not regressing, spying on strangers and contemplating violence. I've forgotten who I am, and who we are, and whenever possible I check Mark's messages to find a sign that he's had enough. I find nothing but am convinced he must be disgusted by the woman who's hijacked his wife.

Secretly finding out if I have any affiliation with this man on the bus becomes my drive to get up in the morning. An escapist investigation, something to work towards. Since my body has removed everything that normally helps boost life from point-less to liveable – laughter, libido, imagination, daydreams, ambition – there is little to motivate me to get out of bed. I feel as if I am fading away from friends because I'm bad at being honest about my sinking sanity, and after all, the condi-tion is far from fatal. It's not like cancer – there is no urgency or fear of dying. It's just withering my soul.

Then one week there's a flurry of activity, as if someone's hit the side of the TV and jogged the signal. The bus guy gets on the bus, sits down and pulls out a small green book. The words on the cover are blurry from where I am standing. I google the words 'small green book cover' to no avail. The next day I hear him talking to a woman. She's sat down and he's stood up. He is making her laugh but his voice is so quiet. Hers is louder so I survive off her replies: ' . . . the buildings around Tottenham Court Road', 'development' . It's not much but it's enough. Combined with the fact I've noticed him observing building work when he's waiting for the bus, and the neat clothes he wears, I suspect he is an architect. I watch him caress the Oyster Card machine nervously with his small, spindly hands as they speak. I suddenly feel protective of Bus Guy – a man who clearly needs downtime before he starts work every day but is now locked into idle pleasantries with this woman. I plan to give her a surly look that says 'back off' when I get off the bus. When the moment comes I lose confidence and bustle out with the others.

As well as the bizarre physical and mental changes I am enduring, my internet habits have shifted dramatically too. I've abandoned the usual obsessions with pretty, clever women who've previously had sex with someone that I have, and am now primarily:

a) seething at celebrities or normal humans who have just announced pregnancies
b) inspecting the team photos of architect companies in London
c) visiting messageboards full of women who also presumably have dry vaginas.

The POI Facebook group and messageboards are an incredible source of information when it's so hard to access an appointment with a specialist. At times my fellow sufferers' stories can knock me sideways: I am on a cocktail of hormones to prepare my body for the donor egg treatment – progesterone and oestrogen, thickening my womb lining, but riddling my brain with surges of depression and voracious hunger – and it doesn't take much to send me over the edge. I often want to validate how bad I feel and submerge myself in other women's sad stories; pure, unadulterated wallowing. One night Mark catches me in bed crying while hunched over my laptop and asks me to come downstairs to watch TV. On the plus side, observing this community makes me realize that I am one of the lucky ones. There are women in their teens, some who've endured decades of fertility treatment, and others who have been diagnosed in their forties, have no partner and have lived with the destabilizing symptoms for most of their adult lives.

Lately I've been coming close to considering doing a vlog. In the months since my diagnosis I have discovered a network of micro-influencers talking about their struggles with the early menopause – sunny girls sporting cheery makeup and bathed in the glow of a ring light while doing demos of how best to apply HRT patches, or describing the process of doing donor-egg IVF in less clinical terms than medical professionals. It's an amazing source of information and I am so thankful for the people with conditions formerly considered shameful that are helping others on such a public platform. But there is darkness in turning your insubordinate body into a commodity. Algorithms reward trauma, and it's apparent that the more you're willing to share, the larger the audience, and the more your entire identity is defined by being unwell. I worry about what their lives are like when the camera's off; the burden of being professionally weak; the dopamine hit of being celebrated for your sickness. If they get better, do they relinquish control, allow more poorly candidates to pick up the mantle? Maybe I sound bitter. Because I would absolutely love the attention. The only thing stopping me is the thought of my family; how confused they would be if they saw my cry for help on social media when I can barely pick up the phone.

The parallel mission of getting pregnant rumbles on in the background of my emotional descent. Yet in spite of my own private turmoil, I am comforted by Libby and Mark, who have both been prodded and tested and are ready for the next stage of the donor egg process. I can't believe my luck to be flanked by these silly, stoic humans. Especially because IVF clinics are bleak. People aren't hot in the IVF clinic. The rooms are grey and the tension is high. The posters are miserable: infertility support groups, flyers that read 'ANXIETY AND DEPRESSION? CALL US!' The one time I did see a cool couple, their charisma faded pretty fast. There's a unique distress to be found in two vintage-clad hipsters sat on a plastic bench wearing suede tassels and flares, staring morbidly into space.

Nevertheless, we plough forward. Mark manages to successfully masturbate some healthy sperm into a plastic cup. Libby's eggs are healthy and my womb is hospitable. We've been in multiple meetings with a brilliant woman named Debbie who's got ringlets and a maternal temperament. She talks to us as if we aren't idiots. She's told us about blastocysts and egg transfer dates, and other fertility terms we've not researched. I watch on with amusement as Mark gesticulates in time with her proclamations about intricate biological explanations, knowing full well he barely understands what a carbohydrate is let alone an endometrial lining.

A year after our first appointment with Debbie, we are ready for the egg transfer. There are daily injections for two weeks that'll pull the pin on a grenade of intense emotions and stimulate the eggs to prepare them for removal. Libby does this part; her default setting is passion and the rapid bursts of hormones are overwhelming. I feel so bad that she is suffering because of my physical impairments. In conjunction with this, I am having daily ultrasound scans at the hospital, each time hiding my pants in my coat pocket when I'm asked to take them off, despite the fact they're about to look all the way inside my vagina with a torch.

You get really good at lying back and having objects inserted into you when you do IVF. Each time you visit a doctor the sensation is different and unexpected: cool, long lubricated probe that glides across your insides and makes you feel haunted? The scratchy stick that feels like it's barbed? Or the slow crank-it-open process that stings for days? I get good at rubbing a pressure point on the side of my thumb to brace myself. I have pressed it so much recently that there's a dent in my skin. Mark occasionally takes a Wellman supplement.

After fourteen days of intensive preparation, Libby goes into theatre for a general anaesthetic – it's here they remove her eggs and put them into a lab so they can fertilize with Mark's sperm. We wait for the procedure to finish under the blinking lights of a bleak hospital cafe, while Mark manages to make room for a soggy full English and I eat half a banana.

We get a call to say she's ready to be collected, head to the ward and pull back a curtain to reveal Libby's body, grey and lifeless. When she comes to, her lips are dry and pale and she is drowsy, but still offers us both a Milk Biscuit from her rider.

Her husband Patrick comes to take us all out to Carluccio's to celebrate. On the way out I bump into Debbie. 'We got three eggs,' she says with a conciliatory smile, and a defeated nod. 'We'll give you a call tomorrow to let you know how the fertilization goes, and then we should be able to do the transfer.'

I keep the foreboding exchange a secret so as not to lower the mood over lunch. Spirits are high, even though Libby's skin is still the colour of an artichoke. I know we've not got enough eggs and every day they will diminish.

At 7 a.m. the next morning I get a call from an unknown number. A nurse from the hospital. She has bad news. None of the eggs have fertilized.

We are all broken; Mark and I spend the day walking around our local park, an endless parade of buggies and buoyant families attacking us from every direction. In the end we seek safety in a pub and I order an Old Fashioned, finding a small glimmer of joy in the fact I can drink. 'Maybe we could get some heroin in?' I joke. We do actually momentarily consider buying some drugs to take the edge off the grief, but decide against it.

The next morning I get a call at 7 a.m. It's a nurse – she's happy.

'As a precaution we kept your eggs in the lab overnight, and one has fertilized,' she explains.

It's a miracle. I imagine how the news would have gone down if I'd received it splayed out on the floor of a crack den.

Two hours later they implant the embryo into my womb. Two weeks pass. On the fourteenth day we do a pregnancy test. I'm not pregnant. We're hit with the heavy grief again. I call my sister to tell her the bad news.

'I'm so sorry, Hat,' Libby says, her words strained with sorrow. She really means it. I reassure her it's not her fault, then she says she wants to go again, motivated like a sadistic PE teacher. On the cusp of crying, I quickly thank her, tell her I love her and say goodbye.

I am so broken. Mark is too but wants to try to fix it. He arranges a meeting with another NHS doctor from the same clinic. A clear, bold, pragmatic Italian man, who is a consultant obstetrician and gynaecologist. We have some options, he says. Try again with my sister, or go and get the eggs of a younger woman, a stranger. 'It's not a big deal. The baby's still yours.' Mark agrees. I nod, but I am horrified. I've been prodded and penetrated by needles and cold instruments for eighteen months. I need a break.

It's a relief to have a brief window of no medical obligations. I can roam around as I please, knowing that I'm not supposed to be willing my womb lining to thicken. I have a big decision on the horizon, so bat off any chance of thinking by becoming completely fixated with screens. It's a new phase of compulsion; rather than finding a specific person or subject interesting, I am plunging into the internet directionless and hoping for distraction. There is no downtime, overstimulation always; podcasts playing at the moment I get up from watching the TV, phone on the loo, every silent second filled with the hum of light entertainment and arbitrary footage of other people's lives.

One evening I am on the bus home from work and have a lonesome, nagging feeling. My usual social media scrolling isn't filling the void and I am keen to get a hit of something before my brain catches up with its cue to feel sad. I avert my gaze and look around the crushed bottom deck of the bus and see a cream tote bag. My stomach flips. It's not him; it's an elderly woman holding a Lidl bag for life. But it's enough to jolt me back into my former hobby and neglected duty. I take a stab in the dark and google the area of London I believe he might work in based on the bus he gets on, where it goes to, and search: architects. I begin to tap on each website, checking the team photos. I am hungry now, perversely driven by an achievable goal, one not revolving around ovulation. There are maybe thirty architects that come up, many of which I have looked at before. It is nearly time to get off the bus – two more stops. I go on an architect's website I've not visited yet and on its homepage is a slideshow of photos set on the fadeout function: a shot of the team doing marathons disintegrates into a shot of the team standing outside a building, then on to a team trip to Bulgaria. It's in Bulgaria that I notice the hair. Stood at the back. The eyeline. He looks tired, pissed off because he's having to socialize, probably. But it is him. The image fades into a shot of a hotel. I am lightheaded. It's time to get off the bus.

I speed-walk home, enter the house, fire up the laptop and neglect to turn on any lights. I have found the Bus Guy's place of work and for that I am remarkable. The website has a page dedicated to its staff. With one scroll I see his face and see his name for the first time. I click on his profile and read about his backstory: been at it for ten years, started this job in 2017.

Click here to email William. Click here to email William. I click on it and it opens an email template. I quit the tab and go downstairs to recover. I found a stranger online. This has boosted my ego in a way that no compliment or work accomplishment ever could.

Now sat in the living room in complete darkness, I search his name on Google and find a Mixcloud page which reveals to me his recently liked playlists: jazz, bossa nova, left-field hip-hop. Classy. Perfect soundtrack to the great exploration. There is a Facebook page with a really old photo of him on a boat. He looks different – bigger, baggier, less urbane. We have no mutual friends; he never knew me but now I know him. He grew up in Wales. I can see a few posts, some YouTube tracks. Wedding photos. His wife is a tall, slender woman with a wicked smile – gift of the gab, no doubt. There are photos of them on holidays: American road trips. I wonder if they had sex in the eerie pink motel rooms or felt too pressurized by the overbearing sleaziness. I click through her pictures, from scrappy early photos with vintage filters to the more poised recent ones. No children. There's an important comment from an old school friend named Rachel under one of her selfies. 'I can't wait for you to have babies! Hurry up pal!' 'I would if I could, pal,' William's wife replies, curtly. And there it is. That's why we've been pulled together. The magnetic tug of infertility.

Two months have gone by since our failed IVF. Time is ticking, and I've exhausted William's sister's Instagram and his wife's best friend's YouTube. No more distractions. I am still grappling with the thought of inserting a young fertile woman's body part into mine. But, as Mark and I have discussed, every other hour, we either want a baby, or we don't. And we do, so desperately, so I decide to shut that part of my brain down and do whatever the Italian doctor tells us. He suggests a clinic in Spain. We agree. They are fast and they have an excellent success rate.

The Spanish clinicians are incredibly slick; we have video chats during which we explain we have no specifications for the baby other than similar colourings to me – dark hair and light eyes. They find a donor quickly, and two months of hormones and tests later, we are in Spain for the procedure. When we get there, we try to do touristy things – sit on a rooftop, try local delicacies – but the intention of our trip muddies every second of attempted pleasure. Lightening the load is our hotel room; Mark books us into place in the gay district; our room is decorated in purple leather, pink fur, black silk and bedside bowls of condoms. The trip is a pressure cooker: full of phone calls that tell us the status of our donor's egg collection (we get nine), the embryo's fertilization status and whether we want to jump in early and try implanting two eggs to get twins, or wait a few days more and get a good healthy blastocyst for one. We choose the latter, the blastocyst is implanted, then we head straight back to the hotel, avoiding busy crowds. There's no bleak breakfast. No sad Debbie this time. No suggestion of heroin.

For the next two weeks, I barely move and avoid baths, heavy lifting or operating machinery. I am so still. Every twitch and ripple my body experiences could be a sign of life or death. On day 14, I have a blood test to see if I am pregnant.

At 12 p.m. I should receive an email with the results. At 11.30 a.m. Mark and I walk in the park, buggies ram-raiding us at every turn. I keep refreshing: newsletters, PRs. Not now. Mark says we should wait until 12.10 to look again. We stare into the distance and say nothing but are telepathically sharing our fear. At 12.11 it's time to check, and we see an email from a complicated medical address – 113523@nuca1J_e44 – that looks like spam. It reads: 'Please find attached a copy of your results which confirms a positive pregnancy test.'

I tell Mark the results and we hug tightly then waggle our bodies with relief. I am stunned, yet far from happy. In fact, it takes around three months to feel as if I can breathe. The desperation to maintain this pregnancy is overwhelming – it feels as if we've cheated the system. During our first ultrasound scan, I go through the motions and get completely naked from the waist down, butterflying my legs open on the bed, only for the startled midwife to say: 'Sorry, it's not one of those sorts of scans.' At least when you're finally pregnant you're spared one strand of indignity.

The pernickety HRT regime continues during the first trimester – applying suppositories and taking tablets at the same time multiple times a day to keep the baby alive. I also carry on with the slow and considered approach to movement, which means I start going into work later to avoid rush hour and stop seeing William. He feels part of a past life, in which I felt freakish levels of isolation and distance from my loved ones unlike anything I have experienced before. Pregnancy hormones have made me neat and complete. Still, I hope his work website doesn't track my IP address.

One Saturday morning a few months before I give birth, I see William's frame in the distance as I head to the supermarket. He is carrying a house plant and is with his wife; sure enough, her belly is big – full of baby, ready to go. Fantastic news, guys. Rachel had better bring a Bugaboo Bee 5 to the baby shower. Look at us! Who'd have thought. Not me.

As we draw closer together on the street, I prepare to acknowledge him and our spiritual union with an ebullient facial expression. Even if the poignancy of my smile is lost on them both, surely it's customary to acknowledge a fellow pregnant person? An obligation even, like waving at other people on a boat. Not creepy at all. No.

So I send the smile, tight yet warm, out into the ether, hoping for recognition. To my surprise, his head turns the other way, almost witheringly, as he ushers his wife across the road. 'No worries. He probably just thinks you're a stranger,' I tell myself, tootling off down the street with my unborn son in my belly, and for a moment I swear I can feel him crossing his tiny unformed fingers in there, so tight that they turn blue, as he hopes against all hope he doesn't turn out as odd as his mother.

CHAPTER THIRTEEN

Well Done Harriet

Bodies are beginning to drop like flies. 'Don't forget child's pose is always there for you, when you need it.' Thanks very much, but it's not for me: I'll push on even though my expression resembles that of a Bond villain passing a gallstone, and my arms are weak and visibly trembling. I've got to prove to these bitches that while I'm the only one in here rocking some old school VPL as the result of my unforgiving leggings, I am here to win. I'll be doing this downward dog until the last polar icecap has melted, with the freezing water lapping into my upside-down grimace while my friends and family are Zorbing on Mars.

Before my pregnancy, I would do some form of strenuous workout five times a week. Often it's just running, turning up with an unsightly camel backpack everywhere I went in case I decided to jog home. Other times I'd visit an exercise class. In the aftermath I was steadier, more confident. It was far from relaxing, however. The only space in which I am truly relaxed, where I really succumb to the emptiness, is alone in bed while watching a structured reality show while simultaneously looking up every new character's Instagram profile. It's in that space and that space only in which I am tapped out: the mind empty, clarity resumed. I know that some go to yoga for a similar form of mental enema, but for me it is a battle – a battle to be the best and a battle for the love, respect and time of the teachers.

It's not even my fault, entirely. It's the industrialization of yoga. They get you hooked on the idea of finding your 'tribe' and joining a reliably expensive 'community'. There are score-boards on the wall with points given to the yoginis who visit the most days in succession. The intention is to create a touchy-feely family, but you can feel the cold wind of capitalism inevitably gusting into every modern Western studio as soon as you yank open its heavy iron doors. Without even addressing the implications of endorsing and perpetuating the ongoing cultural appropriation of yoga, I am mainly appalled by the way in which I personally engage with the ancient practice – which, partly because of the internet, has become far more about following the teacher than it has about the teaching itself.

Before I had the guts to walk into a real studio, I started out practising online. The benefit of doing yoga online is that you can pause the videos to stare at their homes – those empty, spotless homes. I'm far from the first person to admit to having a fixation with Adriene of Yoga with Adriene. I liked that her jokes are bad – dorky; that she is so free in herself and that she treats her body with respect, like it's a body rather than a lump of clay to be chipped and sculpted into perfection. I even liked her dog, which is crazy because

I hate dogs. She was nurturing to me for a while, but I soon got bored. I ached for the 'flat ab tummy in ten minutes' videos that promised a 'fat burning vinyasa'. I yearned for speed and vigorousness. Discipline and pain. Adriene's style was hushed, tender and precise – pausing in poses for so long that I was forced to come face to face with my domestic inadequacies. The cold hard clutter and debris that exists under the cosy sofa. The clouds of dust and kirby grips, discarded bills and the small snips of tissue used to kill a clothes moth and then left on the floor afterwards.

I am of the opinion that if it doesn't hurt – if the exercise doesn't make my limbs burn or make my throat taste of blood – it probably isn't working. So I moved on to some YouTube babes who promised fat-busting yoga. The video was in its essence a fitness tutorial in which three exercise enthusiasts from the US squatted, crunched and clenched their way through thirty minutes of gruelling muscle workouts. Fronting the video is Lean Lisa, a refreshingly mature woman with a corporate smile and faraway eyes; the type of lady who might unwind alone each night dressed in a long beige cardigan with a large glass of Chardonnay and a stunning sea view. The other two enthusiastic, unnamed women respect her – they spout fawning comments celebrating her methodology but appear to have misjudged their leader's ability to accept compliments. 'We love you, Lisa!!!' they scream, only to be met with a meek: 'Thank you.' Wow. Who hurt you, Lisa?

By the time I've plucked up the courage to visit a real class, I have become hooked on the teachers before their hands have even adjusted my hips. The standard practice for stylish studios is to include a large introductory bio accompanying a photo of each teacher, so you can see if you might be compatible and perhaps form a bond. It includes where they are from, why they started teaching, alongside some more general stuff about good vibes and nurturing energy. If you enjoy their CV, then you can take a look at their Instagram account too, in which they often post photos of tree pose and holidays, stuck in a perpetual wellbeing aesthetic of pretty latte art and hazy sunset shots. Many of them leave little clues as to why they might have taken up the profession – there are eating disorders, broken homes, and soul-destroying break-ups. They don't say that explicitly, but once you've spent a good forty minutes going through every blog post and picture caption, you pretty much get the gist.

Eventually it's time to meet. Usually this is in a disused office block filled with succulents. Every Wednesday I will leave work three minutes early, shrouded in guilt and secrecy, in the hope that I will get the exact same place in the room, and that the teacher that I've invested in so desperately might say my name or adjust me in a way that will suggest I am their possession and also the best in the room at yoga.

Once inside the space, all the Sanskrit bangers are there: the words '. . . and breathe' in neon lights, a fridge full of coconut water and turmeric shots, and flyers for flat-bread-making workshops and deep-tissue massages. One thing you can guarantee: it will always slightly stink. Entering any new studio remains terrifying, with first-day-of-school levels of paranoia and the childlike fear of doing something wrong. It's a constant worry that someone will tell you off for not cleaning the sweat off a mat properly or, worse still, taking a long-term member's mat thinking it's a communal mat, but they're just there so often they leave their mat in the cupboard and everyone else knows not to touch the mat, but you've touched it and now someone else is telling you it's not for you – she travelled the world with that mat, it's soaked with sweat from her honeymoon in Goa and tears from the grief of her late sister – and now your grubby novice fingers are all over it. There is no humiliation like it.

Having now established the correct mat, however, my job is to not upset the teacher. My deepest fear is that I will do a move before they've said it out loud and they'll assume I'm arrogant; or I'll do a move so wrong they'll have to do a demo of how to do it right, for the benefit of the whole class but it's pointed at me. Quite a lot of teachers are really uptight.

Trusting your body and the other person in the room, silence or occasional deep breathing, the sensation of slow release – there's a thin line between a yoga class and sexual intercourse, when you think about it. It's not the teacher's fault but I am often left post-class feeling as if I have exchanged something intimate with them. Perhaps it's also because they can be so nurturing and physically impressive. First there was Ariana – a former ballet star whose body danced like sunlight across the mat. She was the first teacher I had the courage to talk to, and we vibed so joyfully before class I wondered if we were flirting. But then the next person would sign in and she'd do the same; turns out she was just friendly. Then there was Annabel, a muscular fifty-something teacher whose arms were like a pair of nude tights packed with popcorn. She had the vibrant, earnest energy of a healer and the most impressive glutes I'd ever seen. Or Franchesca, who I suspect was Dutch, and for whom everything was 'lush', 'juicy' or 'releasing pressure'. A short time into our sessions together I saw her on a train crying on the phone and it punctured the dream. I cursed whatever person had broken this courageous warrior's heart. Then there was Cleo – one of my all-time-favourite teachers, northern, covered head to toe in tattoos and with the wise and humbled face of someone who's in the process of leaving a difficult relationship – who was the first teacher I'd met who requested 'we keep our groaning to a minimum'. I bookmark her Instagram on Desktop as soon as I'm out of the class.

The yoga bros are truly fascinating too. The Boys of Yoga. Their classes are always over-subscribed and they've got the physiques of rugby players. They often have interesting back-stories, such as being brought up in the south of England and then travelling to India once. I'm sure they had some wild summers at Secret Garden Party, but now they are rinsed of dirt and ego and ready to spend their days in front of a room full of rich white women who'll do literally anything they'll say.

Nevertheless, my whole body shudders when they call my name or touch my arm. There's an exclusivity to their atten-tion that I can't quite get a handle on, and I am jealous of others who have more personal relationships with their teachers. I can't tell if they've all been on yogic excursions, retreats together, or if they've all just gone to the same classes every night for the past ten years. Part of me wonders if it's time to stop hiding in the shadows and step up to the challenge – to fight for the right to become a teacher's pet.

Nathan's classes are my current favourites. His hour-long sessions are febrile, incessant and forehead-throbbingly intense, to the extent that my teeth are chattering on the bus home and I am too weak to eat my dinner. But the real draw is the man himself. He is a matter-of-fact Irishman who has curated an indie playlist filled with music from the last fifteen years. Most of it is from 2009 to 2011, and I wonder if this was his time – the years in which he blossomed, fell in love and found himself, experimenting with women, men, drugs and hygiene. 'Me too, Nathan!' I try to tell him with my attempt at eye contact during Sharon Van Etten's song 'Kevin's' and a wobbly Chaturanga. I admire his boldness and desire to assert his identity. The confidence to put himself out there when most of the other teachers opt for the generic modern ambient playlist. There is a bit towards the end – when we are all exhausted and nearly puking – when a folk cover of 'Smells Like Teen Spirit' comes on. The whole experience is so heightened and uncomfortable that I can't help but sign up for more.

After a few weeks of going to his classes and trying really hard, sometimes lip-syncing to Modest Mouse in the hope he might notice, Nathan starts to remember me. He gives me a curt nod when he says he can see 'a few familiar faces in the room'. I take this slight acknowledgement as a gesture towards us potentially being best friends and find him on Twitter as soon as I get out of the class. To my utter joy I see that he is often tweeting about gigs that I've been at too – or about albums and bands that I like. So I do what any self-respecting member of society would do in this situation, and make him a Spotify playlist of songs he might like. He's seen me at my most desperate and I want to tell him that I've seen him too.

As I drag the last of the tracks into the Spotify playlist, I am struck by a moment of self-doubt. 'Are we sure we are about to send a yoga teacher a compilation of songs based on his yoga playlist and tweets?' I ask myself. No reply, so I sleep on it. I wake in the morning then play it on my way into work, imagining him listening to it while trying to picture his expressions during each of the selections. I'm pretty certain this is all fine, and not too weird, or too sinister. And what's the worst that could happen? He could block me on Twitter? Shame me in front of the rest of the class? Send it to his wife, who then breaks my legs or puts a curse on me? Who cares. This feels right – like the only logical way I can get close to a teacher without dropping £2,500 on an Ayurvedic yoga retreat in Austria. I press send on the tweet.

The next morning I go to Nathan's class. The message was read but my inbox is still empty. I am filled with utter disgust and dread. As I queue up like all the rest of the nobodies, I feel him look at me as if in recognition. And as I say my name and he marks me on the register, and he puts two and two together, he turns and holds me by the shoulders, looks me dead in the eyes and gives me a hug. Who cares if we keep the rest of the queue waiting! If anything, it's all I've ever wanted.

We chat about the playlist, what he likes, what tracks he'd never heard before – I am careful to move it on to broader conversation so fellow students don't find out about my corrupt attempts to win brownie points. Following on from the playlist incident, we go on to occasionally message about music and I keep attending his classes, but when I bump into him in the park one morning it turns out his life is tumultuous too, that he has a story far beyond visiting India on a gap year. I love his openness, but I am wary of breaking the buzz – scared of spoiling the sacred unspoken dynamic, of us becoming equals when I'd prefer him to be my master. I yearn for those intimidating all-seeing authority figures, the ones that give feedback, the frightening teachers from school. As I've grown older, I must read between the lines – or the punctuation in my bosses' emails – to find out if I am flourishing or flopping at work. I belong to no cultural tribe, and have no real community leader to tell me all that I need to know – that I am a good girl with open hips. Nathan has unwittingly filled a role, where I am his baby, his disciple. And here he is, so ordinary, leaning on a bench, holding a flat white in a reusable cup with his wireless running headphones dangling around his neck. I avert my eyes and remember the time he cradled me from crow pose to headstand.

Normalcy is resolved, however, when we are back in the studio, back in his class. My limbs ache, I'm drenched in sweat and at one point I am adjusted for doing something wrong. I get a 'Well done, Harriet' and a hug on the way out. I breathe out through the nose; I breathe in through the nose. And finally, I feel relaxed.

CHAPTER FOURTEEN

Literally Never Ever Been Happier

Cheeks pink with a post-orgasmic flush, her hair damp and tangled, the woman in the small square photograph is surrendering to an expression of total euphoria. In her arms is a tiny creature, so new and unformed it is still practically an internal organ turned external. It's a special baby. A healthy, happy baby. It's Deliciously Ella's baby.

It is six months before I give birth and my interest in the wellbeing influencer's Instagram is starting to become more pronounced. Ella had a positive birth experience, one of spirituality and inevitability, and obviously I'd love the same: a gentle evacuation before breastfeeding into oblivion. Unfortunately our schedule is already deviating from Ella's: NHS categorizes ours as a 'high risk' pregnancy because of my underactive thyroid, POI and donor egg IVF process. The midwife reassures me they're just being cautious but advises to opt for a full bells-and-whistles medical set-up anyway. I relish telling friends and colleagues about my high-risk status, and I delight in hammering home what a delicate little angel I am.

A few months pass, and at my 28-week appointment my

midwife generously asks about a birthing plan. There's a lot of chat in mostly middle-class white-lady circles about the mother having more agency throughout the birthing process, and we are encouraged to draw up a list of requirements to ensure tranquillity and focus, like a projector showing a Glyndebourne live stream and access to a qualified Reiki instructor, for example. But not me. Not little old low-maintenance, delicate angel me. 'Just get the baby out of me alive!' I jest, nervously, and she looks relieved.

Things are getting more dictatorial in the kitchen, however, as I've recently downloaded the Deliciously Ella app. It's filled with plant-based recipes: I make her nut butter, sweet potato and quinoa salad and drink big cups of thick purple and green smoothies filled with hemp, chia and other supplements from the supermarket that look and taste like dust from a carpenter's workshop and cost £12. Subscribing to someone else's way of life amid a time of such health-based scrutiny feels like an easier option than relying on my own instincts, however, so I plough ahead.

For the next few months, she is my secret guru. This steady, nurturing approach is essential for the baby's growth, but it's unfamiliar to me. After many years of using food as some form of punishment, restricting it, removing it from my body, and having very little faith in my ability to look after myself, or that my body even works in the way it should, I am depending on Ella to teach us both how to survive. I google 'mild eating disorder cured pregnancy' and find nothing I relate to, but know that the mere act of searching is an affirmation in itself. I buy an almond croissant for the first time from the bakery in the park and consider tweeting about it, about the croissants and how they are my spirit animal, as if I do this all the time. But then I remember that a friend once said that it's only ever women who post about loving food with so much enthusiasm, as if to tell the world they're adjusted, unlike the others; that their small body is a result of genetics and digestive victory rather than dieting. I don't want her to see it. Because my friend will know, and I'll know, and I really just want to enjoy this croissant.

During my first trimester, Ella makes her Instagram inbox open to her one million followers. I immediately DM her to ask if it's OK that I am eating so many Hula Hoops.

'Huge congrats, so happy for you!!' she begins. 'I totally abandoned my normal diet in favour of crisps, chips, bread and potatoes all day everyday. It's all my body wanted so I just listened and accepted it was part of the process xxxx'

I am touched by her speedy, warm and honest response but a bit perturbed as to why I sent it in the first place. Days before, I'd listened to an episode of her podcast in which she reassured listeners that it's fine to feed your body whatever it asks for in the first trimester, and that she just ate potatoes. So why did I send the message? I then vow to keep her at arm's length, painfully aware that I'm never more than one G&T-in-a-can away from becoming the type of person who writes 'Well done hun, you're stronger than you'll ever know' underneath a post from a former *TOWIE* cast member whose Miniature Schnauzer has just been diagnosed with diabetes.

While it's a huge honour to have this baby inside me, I am disconcerted by the feeling of being somebody's home. Not only is having a serene and clean pregnancy and birth a new set of standards to contend with, my body is also under medical surveillance. If there is an unexpected bleed, I have to tell someone. If something hurts, I need to see a doctor. If I'm hungry, I have to eat. It's all regulated. Down to the colour and smell of my discharge. I long to be left alone, and to suffer with my minor ailments once again, quietly hindered without major repercussions.

I do enjoy some precious moments of intimacy, however. I take him swimming most lunches; it makes me smile to think of my baby suspended in water, floating blissfully within my pendulous stomach. I wish it was just us, but the slow lane often has at least one man in it, with no spatial awareness and experimenting with the butterfly, emboldened by our own slovenly pace. It's worth the frustration if my belly gets touched by an old lady in the changing rooms afterwards, however. A gentle pat of the tummy, both a 'well done for coming so far' and 'just you wait'.

Ella speaks a lot on social media and on her podcasts about the benefits of hypnobirthing – a method of pain management which involves mindful breathing and visualizations – and a woman I work with claims her baby slipped out like a bar of soap thanks to breathwork alone. I google local classes and sign up for the nearest session.

Along with fourteen other couples, we sit in a circle on the top floor of a stuffy pub filled with the muffled cacophony of carefree young people eating £20 roasts downstairs. During the hypnobirthing class, we do a range of exercises, the central one being when the non-pregnant partner massages the pregnant partner while repeating various calming phrases. Mark and I find the sincerity a bit embarrassing and laugh quietly. But as I peek around at the room I'm struck by the seriousness and borderline sensuality of the other couples.

'Let's do it properly,' I whisper imploringly at Mark. It's not his fault – he is healthy and strong but his hands were not built for massage. Just a few seconds of kneading my back has ravaged his energy resources and now, perspiring and defeated, he needs a break.

After the session we go to a high-street bakery for a treat. The woman behind the counter congratulates me on my pregnancy and while jimmying two donuts apart says I need to massage my perineum 'every single night, with Vaseline', so it's flexible enough to avoid a bad tear. She did it with all three of her pregnancies and 'it' is as good as new. While I can't quite imagine Ella posting 'just vigorously rubbing the bit of skin between my vaginal opening and back passage' on Insta, I'd bet both my legs she was at it too.

I realize there is a lot more I need to learn if I want to escape this process with my genitalia intact, and I am told by a new-mum newsletter that three moderately expensive NCT classes will do the trick.

The National Childbirth Trust is a parent charity known for both educating pregnant people about the pandemonium on the horizon and connecting local mums and dads to make for a less isolating experience. And I do need to make some new friends; the majority of mine have made the sage choice to not have children, what with the climate crisis, food shortages,

fear of mental and physical injuries, and home and job insecurity, so my fellow idiots in the NCT crew will be a lifeline.

The week before our classes begin, we get sent a spreadsheet
with everyone's full names and email addresses on it. Needless
to say the sheer volume of information and internet search
potential gives me a head rush.

Some searches lead to dead-ends – private Instagram
accounts and profile pictures I have to screen-grab and zoom
in on to analyse. One particularly fortuitous discovery on
YouTube reveals an acting showreel, aka the jackpot. Others
have fairly neutral Twitter accounts and standard Facebook
profiles. It's reassuring to know there's no curveballs in the
mix – a ten-months' pregnant Anne Hathaway isn't about to
rock up in dungarees. That's what I'm telling myself, anyway.
The truth is I just want to figure out if they're the sort of
people who might like me.

I feel a bit guilty when we arrive for the first class. I've neatly
ordered everyone in my head in terms of what genre of person
they are: reads *The Guardian*, likes exotic holidays, extreme
sports. But they are all their own people in reality: diluted,
nuanced, textured humans. Nobody is a nightmare. Not even
the one with the showreel.

We sit in a circle and introduce ourselves. 'My name's
Harriet,' I say, my neck turning completely red. I am hoping
for a few titters but the pressure gets to me and I forget to say
something funny. 'I'm just keen to find out as much information as possible to make sure birth isn't too scary.' Pathetic.
They then skip Mark, much to his joy.

I take notes on how to resuscitate a baby. What being

induced is. New words like 'colostrum', 'Braxton Hicks' and 'black, tar-like poo' embed themselves into my lexicon. There's a lot of discussion about breastfeeding – how it helps with mother–baby bonding and ensures that the baby has a boosted immune system, excellent gut health, spotless credit rating etc.

At the end of our final session the girls are separated from the boys so we can explore more 'sensitive' areas of discussion. 'How long after birth is it safe to have sex?' asks one woman, who I immediately see in a completely new light. 'Two weeks should be fine,' says the NCT midwife casually, as if this wasn't the most horrific concept possible.

I spend the last three days ahead of the due date swaddled in a secret utopia: watching *Escape to the Chateau* and sorting through piles of pennies and loose change I've found in jars around the house. Every day I carry the collected coins in plastic bags down Bethnal Green High Street and get it converted at the bank. I get £63 in total, which I mostly spend in Iceland, where I bulk-buy frozen fruit and Gino D'Acampo seafood ready meals for Mark. I am off-grid and the happiest I have ever been, even if the pregnancy bump has pulled my ass into non-existence.

The baby is happy too. He is now seven days late and not budging. I've been told by my midwife that I should go in for a sweep to get things going. This is when a doctor waggles their finger around your cervix in order to release a hormone which should kickstart labour. Lying on the doctor's examination table, legs in stirrups, with what feels like her entire arm inside of me rotating in a circular motion, I swear to God I hear something inside me crack.

It's the first of many medical interventions. Ones that snap me open and break my mind. And this is where mine and Ella's birthing paths truly diverge:

Ella: 'I had a sense that she was coming on Friday and woke up to my waters breaking early on Saturday morning.'

Me: After writhing in a lukewarm bath for an hour at home, my waters are broken at 3 a.m. by a midwife who is worried about my baby's decreasing heart rate. She sticks an amnihook (as bad as it sounds) inside me and pulls it about while I repeatedly cry the word 'no' until something pops and fluid rushes out of my membranous sac.

Ella: 'We pottered around at home for a few hours, went to the farmers market, made breakfast, watched *Notting Hill* and then as it started to pick up we put our fave calming music on, lit candles, closed the curtains and filled the birth pool.'

Me: Before the bath, before we head to the hospital where they break my waters, we decide to binge-watch a four-part Channel 4 drama about a paedophile comedian, played by Robbie Coltrane. The only music I listen to during the whole birthing experience is 'Black Skinhead' by Kanye West – which sounds a bit like an army of seven million men made out of bricks going to war – on my headphones on repeat, thirty minutes before I tear my arse open.

Ella: 'About five hours later she shot into the world like a rocket.'

Me: About seventeen hours later my baby is dragged out of my body more or less dead after getting stuck inside me. I know he's stuck way before the midwife realizes he's stuck but I've never done this before and don't know if I'm just high, as about three hours ago I mentioned that I felt as if I had two babies in my body, one on top of the other like a double-decker bus. I can't feel my legs as I've had an epidural and push so hard I get a third-degree tear in my aforementioned anus. They end up giving me an episiotomy – where they cut your perineum open with scissors – and pull him out with a pair of forceps.

Ella: 'She came out the water straight onto my chest where she fed for about an hour and a half while we waited for the placenta and our midwife checked we were both ok.'

Me: He is tugged out pale-blue and floppy, and with a very slow heart rate. There is no spontaneous chest movement. He's taken to a table where they huddle over him, rattling off urgent phrases and making hand gestures. Tears form in Mark's eyes as he realizes his son is dying, and we hold hands and I reassure him the baby will be OK, because some animalistic part of my soul just knows he will. Eventually we hear a noise. A brief, husky weep. He is here. I haemorrhage every-where and am given my baby for what feels like thirty minutes while they stitch me up. Something goes wrong and I'm sent into theatre for two hours. We don't master breastfeeding. The milk never comes.

Ella: 'I went totally into my own space during the birth, focusing on every sensation and visualising what was happening during it, thinking of each one as a wave.'

Me: I'm drugged up to my eyeballs and terrified of coming down.

Ella: 'It's a whole other level of surrendering and trusting your body totally, and we spent months focusing on letting go of fear, learning everything we could about birth, so that we felt as educated and informed about every step of the process and every decision along the way.'

Me: My body did the opposite of what it was meant to do, at every stage. On the plus side, at least I didn't waste time massaging my perineum.

★ ★ ★

That night in hospital my body rests on a bed with nurses coming in and out, giving me injections, tablets, and checking up on my wounds.

'How is the breastfeeding going?' they ask.

'I can't really lift my arms,' I reply.

Mark is asleep next to me on a chair and the tiny boy lies in a tiny plastic crib. I am so lucky to have this incredible care, but the bleeping medical sounds, hourly interventions, drip in my hand and my confused, smacked-out state makes me feel like an alien being given an autopsy.

It's impossible to sleep that night, with the disorientation and panic because I now have a son to feed milk to via a syringe filled with a thimbleful of pre-prepped colostrum – the yellow milk you get in the final trimester, before the proper milk kicks in – I'd diligently harvested before he arrived. Hours pass slowly in the night but the breastfeeding clinic at 8.30 a.m. comes too soon. I shuffle down the corridor holding my son and sit down. The other women enter. We are told what to do: the right way to angle the baby's body, the way their mouth should look, how it should feel. Everyone else's bosoms look so maternal; small yelps of joy as they feel the liquid leaving their bodies. After a few minutes of frustration the room begins to get too hot, and I feel so sad, as if I am getting left behind in a lesson. So I stand up, fart and leave the room, hoping it'll all work once we've left the intensity of the hospital. Nobody stops me.

Once we arrive back home, I barely know what to do. I gaze at his face, more smooth and debonair than I thought he'd look given Mark and I have quite busy features. He has a thin layer of hair, an amazing black greasy slick of hair.

But his skin is turning yellow. He's not eating – or rather, I'm not providing.

Health visitors have come and gone, pushy and abrupt, arriving at a moment's notice as if to catch me off guard. They want me to show them how I am breastfeeding and seem dissatisfied, but ask me to keep trying. I am pumping milk using a machine, too, but I only get a dribble. One NCT friend sends me a spreadsheet detailing the volume of milk she's pumping per day. I start to suspect something's not right.

On day two, he cries for eight hours straight. By midnight there's blood in his nappy where there should be wee. Hysterically, we rush to the hospital in a cab, where they confirm he has jaundice and has barely eaten since he was disconnected from my placenta. They admit us both overnight and get him on formula milk. They say it could have been the traumatic birth stunning my boobs into submission, which is particularly annoying because exactly what I need most to calm my almighty nerves is those delicious hormones that breastfeeding triggers: oxytocin, the love hormone, and prolactin, which makes you feel floaty and calm. Like Glastonbury, without Michael Eavis's chinstrap and the constant threat of a UTI, basically.

In the hospital ward, there is a very strict structure for me to follow for the next twelve hours, but I feel a mess – cold, disturbed and unclean. We left our house in such a rush, and I brought nothing with me – no change of clothes for my baby and no toothbrush or phone charger for me. I lie under a cardigan in the freezing ward, wearing an adult nappy that's now soaked and doubled in size. One of us needs to sleep so

I send Mark home to rest, leaving me alone with the spooky noises echoing across the ward of other new mothers with tiny babies; a zombie mother singing a haunting, ad-libbed nursery rhyme every forty seconds to soothe her frightened baby, a sound that jolts me out of my startled silence and prompts me to attempt one of my own. 'Tiny boy, little lamb, please don't cry, you're a lamb,' I sing raspily, as if I were the ghost of a dead child trapped on a farm. Beneath the murmuring of all the harrowing singing is another new mother, this one on the phone to some poor soul, moaning endlessly about the staff. The husbands, all in a deep sleep, are snoring. This is motherhood, I suppose.

My sodden nappy is really visible under my thin joggers. Visiting the communal loos on the busy ward is humiliating – my crotch is wet and extremely padded. I think of Ella's nappy. In fact, it was on her Instagram that I first got the idea. She wore them for the post-birth bleeding, rather than for the incontinence, which I am experiencing. By day three of her firstborn, she was 'emotionally in the best place' of her life, she writes. 'I've literally never ever been happier. Currently wearing an adult nappy, breast-pads and a v sexy maternity bra, and honestly never felt better about myself.'

This is all well and good but alone with my stunned boobs and thin baby, I've truly never felt more unhinged. How could someone so good at athletics – holding a school record for standing long jump and placing third in Welwyn Garden City's 200-metre regional sprints all before the age of sixteen – fail her biggest physical challenge to date?

By 9 a.m. the next day, thankfully his health has improved.

He is getting better with every formula feed. However, today is the infamous day of the post-birth plummet, when your pregnancy hormones leave your body. It is a bit like falling through a trap door into a cruel world in which all of your deepest fears are waiting; up front, in your face, salivating with their potential to ruin you.

A nurse pops by to see how my night went and to give me an assessment. She asks me how I feel, emotionally, and I tell her only part of the truth, which is: 'I don't deserve this baby,' and that 'I don't understand how I will look after him.' There's so much more I want to say but I don't want them to take him off me. It's dodgy enough for them to keep us in for another five hours.

Honestly, though, I'd just love to be sedated and locked in an empty room. I'm aware this sounds a bit like I am actively looking forward to death. Maybe it's because I haven't slept since the epidural four days ago. I don't feel connected to my body, and there's just too much to remember, even though it's quite simple: drink lactulose so I can pass a stool, inject heparin into my legs so I don't get a blood clot. Sterilize a bottle in the microwave, before making up formula every three hours so he can live. Cuddle him, cuddle him, cuddle him.

I take a few photos of me and my baby, in which my eyes are black and I am smiling like a murderer. I send them to no one. It makes me sad: I long to be part of the club, for those lovely maternal images I see so often on social media, like Renaissance mother-and-child paintings evoking serenity, purity and a tender physical togetherness. I know those photos don't tell the whole story, I know they are choreographed, that the entire house was covered in milk and a mess, but to capture just one image – a tiny fragment of light – would feel good right now. I want the attention; I want to know that I still exist; I want someone I worked with in 2012 to tell me that I am lovely.

Eventually we hear the nurse's feet enter the ward – it's game time. Mark, who's returned from home but forgot to bring us both clean nappies, tells me to 'keep a lid on the mad stuff'. I, possessed by the spirit of a cockney gangster, tell him 'I am going to kick your fucking head in,' but internally I decide he's probably right. If I say the thing about death, we are in here for the long haul – and I can't handle any more lullabies. We need to go home.

'Actually I am feeling much better,' I explain to the nurse on duty. 'The whole thing earlier was just hormones.' And off we go.

Being back home is sinister. The house seems dark, dirty and cluttered, and I'm terrified my baby will go hungry again, so I make bottles of formula relentlessly. It's stinging badly where my episiotomy stitches are, and because I spent fourteen hours lying in a wet nappy, it's become a little bit infected. Two days of agony later, the health visitor sends me back to hospital. It's the first of three visits to the same ward where I gave birth, each of which involves a bus ride in which tears fall from my eyes as if someone's just broken my heart, then four hours-plus waiting in a corridor to be seen by a doctor. It's too sore to sit down on a sofa let alone a plastic seat, so I stand in the corner by a window, scrolling through images of my happy NCT friends, who all had some kind of rocky birth but are now full-boobed and doing skin-on-skin with their babies on sofas, surrounded by bouquets of flowers and cake.

It's juvenile but, for a while, my jealousy for Ella becomes all-encompassing. My brain is filled with a whiney new voice, negative but not like Alexa, more like a child who feels entitled to a different dinner. I am weaving a sorry narrative: it's so unfair my baby's conception was fraught and medical, while Ella conceived whiling making sweat-free love on pristine sheets as Chilled Out Flute Compilation #7 played in the background, probably. Her birth was essentially a slightly intense poo in a paddling pool, while ours was murderous. And yet I took care of him during pregnancy just as she told me to; I did gentle yoga, meditation and ate whatever my body asked for, the good and the bad. We never had the bliss or rapture of that photo and I don't think I'll ever catch up, especially as Ella has a nanny (shout out to Janet).

It's not her fault that this is her life. She is just trying to promote positive birth stories so others aren't afraid. But maybe they should be frightened? Women and babies still die in birth, and it's not because they've not meditated hard enough; it's because it's seismic and unpredictable. And once the pain and blood of birth have finished, you are filled with psychological savagery on the other side. The first few days of motherhood are brutal. The level of high-functioning performance required is unparalleled. It's like stumbling on stage at the start of the Oscars, your body bloodied and broken from a plane crash, and you're handed a mic and told you're hosting the whole gig, but if the jokes aren't good enough, the audience dies. Why did we not chat about that in the NCT class?

For the first three weeks, the wheels are fully off. I haven't spent much time with babies other than this guy I now cohabit with. The ones I have met, I rocked and kissed and felt a deep peaceful affinity with. But this one is way too real. He needs me badly; I can't leave the room, and his head is just so heavy, his neck so weak. I've taken to pinching my upper arms and thighs as hard as possible for a feeling of momentary relief.

He wakes throughout the night, which is to be expected; I am getting used to sleeping in confused, sixty-minute fragments. During the day it's a little more turbulent. The advice is to 'sleep when the baby sleeps', but every time I go upstairs to lie in bed, the flashbacks begin; my interior world becomes flooded with violent images, like some kind of horror-film cliché. I can feel it rise: the panic, discomfort and terror. It's easier to keep my eyes open, downstairs with the boiled kettles, messy worktops and my greasy-haired angel.

I take relentless selfies of my baby and me, hoping to capture some flicker of togetherness, some gesture of normality for social media, as if it will cement it in reality for me, but it's hard when I've inexplicably started wearing my hair in pigtails. The whole experience is hallucinogenic and demonic and yet I still do a three-step skincare routine every night before bed. Not that it's working: my skin is crusty in texture, scarlet in tone, and my face deranged in expression. These selfies are exclusively for my own records. Yet there is so much that I want to publicly mark. 'Little boy,' I would write, if I had the courage – if I weren't so scared of being sentimental online, and if I didn't look quite as dishevelled. 'I knew you before you knew me. Presented so tenderly by a Spanish doctor, just a grey-and-black blastocyst on an iPad screen before the lights went dark and your dad held my hand, and we all held our breath and you were placed with magnificent precision within me. I saw you as a foetus on an ultrasound screen eight weeks in and gasped and cried; years of grief and sorrow as the doctor's voice softened from concern to relief. I saw your body grow inside of me, your arms and legs so worryingly still in the morning but slow-dancing by dinnertime and raging by night. I saw your heartbeat on a hospital monitor, its regularity dipping from horizontal squiggle to sharp peaks, until it was shielded by a mass of doctors and unintelligible phrases that all translated to bad news. I saw your dead body lifted into a shining light, your dad's eyes filled with panic and pain. And now I see you here. Asleep on my chest, no longer sickly with yellow, no longer in urgent blue or far away on a screen in grey. It is you in technicolour: peach skin, black hair, eyes like mine. One day you will know your story and may find it confusing, unlike that of your friends or the biology books. Whatever you feel at first, please know that you were so wanted. I didn't make you entirely but I devoted every fibre of my being to ensure you were made. Out of pure love, luck and magic – medical geniuses, kindness, grit, and the instinctive optimism of your dad when you seemed like an impossible dream. While I will moan and embarrass you about the horrors of childbirth for the rest of my life, over mashed potato or during your wedding speech, please know that if I were to do it all again and lose both eyes and my toenails too, I would if I got you. I'd do it all again if I got you.' Probably too long for a caption though, so I might just go for the peach emoji and hashtag 'meconium'.

I might not be posting, but at any given chance, I am scrolling. The fourth trimester is the rockiest ride because you're supposed to be relieved by the healthy arrival of your child, but caring for a newborn, especially when the birth has been tricky, can be far from blissful. Most days I am in a transient state, slipping through extreme boredom and acute stress. Social media has stepped in, taking control in the worst possible way. It is acting the role of a best friend who gets you blackout drunk in a terrible club when you're grieving the loss of a loved one. A temporary distraction – an artificial sensation of intimacy and community when really it is toxifying and exhausting. Nevertheless I check it mindlessly, slack-jawed, closing then immediately opening the Instagram app without a single recognition of the mind-rotting absurdity of it all. My friend Debbie messages to ask what I've been up to.

'Looking at yellow poo and envying a wellbeing influencer?' I type, sending her a link to Ella's rigorous morning routine, which begins with meditation and an alarm clock at 5.45 a.m.

'Jesus, can you imagine how awful it must be to *have* to post that shit *every* day?'

Debbie has a point. I may be full of bitterness, but at least I am free of all online duties. There is no following waiting for me. My career doesn't depend on the regularity of my online existence. It's a tiny triumph but thank God I am not betrothed to an audience who demand my updates in order to exist. The day after leaving hospital, Ella posted a photo of some avocado toast and roasted sweet potatoes. Five days later she was 'recipe testing' falafels for her next book. A month after her baby was born she released an episode of her podcast and posted about having a 'busy day at work'. Meanwhile I can't remember how much formula to put in the baby's bottle. Mark's stuck a Post-it note on our fridge so I don't forget ('four scoops'). If anything, Ella must be more afraid than I am. Of losing who she is, her career, her wealth, her reputation. The fury turns into sympathy; so long as I don't think about the nanny.

There is another option for me. Maybe someday I could join the legions of women who now share their horror stories and postnatal trauma online? They are a febrile new community, the proud antithesis to the Ellas of the social media ecosystem. But I've never had the certainty to commit to a personal cause, to make it my brand. Right now, I'm not sure I am ready to be an advocate, a 'warrior mamma' or a spokesperson. Being #brave and #real sounds exhausting too, and comes with its own veneer of messy, loveable artifice.

Both approaches also involve participating in the world. Sharing your innermost thoughts with others. Instead, I decided to disappear completely. Tap out. Shut down. What could possibly go wrong?

CHAPTER FIFTEEN

I Am Grateful for My Bed

The thing about Issy is that she has a mullet. And it's nothing like the mullets we all grew up fearing: middle-aged men peacocking with their shiny red bellies on German beaches or mustard-toothed 1980s uncles propping up bars. Hers propels the mullet into 2020; an alpha expression of female modernity. She inhabits the swoon and swagger of a romantic poet, Shane from *The L Word* and the heartthrob from a John Hughes film.

Issy is a singer-songwriter on TikTok who posts thirst traps designed to tempt queer twenty-somethings and, unbeknownst to her, a miserable thirty-four-year-old woman on maternity leave with a husband, a tiny baby and PTSD. When the emerald glint of her miraculous face first stops me in my tracks, I realize this is it. There she is. This is the woman I'll design my life on.

I unearth my idol at 8.45 p.m. as I lie on my belly scrolling the app in bed. My son is finally asleep after my multiple failed attempts to crawl out of the room unnoticed, while trying to avoid all creaky floorboards and the tendons in my ankles clicking too loudly. Now I ogle as many of the seven-second videos as I can before I feel physically sick, a pastime I've fooled myself into thinking is a modern form of self-soothing after a day of parenting is over. Maybe it is. It's certainly an escape from my reality. Motherhood has mangled my mind and maternity leave is far from the cosy, languorous utopia I'd imagined. Everyone said it would be far from a break from work, but I'd hoped that my experience would be different; that I could handle a year of staying inside, being calm and loving.

Instead, it's a kind of slow, grinding carnage: the rudderlessness of the routine that I am captain of, the extraordinary fragility of my baby's skull, the lack of personal space, a constant dry mouth, dirty head of hair and filthy nails. How can I sustain this for eight more months? He is an alert baby; decisive and affectionate. While pregnant, I daydreamed about the efficient synchronicity of our lives, him in a bouncer and me and my bounce-back body in the shower shaving my legs, singing Bob Marley's 'Three Little Birds' with the door open while he gurgles in the doorway. What a mother, what a wife! I hadn't accounted for the fact he would remain startled by life outside of the womb; that he'd find a millisecond of broken eye- or skin-contact distressing. So we stick together, always. He hates the buggy and so I strap him to my chest. I buy multipacks of Invisibobbles and stash my long oily hair away.

Rolling at all hours, the TV becomes my neurotic companion, and Piers Morgan and the *Loose Women* chicks my toxic new friends who stoke my belligerence and fear on a daily basis. Mostly it's the news that I watch: the gradual unfurling of coronavirus, a word I hear for the first time while doing a bleary 6.20 a.m. feed in early February, and grow to dread as coverage escalates from mild concern to global emergency. Six weeks after giving birth, the country goes into lockdown and

I'm cut off from my family, friends and health professionals. I stop speaking about my violent birth and surgery flashbacks, so the thoughts of them bulge into bouts of fury and panic, which I suppress and ignore. I know I need to get over it – when you come off the morphine after surgery, doctors are so good at being positive and moving the conversation onto recovery – but my brain can't let it go. It's stuck. The images and the pain are there and imprinted in my mind even if I'm looking onwards, forward, as if walking past a mutilated rodent's body on the side of a road.

As well as the standard fears of bringing up a baby, there are now uncharted pandemic-related complications on the horizon: running out of formula milk and nappies, booking a Sainsbury's delivery slot, slathering food packaging with hand sanitizer, avoiding humans at all costs, the threat of never smelling garlic again, my family dying, losing my job, being too ill to care for my baby or my lungs ceasing to function in intensive care. For the past few nights a wizened woman has banged on our front door demanding to see Valerie, and I wonder if this is finally it: the moment society comes undone. Mark and I are caught in the crossfire of multiple stresses and I have resolved that re-treading the gory events of the hospital is an indulgence and waste of resources, even if the flashbacks are, if anything, getting worse.

Heavier by the day is the longing for my mum. Before lockdown she would visit and reorganize my cluttered home into something more streamlined. She'd sterilize bottles while my baby slept on my dad, and tell me I was doing so well at motherhood, that I was 'looking bonny'. She'd make sure the cupboards were stocked with boxes of oatcakes and that I was eating protein, then she would leave and I'd feel renewed and capable of taking on the long, long days that begin with a shoot of adrenalized optimism at 5 a.m., and then begin to drag around 9 a.m. But now, the metaphorical umbilical cord has been cut and I am struggling to survive without her.

As my baby's body fuses together, preparing for launch, mine is stagnant and stiff. My post-pregnancy belly remains bulbous and not even Beyoncé's juice cleanse would flush out the phantom within me. Then there is the unease of my undercarriage – raw and inflamed, a dead turkey head between my legs that renders me unable to sit down for longer than seven minutes without wincing. The horror, the shame, the lack of preparation.

By comparison, Issy is in full bloom. A student and barista she is using the empty space of lockdown to promote her music, along with her stunning Italian girlfriend, who has the seductive, golden aura of a character from *Call Me By Your Name* and posts only Issy's videos. Is she supportive, or overbearing and insecure? And how long can I sustain this thought before it gets derailed by chores and intrusive thoughts of scalpels?

The Great Pause has benefitted Issy by giving her time to reflect and rebrand: the girlfriend has cut Issy's girly hair off, and the new short style enhances her black pearl eyes. She is also experimenting with sweater vests, leaning into her new androgynous identity. I wonder if she was perhaps freed by being in isolation, and from the day-to-day observations of fellow students or co-workers that may have hindered her from making a radical change. Now she wears waistcoats and cowboy hats, subverting macho male aesthetics and imbuing them with delicacy and mystery. She mimes to popular sounds but does it better than the rest, with irony and sex appeal. She crushes my soul with her seductive spirit – her boyish charm in direct opposition to my frumpy womanliness. Instead of resenting her, I adore her.

It's no surprise therefore that I begin to believe a mullet may be what I need – a 'fuck you' middle finger up at motherhood and the stereotypes I'm subliminally urged to replicate. I am lingering for far too long on ankle-length puffer coats and beanie hats while online shopping – or other extreme weather attire that I never thought I'd own. It's the uniform. Both practical and a sign of status; a symbol of exactly how long you're prepared to stay in the park for in November. I've also started watching YouTube videos on how to self-cut hair and am casually running the concept by Mark to see his reaction.

'You told me when I first met you that if you ever said you wanted to cut all your hair off again, I should say no,' he reminds me. Debbie also begs me to reconsider. She was there for the last 'growing-out phase' in which I resembled James Brown in the '80s. But I'm not so sure. This time could be different! I stare at Issy's face and wonder if our features could be transferable; if my personality or bone structure is bold enough to make the leap. My daydreams become a music video in which I am strutting around the local playground – me pushing my son on the swing as the jaws of mothers crash onto the floor in awe of The Mullet.

*   *   *

Besides bringing me Issy, the algorithm has sensed there is a void in my life, and its solution is to offer me alternative mothers: helpful, relatable, entertaining and sometimes enviable women rearing vast fleets of neat little children. They are known in the industry as Mumfluencers, a term which seems more reminiscent of either a lethal rash-based disease or a memory-foam mattress. The Mumfluencers are a million-dollar community of women whose 100 per cent financial growth year on year demonstrates that centuries of unpaid labour is finally being rewarded by society. Whether you're a former reality TV star or a receptionist, now you can capitalize on the stage of life that's traditionally held women back, by creating a lifestyle brand and offshoot career off the back of a few good-looking babies and a revolving content mill – from espousing bounce-back body wellbeing routines to flogging sporks. Some of them earnestly point at graphics about the key signs of postnatal depression, while others channel their inner child and dance to Megan Trainor's 'All About That Bass' in sunny white kitchens, their toddler an unpaid extra in a fleeting moment of eccentricity. While I'm in no rush to cut a smartie-filled cake in half to reveal the genitalia of my future child, I find that I am increasingly endeared to the infamous Mumfluencer mantra: Live, Laugh, Love. It all makes sense now. It's all I really want. Stick it on my fridge if you like. Above the mantelpiece, or on my grave.

There's a format, a pattern to making it a success in the Mumfluencer world. These women tend to be either religious goddesses with tonged hair and smart methods of inserting broccoli into a birthday cake, or more 'authentic' Gin-O'clock rebels who rejoice in their kid's last-minute, shabbily constructed World Book Day costume. There are the Insta Husbands too – innocent bystanders following the tide, some of them quitting their jobs because of the success of their wives, but whose sycophantic post-birth posts about their other halves currently have the power to make me spit at my phone.

'So in awe of her strength and grace throughout,' they write, as if contractually obliged to post a photo of their angelic wives unhassled by wires and drips. 'The love and respect I have for you knows no bounds!' Birth is the most violent and overt of the female forms of endurance. But did our pain and power not seem main-grid-worthy before fathers were given something physical in return? Show me the fawning post about polycystic ovaries or endometriosis – a photo dump of 2020's best blood clots – and then we'd be talking.

Baby sleep companies get a sniff of my neurosis and incapabilities too. The 2 a.m. googles for 'how baby sleep more than 40 mins' lead to a series of targeted attacks from all corners of the internet. Like the diet apps that promise dramatic weight loss if you follow their process of registering every calorie you consume, for ever, these too are centred around arbitrary data entry – tables in which I fill out the time, quantity and quality of his feeds, stools and naps. I'm never told why; I never re-read the information I input. It's just another task for me to complete, his daily schedule no doubt carted off to wherever data is collected and turned into another £2.50 app for frazzled mums and/or baby robots who will in ten years storm the White House.

I am willing to pay for any old AA-battery-powered box – white-noise machine or portable baby rocker – that might give me ten minutes alone to scream into the abyss or scroll Twitter. Nothing works; the Amazon packages come and are scrubbed and assembled, but my baby still wants me. So I revert back to feverish devotion.

Even going for a walk with him in a sling, enjoying the warm sun across my cheeks for a few moments, fills me with overwhelming guilt. As soon as his glassy marble eyes clock me relaxing, I am convinced I am doing something wrong and head back home, where I will watch a YouTube video on how to fashion a pom-pom out of a plastic bin bag that I then make and waggle in his face for as long as it takes to relinquish that negative feeling of momentary Vitamin-D indulgence.

The Western mothering tribes: where do I belong? Indecision has my brain in a headlock. One option is to follow the modern impulse to micromanage and train my baby into being a compliant sack of skin via the neurotic sleep training blogs, which contain steps that, if followed correctly, will prevent my child from becoming an adult male forever-virgin who requires twenty minutes of breastfeeding to sleep, and allow me to go back to work within weeks. Alternatively, I can pursue the bohemian bloggers who suggest succumbing to the ancient maternal tug to dedicate every fibre of my being to his desperate desires no matter the cost to my sanity. I'd really like to follow the latter: abundant in tenderness and patience, baking bread, boobs bouncing and ready. However, she requires a village in order to maintain her saintliness, and I just have Mark, who does everything he possibly can, but is now working from home – all of us in one room all day – with important, sensitive calls flooding in on his broken mobile phone that only works if on loudspeaker, for some awful reason. A friend at work asks how I am getting on and I tell him I am finding it too hard. He says it gets easier when they go to school. As I fall in and out of a frightening, sweat-drenched sleep that night – unsure if I am still holding my tiny son or not, if I am a baby or not, my lips and eyes swollen and my heartbeat racing – my brain starts counting down the minutes until he is five.

Most days Mark takes the baby out for a walk in the park for thirty minutes to give me a break. 'Don't clean. Take some time out – relax,' he says with a worried smile. I nod and, once the door has closed, rush up to the floor-length mirror on the landing to have a look at my naked body. Pre-baby, my favourite pastime was to have a maintenance bath – to remove hair, bleach additional hair, cut nails, moisturise. I'd look in the mirror and feel clean, deeply clean. Now I see pigmentation. Yellow skin. Water retention, rubbery legs and ankles, unable to wear my wedding rings. Bony clavicle. Unkempt pubes. A new smile: teeth ground so hard and so relentlessly that I now have gaps between them big enough to accommodate the chord of my headphones. It's like I am Mr Burns's mother, or a sundried tomato. Mostly I feel dirty. I start to dance, swaying my hips slowly, cautiously, in case the fluid motion jolts some swollen vein and I internally bleed to death. My movement is unfamiliar – I feel rigid and timid, as if my hips need oiling.

Before I was pregnant I'd do this – the nude dance – and it felt great. Shimmying around the house with no clothes. Freeform, dramatic and like I've joined a cult and am about to do some kind of goat blood ritual which ends in penetrative sex with an Elder. A lot of emphasis on arm motion and hip jutting. It felt good to be free. Now it is as if someone has removed the act of frolicking from my soul. After a minute of trying, I cover up my body and return downstairs to scrape the dried formula milk off the sterilizer base before the boys get back and normal service resumes.

The days are long with a new baby, even longer when you're locked in your home. To fill the time I've been dabbling in online classes, replacements for the face-to-face mother meet-ups I should be having, temporary or lifelong bonds I should be making. I keep seeing the words Baby Sensory on blogs and have become fixated by its absence in my son's life. I don't know what it means but I fear that if I do not do at least three hours of Baby Sensory a day my son may suffer with depression or dementia throughout his life.

Fortunately I find a link to a woman who's doing sessions on Zoom, and brace myself for an overload of cosmic colours, sounds and shapes. When I log on, however, I realize it's just a woman on an iPad with a puppet. There's also a screen with about seventy other mothers, and all of us are waving at each other, like we're a really sad Brady Bunch. The grey living rooms and unwashed hair of other mothers is comforting, however, mainly as it's so unlike the other motherhood I've been absorbing on Instagram. We are all in our squalid little world, scrambling around on our knees. I was hoping it might kill an hour, but my son is utterly disinterested in the puppet singing 'Wind the Bobbin Up' via tinny laptop speakers, and who can blame him when there is a plug nearby he'd like to push his tiny thumbs into.

When he eventually sinks into a daytime nap on my tummy, I use my free hand to scroll through the mummy message boards. It's a cheap and sordid thrill, like cock fighting, and I get a kick out of watching other women snap at each other about the ethics of sleep training. And I've taken to visiting Tattle too, to see what cruelty is being hurtled at the mainstream mummy vloggers today. The messageboard is one of the most visited websites in the UK and trades in trolling, mostly popular influencers and media personalities. It started as a way to discuss the lack of transparency in the online celebrity industry – public figures who were brazenly breaking the guidelines for adverts and sponsored content. Sometimes it raises some legitimate questions about safeguarding young children when parents make money out of their child's poop, fussy eating habits and cute mispronunciations online without their consent. But mostly it has a similar snarky energy to the indie forums of the 2000s, only fuelled by a vitriol normally reserved for incels on 4Chan. They think the rich and famous are all selling us a lie, a conspiracy – they allege the mental health problems of influencers have been faked for attention. They claim romantic relationships are a gimmick. That they only had children for the job opportunities, that they are neglectful mothers who are privileged and lazy. Imagine walking in on the most frightening group of sixteen-year-old bullies in the girls' toilet at school, full of spite and jealousy, relishing in the collective bashing of another human by public humiliation, but magnified by three quarters of a bottle of white wine. It is a hellscape, but who am I to judge? In my moment of vulnerability, I too am just a gossip slug who's basking in the cruel relief that it's not me in the firing line.

By night there are Zoom quizzes with friends. Sometimes fancy dress, sometimes just a chat. The loudest and fastest prosper on video chat, so to avoid being cut into or ignored, I stay mostly quiet. Also it's inappropriate to bring up the savage imagery railing my brain on an hourly basis. 'Sorry, drifted off for a second there. I was thinking of a knife jabbing at my frontbum. I think the answer might be Dame Maggie Smith? Happy birthday, Emma!'

Of course there are many other people like me also trapped in this nightmarish version of maternity leave, in a pandemic. When I see them out there, in the wild, I wonder if I have the confidence to go over and connect. A friend tells me about an app in which you can scour the local area for potential new friends, but Tattle has rattled me and I'm too judgemental of their interests, hairstyles and hobbies to make the next step. So I take to the park, where we all congregate in our daily trundle. I always see the same faces. There's a woman I recognize from school. She was a few years above me and now has twins – every day her body becomes thinner and frailer, and I wonder if she's had time to eat in six months or whether she is starving deliberately. Then there's the mum who walks around with the huge headphones on; she can't hear that her child is crying, or laughing; her expression is just looking forward and trying to get to the end of the day. I try to catch their eyes – imagining a scenario in which we confide in one another on a bench. Ultimately, however, it just doesn't feel right to risk our lives for a quick chit-chat about their prolapse.

When the summer comes, my new NCT friends begin to meet regularly outdoors. To share stories and check in on each other. I can't wait to see them and look forward to finally showing them what I can be, that I'm more than my fraught WhatsApp messages, but each time I arrive at the chosen spot I've forgotten how to interact. I run out of conversation quickly after the basics are covered – sleep, food and partners – and often make an excuse and head home after thirty minutes, which is really not long enough for a scheduled meet-up. It doesn't help that I am terrified of contracting the virus – it's not an attractive quality to flinch when they touch my son or offer me a crisp – but they are more at ease. I WhatsApp the group to ask if anyone is still struggling with what happened to them in the birth. They're supportive but have all moved on, and so should I. It's time to be stoic. I think of the time my mother cut the top of her thumb off, stuck it back on with a plaster and finished off digging out the weeds.

I decide to post a homemade meme onto my Instagram to satiate some need to release. It is the 'expectation' of my maternity leave (babyccinos, going to the Tate, quality time with family, baby massage courses, drinks with the NCT gals) versus the 'reality' (PTSD, rationing, quarantine). I want to tell the world that I am suffering; less than those who are dealing with grief, domestic abuse, poverty and sickness, but more than those who are just bored and watching *Tiger King*.

My friend Charlie messages immediately to say how sorry she is – and that she has a friend who could help with the PTSD. It's via her that I meet a man named Carl Peck. Google Images search results reveal a chipper guy with a small, neat goatee and a suggestion of a wooden bead choker. Over video chat he tells me he can cure my birth trauma, potentially, in one ninety-minute session. 'Like an exorcism!' I say. He laughs nervously and we arrange to meet in the park in two weeks' time.

What happens next does seem like magic. Peck practises Rewind: a form of neuroscientific therapy which sounds so effective it reminds me of hypnotism. I was sceptical initially, having spent two sessions with an eccentric hypnotherapist in 2016 who talked openly about his other clients' problems, offered me brandy and slathered his hands in moisturiser while counting me down into my hypnotic state. Peck says it is in no way hypnotic, but instead a 'non-intrusive, safe and highly effective psychological method for de-traumatizing people' – something to do with the adrenal glands and a reconfiguration of how my brain processes stress. He reassures me there will be no hand lotion involved.

After an hour of talking to this man, who is incredibly enthusiastic and finds fascination in the little things – the sort of guy who's turned on by petrichor and a butterfly's wings – we begin. He puts me into a relaxed state by asking me to think of a safe place in nature – the first three options are abandoned, all of which remind me of my mum and make me too emotional, but eventually I find a memory of a beach in India with cows and Mark. He then asks me to imagine I have a remote for a TV and if I could imagine that I am floating to one side, out of body. He tells me to play the footage of the traumatic event in my mind. Fast forward, slow it down, speed up, slow it down. There's some repeated phrases and gentle reassurance, and after ten minutes I am back on the beach and he counts me into the real world. I feel a relief; as if something has left me. I get back home and Mark says the baby is incandescent without me. Instead of punching my legs as hard as I can and hurling abuse at Mark for not being able to cope without me, I pick the baby up and soothe him and Mark. Finally I can be a mother. In fact, I am so galvanized by being in my right mind that I think it's time to message Issy.

Later that night I type in the TikTok message box: 'Hello, just wanted to let you know how brilliant you are. I think your music is really special. I work in the industry and maybe I could help? Do you have an email?' It's quite hesitant and feeble. I try something more direct, assuming the role of a hard-nosed man in business: 'Hi, you're really great. Do you need management or representation at all? I have a bunch of people who would love to hear your stuff.' It's got big-dick energy but I can't deliver on any of my promises. Before pressing send I consider what I am doing: I sound as if I am an old man messaging a seventeen-year-old model/actress in Hollywood with promises of getting them an acting agent. It's creepy and if she ignores me I can't overcome the embarrassment. I press send anyway and get a message right back.

My heart leaps, but it's just an automated alert from TikTok saying she will never see my message as she doesn't follow me back. So it just sits there in my inbox, as I quickly resume my arm's-length status, watching her videos in awe – her dark, mournful eyes looking straight through the screen, my crumpled face illuminated by her reflection.

The more I get to know about Issy the more I realize how much I need her in my life. She makes me want to kick against the new era of domesticated womanhood I've entered and am doing so badly at. The house is littered with dairy-encrusted muslins, the microwave is splattered with tomato soup and the carpet is accruing twisted lumps of hair and dust. I spend my days desperate to clean but am unable to find the time or energy, and come 5 p.m. I am drinking rosé to take the edge off the witching hour. Issy's life is slapdash and creatively bountiful – she possesses her sexuality and confidence in a way that I could only dream of. I can't help but wonder again if it's the hair that's doing it. If it's the mullet.

It's time for action. I book an appointment with a hairdresser who sounds Covid-safe as she works alone from within her garden shed, one client at a time. As I enter the shed I'm conscious I will leave a different woman, and soak up these last few moments of being average before I am reborn as a young icon.

Once in the big leathery chair I show her one of Issy's videos – a 360-view of the haircut she's recorded for other people who want a similar mullet. It is soundtracked by a song by the Wombats and suddenly the whole thing feels stupid, me sat here showing this hairdresser this silly video with this silly song that plays on repeat, and being met with absolute silence.

'Something like this. I know I don't look like this, but something like this. This sort of style,' I eventually say. I feel so sheepish and naked, and am begging for the video playback to end, but the hairdresser says she needs to spend more time viewing it as it's a bold cut. 'Can I see that again?'

A few more minutes pass of the looping video. 'Okay, I think I know what you mean,' she says, with total uncertainty.

I remind myself that nothing can be as bad as childbirth, so I put my life in her hands. There's a bliss to rescinding all control and I fall into a zen-like state for the next two hours. She begins to open up with some tentative questions about my life and how the pandemic has been and I find out about her story. Born and bred in Plymouth. Long-term partner. House on the market. Fantastic immune system – so good she won't get the vaccine. Brother is such a laugh, but also keeps giving people Covid because he hugs everyone despite testing positive. Ex-boyfriend has stalked her for a few years, it's a bit frightening, she's googled restraining orders but won't tell her fiancé in case he gets upset, so she keeps it to herself. Suspected ADHD, unmedicated.

I used to enjoy going to the hairdressers and watching the transformation unfurl. Now I try to close my eyes for the whole process, embarrassed at my reflection and that I might get caught admiring myself. Eventually I open my eyes and sense that she's slowing down. The process is drawing to an end, even though I still don't see the sassy mullet I asked for. It's heavy and huge on top and very small on the bottom. Like a muffin. I hope that once the initial shock has subsided, once I've told her I love it after looking at it from all the different angles, performing the agonizing ritual of holding the hand mirror and looking at the back, complimenting her profusely and paying £100, that it will all fall into place.

When I leave the shed I catch glimpses of myself in shop-front and bus windows. My first thought is that I look like a loaf of bread or a giant mushroom. It's like all the worst bits of the '80s but also completely groundbreaking and never before seen on a human head.

My friends and family on video chat are taken aback by the new hair, even though they all do their best to deny it. My friend Lucy reassures me that with some styling, a little bit of product, it *could* be sexy. Debbie just can't quite figure out what style it is. She is right. I look back at some of Issy's videos and decide to go DIY – take matters into my own hands – snipping into the highest parts of my hair to try to get rid of some of the volume. It's a slippery slope and the hair mutates into a new breed of unwarranted experimentalism. 'You look a bit like a nineties boyband member,' says Mark. He is right. I've turned into Nick Carter, or Stephen Gately.

To make matters worse I am beginning to feel a haunting sensation returning. It's my menopause. The hot flushes are first, then the ghostly sense of constant unease creeping back into every waking moment. While trying to do some freelance writing, I encounter a wave of overwhelm so strong it leaves me dissociated from my body for a week; I feel as if I am experiencing a constant headrush. I call the doctor, saying that I have burnt a fuse in my brain, and that I am scared to look after my son when I feel so disconnected, but they tell me just to keep on with the HRT, and that it sounds a bit like a panic attack.

HRT works after two weeks. I feel the benefits quickly, but my moods continue to peak and trough dramatically, and there's a new, unusual pain in my organs, until I am rushed to hospital to have my appendix removed. The experience of such excruciating pain and the morphine and the stitches will set me back another few months in terms of feeling normal again, and by normal I mean capable of dancing in the mirror naked without the reflection frightening me.

Exhausted, I decide my body deserves some peace and time to recover. So I stop. I stop the yoga videos during nap time, I stop dancing, I stop trying and let my sorry body grow moss, sink into its murky puddles, and let the cobwebs cover its orifices. I pretend it's not there; cancelling smear tests – when a nurse on the phone asks why, I begin to cry, telling her that I am scared of my vagina and of pain. She tells me that if I want to be a good mother I'll need to be much stronger than I am, and that she's raising her daughter to be independent by leaving her in her cot in the mornings with an iPad playing *Peppa Pig*. I'm not sure how the latter point is relevant but I thank her anyway.

A year and a half after giving birth, a new light begins to emerge. We move into a house with a whole room in which Mark can make his important phone calls and where the bathroom has a window. With my hair and the menopause and the uncertainty of my body, I am struggling to imagine a world in which I ever feel myself again. Everything is new, but somehow second-hand and broken. I am rattled by the past four years of my life, and the converging complications that are inhibiting me from moving on – the birth trauma that has returned and is so mentally obstructive it's become a new kind of personality trait, the chronic condition that has warped my self-esteem, and the ongoing internet addiction that makes it all worse. So I get a talking therapist called Julian who I speak to on Zoom every fortnight. In spite of the screen between us he senses when I am lying, when I am a few seconds from crying or if I am struggling to breathe properly. He can tell when I am trying to please him, which at first comes as a shock, but turns into a radical sense of relief. I haven't even looked him up on Instagram yet even though my body aches with desire to know more about his intimate life. It is too much of a risk: why break the spell when I now have a little space in which to purge all of my obsessions and insecurities and feel better for it?

As well as Julian there is a woman called Imogen from a local hospital who moves me to tears when she calls for my post-natal check-up – an appointment that should have happened nearly two years ago but was pushed back because of the pandemic. She asks me about self-confidence and sex and understands that scar tissue and trauma can contribute to pain and fear around something that should be one of life's pleasures. I am beginning to realize that regular perineum massages may be more beneficial to my rehabilitation than a haircut.

With all of these things, all of these incredible luxuries and clever people surrounding me, it feels as if I can start to heal.

I begin by cutting down on anything that makes me erratic: alcohol, sugar and social media, the latter of which is a challenge. I am still looking at Issy most days but as more of a casual fan rather than a disciple, and I still haven't delved into Julian yet, even though I googled his practice, and shortcut-quit the page as soon as I saw his face.

The first stage of my recovery is setting a 'screen limit' on my phone that stops me from looking at social media for longer than an hour, but there's an option to skip it when I reach that limit, and so I start to skip it every day, with a pang of guilt initially, then after a week I do so languorously, as if it's just a digital inconvenience, a bump in the road, like accepting everyone's cookies. The next option is to delete the apps. But even then I find myself on the weary web browser versions with their tiny fonts and clunky navigation. My last stab at freedom arrives when I change my passwords to something meaningless – a word I'll never remember that I find on the back of a bottle of shampoo. I hide the password on a piece of paper in Mark's pants drawer so I can consider what a junkie loser I am if I am ever drawn to revisit it. After that I log out, and finally I am alone. At first the stillness, the silence, is startling. I go into the garden and notice the small things: blossoms, bees, nettles, new shoots and a Cornus kousa. I walk in the park, admire the sound of a swallow, stare at the sun-dappled concrete on my front porch when I arrive home. Nature is healing, for the first hour. I then just head to two of my sanctioned websites – YouTube and eBay – and begin to google celebrities. Mainly Suki Waterhouse and Robert Pattinson, Robert Pattinson and Kristen, Kristen cheating, Robert

Pattinson interviews, Robert Pattinson bloopers, *Twilight* DVD extras. It's not cold turkey but at least I'm broadening my horizons – I've never even watched *Twilight* – and a small break from the top-tier platforms is better than nothing.

Looking after my son gets easier too. He now likes to sleep in his own bed and his desperate demands for me at all hours of the day have reduced. I can walk out of a room, and instead of waking up to the sounds of wailing, I count down the seconds until I can kiss my baby's soft morning cheeks, carry him around like a giant peach and feed him pouches of yoghurt. I keep thinking about the start of motherhood – when a few people clocked that I wasn't coping and said that I should appreciate the first few months because they go so fast. But you can't fake pleasure when you're in a state of shock. You can only enjoy a situation as much as you are physically capable of doing so at the time. I believe that vehemently; but I also feel as if I missed out on a spectral stage of parenting. I weep when I see a newborn baby bobbing around in a sling or crying like a mewling cat. It is a desire to do that first year all over again, hold my son and drink in his beauty sincerely, this time with more emphasis on deep spiritual bonding, rather than stark panic. All he wanted was food, fresh air and to be close to me. I wish I'd worried less about 'awake windows' and educational Zooms. I wish I'd taken fewer disturbing selfies and more videos of the three of us smiling. I want it all again so much so that I am tempted to approach new mothers on the street to see if I can hold their child – 'You're free to go for a coffee alone!' – just so I can be blessed with that ethereal weightlessness wrapped in a blanket all over again.

A month goes by of my rehabilitation of sorts. 'Doing the work', it's called, which sounds gruelling but just involves downloading apps. There's an app that reminds me three times a day to do my Kegels. A fitness app for postnatal exercises, the meditation app, 10,000 steps app, Ella, Goop. Work is precarious so I've even caved and downloaded the LinkedIn app. Before bed I lie for twenty minutes on an acupressure mat, apply magnesium oil to my legs and a mouth guard to stop the teeth-grinding, and add lavender spray to my pillow. *I am grateful for my bed*, I write in my gratitude journal before closing my eyes and hoping that sentence will make me sleep. It is true; I am full of gratitude. I am also bored.

That night I decide to fuck off the acupressure. I lie on it for one minute and it burns and hurts and I realize I want fun and mischief not virtuous pain. Phone in hand, I walk to the bathroom and sit on the toilet seat, a sliver of the left cheek chilled by the slimy side of the basin. It's good to feel gross. Punishment. For tonight, at this moment, I have decided to give in. To cross an ethical line by digging too deep; not on an ex, a celebrity or colleague, but my therapist, Julian. A man with indestructible boundaries and steadfast privacy policies – a man who barely reacts to my singular, fortnightly question of 'How are you?', yet now sprawls semi-nude in front of me.

Had I conceded at the first twinges of curiosity, in those initial few weeks of our psychoanalytic relationship, then I might have been more restrained in my approach to online peeping. Instead, the weeks of resistance, of *doing the work*, have built up an overspill of energy and onslaught of guilt-driven gluttony, and now I'm hogging down his content with the ferocity of a sex addict who's broken a decade-long vow of celibacy by streaming gang-bang porn simultaneously on a phone, laptop, wall projector and a VR headset. I binge as if frenetically swiping a thumb on a five-inch screen were about to be made illegal.

The goal is to start from the start and explore chronologically. I am, however, hindered somewhat by technology. Having deleted the Facebook app, the erratic browser version prevents a natural flow, and I'm jerked into random eras and albums with alarming force. And yet I persist. November 2010: head gets shaved for charity. Julian's journey from grey curls to full-blown Right Said Fred, sheepish bathroom selfies, pictures of eggs, Mitchell Brothers' jokes and JustGiving pleas. Playful! Raised a lot of cash for refugees with a sponsored bungee jump in May 2010. Cold-water swimming in 2013. Rainbow filter on 2015's profile picture. Good guy. Cultural preferences – Frank Ocean at Lovebox 2017; Julian, I was there! We're the same! Tender exchanges in 2012 with a woman named Anita, and gentle rebuttals with 'friends' amid laboured political debates during the last election. People are tedious! People need to leave Julian alone!

What's next? Instagram. You better believe it's public. I am high on life. For this is what I now call living: barely breathing unless titillated by the tendrils of forbidden voyeurism.

With Julian I had felt it necessary to abstain. In a short space of time he has changed my life: he knows all about my obsessions, the lifetime of internet crushes, imposter syndrome and self-loathing. Plus the ego boost of therapy is intoxicating and I'm loath to give it up any time soon. In no other arena

am I able to take centre stage for fifty minutes so unselfcon-
sciously.

Instead of a blank slate to project my thoughts onto, thanks
to this social media excavation I now know that Julian is also
a human – a man who loves *The Hitchhiker's Guide to the Galaxy*,
outlandish suits, and Ruth, who is prevalent on his Facebook
profile right up until 2018. She's funny, brash – a woman who
knows her mind and lives life to the fullest. Someone who'd
stand up for a stranger in a bar brawl, jump out of a plane for
Alzheimer's or show you how to use a Shewee in a Portaloo
queue. No sign of Julian on her Instagram, however. Instead,
there's someone else. He looks just like my therapist – only
projected from a parallel universe. Curls and kind eyes,
outdoorsy but called Carl. I scour Ruth's page to find some
answers: who was the hurter and who the hurtee? Not that it
matters – Julian is my priority – and I will not be swayed by
Ruth's propaganda. Even if she does look like the sort of
woman who'd smuggle a pet rat in her bra onto a flight if
you asked her kindly.

As I sit here and plough through the data, I sense myself
slipping under, the information pre-programming my responses
in future interactions. Must let him know I love Frank and
assure him that I too believe romantic relationships are far
from a fundamental aspect of leading a fulfilled life. 'Harriet
the empath,' he'll think. 'She's not like the other clients. We
vibe like equals. She should be MY therapist! I wish she
wouldn't pay!'

Finally I come to, peel my buttock off the slime, and shift
back onto the careening seat, placing my phone on the cistern;

preparing to re-enter society. Leave the creep emporium behind. Wash hands, adjust fringe in the mirror. I bare my teeth like a dog – clean yet a shade of tea that I'd rather not see. Could I self-bleach? I couldn't pull off a bright white, like I can't pull off a leather jacket, but there's got to be a shade less offensive than this. I'll call my hygienist and google 'veneers' while I'm at it.

I turn to the toilet to pick up my phone with the intention of erasing the memories of the past ten minutes from my history. As I unlock the screen a spike of adrenaline jolts my brain as it registers danger: the colour red. A love heart under a shot of Carl at a Kings of Leon concert in 2018. I liked it. With my finger. Three minutes ago. I liked a selfie of my therapist's ex's new lover at a Kings of Leon concert. I'm a notification on the phone of a man I don't know. I retract the Like. This is the worst thing that could have happened. It's worse than your mother walking in on you trimming your pubic hair while sitting legs akimbo in a swivel chair. Worse than faking a panic attack in the middle of a uni presentation you haven't prepared for. Worse than a lover telling you to stop moaning so loud or an old friend saying they were standing behind you when you said that nasty thing about them you just said.

I leave the loo and skit about until bedtime, a throb of humiliation derailing every attempt at relaxation. 4 a.m. cold-sweat wakings, frightened of what the Like might mean for my future. With every new morning, however, the world renews and the sensation of horror begins to fade. The likelihood of being arrested reduces. For all Carl knows, I could be an innocent KOL fan led to the image by the hashtag. I could just love the amateur gig photography.

I begin to believe I've gotten away with it again. Haha! I've danced around death, an invisible participant in the internet. A ghost in the machine.

Two days later I'm brought back down to earth with a thud when the triumph escapes me as Julian battens down the hatches, shuts up shop and sets all profiles to private.

CHAPTER SIXTEEN

Is This OK?

We never speak directly about the Kings of Leon Like Button Incident, but a few weeks later I get an email from Julian, who suggests I visit a group, specifically a group for people who are stuck in bad habits. At this point, if Julian sent me an email suggesting I wash my nostrils with Swarfega, I would do it without a second's pause, so I book myself a place and prepare to be humbled.

It is the hottest day of the year when we congregate – the hottest day in modern history; so hot it hurts to feel the heat on your skin for even a second, as if the sun's molten breath is a metre from the earth. Nevertheless, there is The Group to attend and quirks to fix, so all nine of us assemble in a small room on the top floor of a thin building, filled with purple velvet pillows and noisy fan propellers. Everybody quietly rolls into their preordained place in a circle, as if we're pebbles thrown onto the floor. We sit here cross-legged, clammy and shifting in our child-like positions, and it's here that I begin to cry.

I was not prepared for such an instant reaction to revealing the terrible thoughts I have had about myself. I'd expected the group to be more of a conference, a TED Talk without the head mics and assertive hand gestures, in which two group leaders discuss neuroscience and breathing techniques, maybe followed up with a bit of a bongo for prosperity, and then we all leave temporarily nourished, armed with the 'tools' to banish a negative thought pattern – but only for three months until we fall back into scab-picking or fentanyl snorting. Instead, we are asked to talk about our insecurities, the things that make us feel trapped and disconnected in life. I bowl into my contribution with some hearty jokes about my inner critic and how she's a hateful 'mega-bitch', but no one laughs and so I take the hint and say that I should stop talking.

'Sorry,' I look down at my shoes, 'I probably sound like a four-year-old.'

I assume everyone will smile courteously, nod, and we can move on to the next person, but instead there is silence and an atmosphere of concern.

'Why do you think you sound like a child, Harriet?' asks Selina, the female course leader, who has hair like a conker and her arm in a sling.

'Oh, umm, because I just sound like a little baby talking rubbish.'

'Is that what you think everyone is thinking about you, Harriet?' responds Adam, the male course leader, who resembles a kind of ethereal Lewis Hamilton.

'Yep.' Blunt, but only because my face now hurts in its attempt to hold back the tears, and because I am conscious of my nervous stutter kicking in. 'I think everyone here p-probably thinks I am just really stupid and that I look disgusting.'

Selina looks crestfallen. She pauses for a moment. 'Harriet, would you be willing to have some feedback from the rest of the group? They could share what's actually on their mind?' I shake my head. 'Okay, well how about you look around the room, and look at everybody's face. You don't have to speak to them, but you can just look at their expressions, and that might reassure you.'

Looking at people's faces. That's something I am qualified to do. I've had interesting moments in my face-based exploits over the years but nothing as agonizing as this. The strangers are looking right back at me, into my core. I sense Selina won't let us move on until I take some kind of action, so with a huge breath in and a lick of all the fluids – tears, sweat, snot that have now trickled onto my lips, I decide to do it.

I start with the girl next to me – a gothic Kim Kardashian whose hair looks like it should smell like black cherries. Her eyes gaze right back at mine, full of sorrow and affection. And the boy next to her, who has kept himself quiet and small but is remarkably tall, and is smiling for the first time today, with tenderness and encouragement. The earthy forthright funk-band flautist is nodding at me and crying. I keep going, methodically making eye contact with these contextless humans, all of whom I assumed were here because they wanted to quit smoking, but are now just sweet souls blinking pure kindness back at me. Most of all I am struck by a flicker of recognition in their expressions. They are moved not just because I seem so vulnerable, but because they feel the same as I do. Each of them cascading through people or pretending to be a solid block, always in some way humbled and hindered by shame and loneliness.

The session ends after three hours of devastating revelations. Drained and ruddy-faced, we all stand up. Some of my coursemates begin to chat to one another, snapping back into small talk about the heat and the best route home. I just run. I run down the stairs and all the way to my house, my skin sizzling in the afternoon sun. I don't care; I just need to get away from these people who have witnessed my bleak, primitive self.

When I get home I pass Mark in the kitchen with a cheap 'hello!' and head upstairs, to the furthest possible room, to open my laptop to embark on my usual slobby procedure. I pull up the email confirming my place at the group, the email that includes each course member's first name. I now know small details about their lives – jobs, hobbies, local haunts – so it shouldn't take too long to find out who they are. I have had harder assignments.

I start with the gothic girl, pasting her first name into Google and a few key words that might help me bridge a gap into her reality. The page loads and there are many different options, paths that I could go. It is anticlimactic. There is no thrill; I'm faking my enthusiasm. Because what more is there to find out, now that I know what thoughts haunt her before she falls asleep, now that I've seen a crayon drawing of her hopes for the future, and a list of all the cruel ways she tortures herself? That is all I have ever wanted. Those clues that connect us all. That reassure me that I am fine, normal, that we are all jettisoned on the moon together.

In the days that follow, I am struck by an emotional hangover from The Group – an uncanny daze of enlightenment and exhaustion. I am finding social media too aggressive, and instead microdose throughout the day rather than the usual sickening binge.

I start off with the soft stuff: Facebook. I log on and feel upset within seconds. I've no idea who any of the people on my feed are. Suki Mortimer? I've never even seen that name before. Or that face. Who are you? And why am I looking at a scan of your womb? Maybe it's a girl I knew at uni who got married, changed her hair and moved to Australia. Then there are journalists who I barely met on press trips a decade ago and whose drama-filled statuses are filled with insinuations about people and events that I now feel inclined to care about. There are temporary fun friends from my early twenties who've faded from my memory now sharing earnest sermons about dead grandparents or news stories about mass shootings. It's like revisiting a local pub from your teens: awkward and sometimes unfriendly, but there's a desperate spirit driven by its clientele, who depend on such establishments for social interaction. It's Gen X and Boomers mainly performing for a micro-community of mates; doing stand-up skits about the neighbour's cat puking on their dog, and the dog barfing on the Christmas presents. At least they're getting something good out of this godforsaken place. Somewhere in there among the shouting, ranting, quipping is my dad, and his beautiful face, which he's presented in the form of a selfie. Dad is letting his Facebook Friends know that he had a heart aneurysm. He nearly died – my mum told me he was going to die. But he didn't and so he's here, on Facebook. I sigh and give a weak smile, and click the emoji face cuddling a heart.

I reluctantly move on to Instagram. There's a tragic sensation that everyone is still playing along with a game that ended a long time ago – the one in which we all pretended our lives were relentlessly fabulous and our skin was naturally that smooth. All the old hot girls have had babies or have become doulas or business women and their brands are too curated to reveal any grit or dirt. Sometimes they'll do a post about their cellulite and tell you 'not to believe everything that you see on the internet', but a few hours later it's back to the bikini shots and handstands at sunset. The old boys don't upload any photos of themselves or their partners – just overfamiliar dogs or a pint glass on a bench in front of a sunset on a campsite. You have to plough through their tagged photos just to get a slight glimpse of their current appearance, but even then it's nothing to get the juices flowing; it's all far-away pics of bike rides or some kind of new domesticated tedium involving homemade crisps or a renovated shed. Then again, straight cis millennial men have never been particularly adept at advertising their lives in an alluring way online. I suppose they've got to be at the bottom rung of something.

Meanwhile, the young cool girls I would normally find intriguing appear so maudlin and deadpan in their posts that I am almost glad to be thirty-six – their makeup is good and they are smarter than me, they are more conscious about what's really going on, achingly so, but they speak in a foreign tongue layered in irony or in frantic Textsprawls that make me feel too excluded to keep up with. Anyway, I know how it feels to be snarky and twenty-one; the moody nihilism isn't quite as sexy when you've got the chronic stomach-acid issues to contend with a decade later.

I wonder if Twitter might stir something. But as usual it's just front row for the dregs of humanity, the same jokes, the same jokes about people making the same jokes. The good people left a long time ago. Now it's just bigots or the dying throes of millennials who once ruled the internet. Every tweet reads as if written from an ergonomic desk or while walking down a carpeted corridor in suede trainers, holding a tiny paper cup of macchiato. Just an air of depression and desperation hanging over every moment. And when it's not 'personal news', it's suicide notes. Conspiracy theorists. Brazen declarations of transphobia. An egg posting racist replies under a link about the casting of a Disney adaptation. A photo of someone's uncle who got blown up in a war. A guy who says he's got scientific evidence to back up the fact that this time next year humanity will be eradicated. Threads – so many threads. When we run out of water I'll take a thread about how to burn the piss smell off a pint of urine so it's drinkable, but otherwise please keep your twelve-part breakdown of the history of rice to yourself. Within fifteen seconds I am resentful and bitter and I log myself out.

Where I yearn to be is TikTok. The party is raging but I'm too tired to keep up. It's like Vegas on a stag do – there is no sense of time passing, of how to get out, the lights are dazzling bright or flashing sinister, the drugs are too hardcore for a Tuesday night and after a few hours of fun I just want my bed and a hot-water bottle. Most addictive of all is its intelligence – the algorithm knows me better than I know myself and when it's good it is a never-ending cascade of offbeat humour, gossip, philosophy; interesting, unusual beautiful people, outsiders and enlightenment. 'Not until we are lost do we begin to understand ourselves,' says one woman, quoting Henry David Thoreau, and as I begin to consider those words it's kiboshed by a video of a guy dancing to a Fiona Apple song, in what looks like the world's grimmest hospice. Then it's a psychologist analysing why childhood is now shorter through relentless internet consumption; now it's little girls dancing in a style that's too grown up for someone who's technically not allowed to watch *Pirates of the Caribbean*. Then the app whisks me off my feet to show a granny in a low-cut top star-jumping in slow motion, then to tell me that I am neurodivergent, that I'm a bisexual with a parasite living in my gut and that's why my jaw is always clenched, that I should consider polyamory and the same diet as an eighteen-year-old ballet dancer. Forty-five minutes have gone and my hippocampus has burned itself to cinders.

What is quietly prevalent on all platforms, a dark thread that joins them all, is the apathy towards other humans. There's a nihilistic anti-everyone trend, an upspike in the type of internet personality who is a proud loner disdainful of real-life socializing. I can see why, in a way: if you spend too long online, it rarely leaves you with a sense of optimism about the human race. We're a lot to handle in high doses and it's not right for our brains to see so much of the world at once: the vicious, deadly trolls, alongside the attention-seekers airing their trauma over breakfast, alongside the news cycle of terrible stories about humanity. If all you consume for eight hours a day is the chaotic side of civilization, I can see why socializing might seem like an ambitious exercise. But there's a lot of sweet and easy people out there too. They just rarely go viral.

We were already lurching towards sci-fi levels of disconnect, but the pandemic has accelerated a type of snobbery about face-to-face contact that I worry is lethal: one where being in the same room is a nuisance and so we never meet but speak on video chats instead – *Thank God Christmas is cancelled! Being with people can be so exhausting!* In which we chat all day to our friends but the constant flow of gossip and chatter and links to Reddit threads about Harry Styles's hair prevents all chances of a genuine caring question that could cure a week's worth of pent-up anxiety. It's what they've always wanted, the biohacking tech-bro demagogues who are creating this tech- nology, malevolent forces who hope to push us all into a solitary state of inertia in which we wear headsets all day, and have holograms of dead celebrities visit us on our birthdays, and we type 'screaming' in the group-chat in response even though we haven't moved our forehead in years, and watch political deepfakes that send us into a spiral of conspiratorial depression that makes us scared and angry and even more susceptible to buying into microtrends, and food we haven't ordered arrives at the front door as soon as our stomach gurgles, and we all wear pleather, like we're in a futuristic music video from the 2000s, only without the relief of a rap interlude from Timbaland.

A future without the healing benefits of true connection is something I am fearful of; partly because of all the aforementioned prophetic, technological reasons, but also because of the natural slowing down and dulling of life as you get older anyway. It wouldn't be manageable to carry on with the same emotional velocity as your teen years for ever, but I can't help but slightly mourn the gradual spiralling away of those moments of candour and hushed intimacy I once had such easy access to. With every year that passes, the people you once stayed up all night with begin to get busier and talking becomes a luxury. Sometimes partners take the entirety of the load, and opening up to others therefore becomes harder and scarier and more of a burden. The more time that passes, the more layers of silent suffering builds and it becomes much more difficult to start chipping away at it when you finally are united. Loved ones move to far-away towns as soon as the cities get too chaotic; others get ill. Some will die.

Then there is the oddness of my body. This chronic menopause I am wading through until I am in my fifties, a deeply uncool condition that I'm struggling to medicate and that brings with it a constant mistrust in myself and with that an alienation – a paranoia about falling apart that makes me awfully self-aware and self-reflective, and sets me adrift from anyone who asks, who hears me grumble about mind-altering hormone crashes but has no frame of reference for what that means. And motherhood: the isolation that new mothering brings, the skewed sense of identity, and the social events that drift away because it's a battle to stay out after 8.30pm on a Thursday because of exhaustion, and when you do manage to make it out you have nothing else to talk about other than the fact you've been up for nineteen hours and your eyes are dry.

Recently this dystopian disconnect has manifested in a very physical way: disassociation – a word I am loath to use in the same way any description of a mental disposition can feel self-appointed and identity-shaping rather than genuine. But who cares – I feel it, this temporary state of being, a symptom born allegedly of my underactive thyroid, a recurring hormonally induced migraine or of birth trauma – I don't know which, but I'm stuck in this idiotic state too often. When different pressures or panic stack too high, and inevitably there is no time to decompress, my head goes into flight mode. I even hear a whomp in my brain as it happens, as if I am a laptop overheating. And then that's it for a week or two – wheeling around like a robot, silent, vacant, slow and sad. I find it frightening – the fragility of my brain and its inability to handle multiple feelings at once. It frightens me to look after my son alone, even though the love I have for him is the only thing that can come close to cutting through one of these episodes. Cold showers and ice can help, or acupuncture, or a sleeping pill. But none of that is possible when you're pushing a two-and-a-half-year-old up an inflatable slide in a three-storey soft-play zone. Worst of all, during one of these episodes I avoid Mark at all costs. I can go for days without making eye contact with him, because I am so concerned that he will look at my face and see that I'm not there.

To break myself open, to snap out of this daze – I long for it more than I've ever longed for any person or item of clothing or haircut, and being in The Group was an antidote to that nothingness. It felt good, even though it felt pretty awful crying so brazenly as well. So I google local groups, and I ask Julian with the black-eyed enthusiasm of an addict if there are other ones similar, and he tells me he'll keep an eye out. I find a couple that look OK but I hesitate before signing up. Because I know that I am avoiding something more profound.

Why am I so desperate to share myself with strangers when I am privileged to have people I know who are ready and willing? My parents, my brother and sister – architects of the greatest childhood, and a safety net of love in adulthood. My two housemates: my son, a magnificent human – a yellow pudding and avant-garde jazz performer catapulted from the early '70s and into the present day by sheer force of humour and charm; and of course Mark, a man whose walk alone is enough to nudge me out of a deathly sorrow, whose shadow has sass and vigour, whose absence in my life gives me a haunting sense of displacement unlike any other I could comprehend. And my friends: we're playing the long game – always quietly in each other's orbit, and requiring no stilted transaction of sex or money to affirm our union; just presence, pure presence, and sometimes a round table in the corner of a room with a basket of bread.

I've always been told that most people are too inward-looking to judge anyone else's actions – that nobody out there is sat at home reflecting on the way you tripped into the room or opened the door with your elbow because they're busy thinking about the way they pronounced hyperbole in a meeting three years ago. The tragic truth is that I am always thinking about someone else. Everyone who has a phone with social media is doing this – staring at others, mind whirring as we categorize them, judge them, marvel or scathe. It's definitely tiring, but is it acceptable? To view other people as I'd so hate to be viewed myself – ranking everyone on their beauty and surface-level achievements? Assuming so much about someone's childhood and present relationship status based on the time of night they've posted, and the way in which they've used a comma?

I've come to realize my relationship with the internet is an infidelity – a remorseless, ongoing affair with the fringes of humanity while I am in a stable relationship with all of my friends and relatives. I find it impossible – with my son's school WhatsApp groups on the horizon and a host of new profile images to feast on – to believe that I will have the strength to give up this habit forever. But at least now there is a growing awareness of my fortune, and of the dangers of wasted time.

Something has awakened in me, the emergence of a surlier version of myself, someone more weary in the face of such temptations. This is not the voice of Alexa, but the voice of my long-suffering, baseline soul, and it is assuring me of some facts.

She says that it is alright to sometimes feast on the contemporary wonders of global connectedness, as long as it is in small doses, and if I've slept for eight hours and have been outside for a walk.

She says that it's natural to feel jealous and obsessive, when so much of being a woman is mandatory social voyeurism, where you are forced to absorb a revolving billboard of other tantalizing lifestyles pioneered by better girls that could be you if you work hard enough, collect all the right tokens, and stop eating crisps.

She says while capitalism is ultimately too tall to topple, the nagging need to rot in despair while neglecting the pure brilliance of simple existence, and to sink further into fantasies in which you are the lowliest rat on the planet, is simply too tiresome to continue. That's what she says. And also to chill out on all the Chris Martin stuff because the whole disabled toilet thing was weird.

I believe it, all of it, with great urgency. This is not a makeover or rebrand but a new perspective, one which I'm going to hold onto as I stand on the precipice of the rest of it all, the rest of life, the hard bit – which brings with it a body that will rebel, a mind that will slacken, and loved ones who will no longer be around. It is scary, but also affirming. The sun is getting hotter, the end may be in sight, but I want to feel every moment of it.

ACKNOWLEDGEMENTS

To Picador. What an honour. To Siobhan Slattery for your tenacity and razor-sharp PR and marketing skills. Tiana-Jane Dunlop for translating a sprawling collection of thoughts into that neat, eerie cover concept, and Anna Isabella Schmidt for the devastating illustration. To copy editor wizards Victoria Denne and Marta Catalano, proofreader Alex Drew, the amazing Rosie Shackles and Orla King in editorial, Jon Mitchell and Mairead Loftus in rights, Rory O'Brien and all of the sales team and to anyone who ever had to schedule a Zoom meeting about launching this book into the world.

To my beautiful readers: Lizzie Adams, Anna Mears, Tshepo Mokoena, Debbie Scanlan, Lucy Youngman. Thank you for the encouragement. To Wolf James Creative, for wisdom via voice note. Thank you to Nicky Baker, Michael Cragg, Hannah Debnam, Priya Elan, Hannah Ellis-Petersen, Nosheen Iqbal, Tim Jonze, Michelle Kambasha, Tim Leslie, Tony Links, Greg Pittard, Joe Rush and Cat Wallace for the love and support over the decades.

To anyone kind and loving who was in my life during any